'Adam Ockelford is no ordinary music teacher. He is as accomplished in the field of linguistics as he is in music, and has analysed both language and music to identify their common deep structures. Few people could claim expertise in both domains. Even more unique, he has used his insights into how we respond to hearing words and musical notes to support the teaching of children and adults with autism. It was a privilege to hear Adam's blind savant pupil with autism, Derek Paravicini, playing a piano duet with Boogie Woogie king Jools Holland in Cambridge. Derek's talent is in part his own and in part the product of the special relationship with his lifelong piano teacher Adam. But this remarkable book also reveals the highly original theory that Adam has developed that informs his novel teaching methods.'

– Professor Simon Baron-Cohen,
Autism Research Centre, Cambridge University

MUSIC, LANGUAGE AND AUTISM

of related interest

Islands of Genius
The Bountiful Mind of the Autistic, Acquired, and Sudden Savant
Darold A. Treffert
Foreword by Daniel Tammet
ISBN 978 1 84905 810 0 (hardback)
ISBN 978 1 84905 873 5 (paperback)
eISBN 978 0 85700 318 8

Developmental Speech-Language Training through Music for Children with Autism Spectrum Disorders
Theory and Clinical Application
Hayoung A. Lim
Foreword by Karen Miller
ISBN 978 1 84905 849 0
eISBN 978 0 85700 415 4

Roots of Musicality
Music Therapy and Personal Development
Daniel Perret
Foreword by Colwyn Trevarthen
ISBN 978 1 84310 336 3
eISBN 978 0 84642 090 0

Pied Piper
Musical Activities to Develop Basic Skills
John Bean and Amelia Oldfield
ISBN 978 1 85302 994 3

MUSIC, LANGUAGE AND AUTISM

Exceptional Strategies for Exceptional Minds

ADAM OCKELFORD

FOREWORD BY FRANCESCA HAPPÉ

Jessica Kingsley *Publishers*
London and Philadelphia

Permission has been granted for all case studies and photographs.

First published in 2013
by Jessica Kingsley Publishers
116 Pentonville Road
London N1 9JB, UK
and
400 Market Street, Suite 400
Philadelphia, PA 19106, USA

www.jkp.com

Front cover image source: Evangelos Himonides.
Front cover image: Romy and Adam share a musical joke.

Library of Congress Cataloging in Publication Data
Ockelford, Adam, 1959-
  Music, language and autism : exceptional strategies for exceptional minds / Adam Ockelford ; foreword
by Francesca Happ?.
    pages cm
  Includes bibliographical references and index.
  ISBN 978-1-84905-197-2 (alk. paper)
  1. Music therapy for children. 2. Autistic children--Language. 3. Autistic children--Education.
4. Autism
in children. I. Title.
  ML3920.O25 2013
  618.92'891654--dc23
                                    2013004563

British Library Cataloguing in Publication Data
A CIP catalogue record for this book is available from the British Library

ISBN 978 1 84905 197 2
eISBN 978 1 85700 428 4

Printed and bound in Great Britain

Contents

Foreword

Living or working with people with autism spectrum conditions (ASC) often illuminates peculiarities of the 'neurotypical' (non-autistic) mind, which might otherwise have evaded our attention. For example, people with ASC are free from the obligatory attention to others' minds that makes it so hard for neurotypicals to think truly original thoughts, avoiding the herd. In the same way, the many beautiful examples in this book of the intense relationship many people with ASC have with sound and music remind us how deaf many of us have become to our auditory environment. One is led to ask, why don't ordinary children mimic the sound of water dripping into the bath, or become distracted by the different timbre of people's voices apparently saying the 'same' thing? Imagine listening to all the sounds around you as you listen to music. Imagine being the talented young man with ASC who spontaneously names the pitch of a cork pulled from a bottle, or the ping of the doors-closing alert.

What you will read in this book will awaken you again to sound. Adam Ockelford is a truly gifted teacher, and as readers we can appreciate that talent as he guides us into the heart of music, with simple explanations of aspects that those without musical training may have assumed were closed to us. This is essential because, as Adam makes clear, music is a space where people with ASC and neurotypicals can truly meet. I am reminded of the old expression 'a bird and a fish may fall in love, but where would they live?' Music is an important common ground for people with ASC and neurotypicals; research by Pamela Heaton and others suggests we share very similar emotional recognition and response to music. Adam explains the natural synergy between the structure inherent in music and the cognitive style of the

ASC mind. Music is 'in tune' with the ASD mind because 'music is typically supersaturated with far more repetition than is required for it to be coherent'.

And for all its deep theoretical insights, this is a supremely practical book. It is full of advice and guidance: how to gauge the level at which an individual child is ready to engage with music, how to develop each child's musical ability, how to recognise and teach the 1 in 20 with absolute pitch, and how to use music to enrich communication. I particularly treasure the inclusion of so many evocative examples from Adam's work with children with ASC who have little language and who are often mystifying to those around them. We may jump to the conclusion that such students are solely 'visual learners', neglecting the importance of sound. I remember clearly one of the first children with ASC I met, who wore his hood up whenever he could, spoke scarcely at all, but showed a store of vocabulary if you sang an incomplete line to him – he couldn't resist singing the ending, beautifully in tune. Adam's advice, like that of all really good teachers, is also tinted with humility and wonder: 'If there is one golden rule in working with children with autism, it is that there are no golden rules', except perhaps 'don't talk too much'!

This wise and original book is essential reading for anyone working or living with a child with a passion or talent for music – it is a guidebook to enter their world of sound.

Francesca Happé
Director, MRC Social, Genetic and Developmental Psychiatry Centre,
Institute of Psychiatry, King's College London

Acknowledgements

I should like to thank the children and families whose stories are told in this book and all those who helped in its production: particularly Kim Ballard, for her insightful comments on Chapter 2; to the team at Jessica Kingsley, especially Lisa Clark, Bethany Gower, Victoria Nicholas and Christine Firth; and to the AMBER Trust, www. ambertrust.org, who funded much of the research that is reported here.

Opening Notes

Unlike fickle language,

Music,

The fine art of repetition in sound,

Could have been designed

With me in mind.

For Freddie, every note on the piano is like a familiar friend.
Photo courtesy of Felicity Ockelford.

Introduction

'WHY...?'

During the thirty-something years in which I've been engaging through music with children on the autism spectrum, it's hard to remember a conversation with parents where that most challenging of questions didn't crop up sooner or later: *'Why...'*

'Why is Jack obsessed with the sound of the microwave? He can't bear to leave the kitchen till it's stopped. And just lately, he's become very interested in the tumble drier too...'

'Why does my four-year-old daughter just repeat what I say? For a long time, she didn't speak at all, but now, the educational psychologist tells me, she's "echolalic". I say, "Hello, Anna", and she says "Hello, Anna" back. I ask "Do you want to play with your toys" and she just replies "Play with your toys", though I don't think she really knows what I mean.'

'Why does Ben want to listen to the jingles he downloads from the internet all the time? And I mean, the whole time – 16 hours a day if we let him. He doesn't even play them all the way through: sometimes just the first couple of seconds of a clip, over and over again. He must have heard them thousands of times. But he never seems to get bored.'

'Why does Callum put his hands over his ears and start rocking and humming to himself when my mobile goes off, but totally ignores the ringtone on my husband's phone – which is much louder?'

'Why does Freddie flick any glasses, bowls, pots or pans that are within reach? The other day, he emptied out the dresser – and even brought in half a dozen flowerpots from the garden – and lined

everything up on the floor. I couldn't see a pattern in what he'd done, but if I moved anything when he wasn't looking, he'd notice straight away, and move it back again.'

There seem to have been as many questions as there have been children. *Why* does Romy sometimes only *pretend* to play the notes on her keyboard – touching the keys with her fingers but not actually pressing them down? *Why* does Bharat (in contrast) repeatedly bang away at particular notes on his piano (mainly 'B' and 'F sharp', high up in the right hand) until the string or the hammer breaks? *Why* does Rachel cry whenever she hears 'Twinkle, Twinkle, Little Star' (the first three or four notes are enough to evoke a strong emotional reaction)?

For a number of years, apparent eccentricities such as these remained for me just that: behaviours beyond the usual orbit that readily attracted vivid description but resisted any explanation that could draw them into broader accounts of human motivation and intelligence. Yet the children's actions didn't appear to be *illogical*, they were just *different* – apparently driven by *different* goals, *different* priorities, *different* ways of relating to the world from those of the majority. So, unpack the difference (or differences), and the behaviours should be explicable, and therefore potentially able to serve as resources for teachers and therapists to use in supporting children on their unique developmental journeys.

The emerging theories of autism initially seemed to hold out the prospect of explaining why the children acted in the way that they did. For example, maybe the notion of 'mindblindness', in which people are unable to put themselves in others' mental shoes, could explain, at least in part, why Anna didn't seem to understand the social ping-pong of question and answer that most children grasp intuitively. Perhaps the idea of 'weak central coherence', in which information is processed in detail rather than as a bigger picture, could account for Ben's love of jingle fragments. And it could be that 'impaired executive function', with its implied absence of an overarching cognitive control, meant that Bharat was unable to move on from repeatedly playing the same notes on the piano.

While these accounts all seemed to make perfect sense, I was nonetheless left with the feeling that they were factors in an equation in which at least one major variable was absent. For example, why was Jack so attracted to the humming of domestic equipment? Why should his mother's mobile phone so agitate Callum? Why did Romy sometimes only *pretend* to play notes? Why did Rachel react so intensely to the opening of a nursery rhyme? The main theories of autism seemed awkwardly mute on these topics. So what was the element missing from our understanding?

INSIGHTS FROM THE BLIND[1]

My route to working with children with autism was somewhat unusual, in that it came through the world of young people who were blind: my first pupils with special needs were severely visually impaired. I subsequently discovered that a number of them had autism spectrum condition (ASC) as well, though at the time (the early 1980s), this wasn't generally recognised and accepted in the way that it is today. Irrespective of whether the children had other learning difficulties or not, though, it quickly became evident that sound provided them with a hugely important channel for gathering information and communicating with others, for learning and for recreation, and I soon learnt to follow my pupils' auditory instincts, not only in music, but in their wider education too.

This aural approach, I discovered much later, did not align with most of the pedagogical strategies that had evolved in relation to children with autism, which were predominantly visual in nature: augmentative communication systems, timetables and enabling environments were largely constructed to be seen but not heard. And visiting schools for autistic children today, one is still frequently struck by how much attention is paid to pupils' visual surroundings, while relatively little emphasis is often placed on what they hear (whether they choose to or not – it's hard to cut out unwanted noise), and the potential impact that sound, both planned and unplanned, may have, positively or negatively, on their well-being and capacity to learn.

MAKING SENSE OF MUSIC AS A LANGUAGE

Hand in hand with my developing interest in special abilities and needs was the wider issue of how music makes sense to us *all*: how is

---

1   The title of Selma Fraigberg's classic text on the impact of blindness on children's development (1979).

it, simply by listening, and without the need for any formal education, that just about everyone can understand and enjoy music? The way I thought of it was like this. Music is a special kind of language, but instead of having words, it has notes. Notes don't generally *mean* anything in the way that words do, pointing the mind to things beyond themselves. Rather, notes just 'point to each other': and the meaning of music is in these abstract relationships that we hear between sounds – usually without making any conscious effort.

But we can make ourselves aware of these connections, and if you want to know what they're like, just sing or hum to yourself the opening two notes of, say, 'Over the Rainbow' (in its original version, as Judy Garland sang it – see, for example, www.youtube.com/watch?v=PSZxmZmBfnU). Do you hear the jump up from a lower note to a higher one?[2] So, ask a child who's never seen, to sing 'Over the Rainbow', and it's quite likely (if he or she is familiar with Garland's classic interpretation) that it will start on an 'A flat' (equivalent to the note that would sound around the middle of a keyboard – see Figure I.1), and jump to another that has the same name, though it sounds higher. Do you hear the jump up from a lower note to a higher one? Two quite different sounds, yet somehow they seem to have a natural connection; in retrospect, the second may seem to derive with a certain inevitability from the first. If it seems that way to you, then you're hearing musical syntax in operation – the structural glue that binds the notes in a musical narrative logically together in the mind. You may even feel a tiny tingle of emotion – a minute burst of rising excitement – as the second note takes over the first, echoing yet also transforming what has gone before.

ABSOLUTE PITCH

That, in a nutshell, is how music works, and anecdotal experience, now supported by an increasing amount of research, suggests that a high proportion of blind children intuitively seem to 'get it' very early on – usually in the first two to three years of life (see e.g. Ockelford and Matawa 2009; Ockelford *et al.* 2006). A key factor in this precocious musicality is a special ability that most musicians call 'perfect pitch',

---

2   Later renditions, such as those by Eva Cassidy (see www.youtube.com/watch?v=fMfBKwCBgGI&feature=fvst) and Leona Lewis (see www.youtube.com/watch?v=QLr1sBQ5gpE), avoid this leap.

which psychologists term 'absolute pitch' or 'AP' – but it's exactly the same thing. To understand what this means, think again about your rendition of the opening of 'Over the Rainbow'. How did you know which note to start on? You probably didn't, and the chances are that you didn't even think about it, though you may instinctively have picked a pitch that was quite low down in your vocal register, since part of you knew that a big jump up was coming. But the exact note didn't really matter, because, as we have seen, what makes a tune a tune is not the notes themselves, but how they stand in relationship to one another. Try starting 'Over the Rainbow' again, on different notes. Some may be easier for you to sing than others, but it is still recognisably the same tune, wherever you begin.

However, for around one in ten thousand of people in the West, about one in twenty professional musicians, and an astonishing four out of ten blind children, things are very different. Often, by the age of 24 months, they will have learnt to recognise (and re-create) individual notes. To these children, *they all sound different*. That doesn't mean that they necessarily know the musical names for them all (C, D, E flat, F sharp, and so on), but each is like a special friend with a unique character. So, ask a child who's never seen, to sing 'Over the Rainbow', and it's quite likely (if he or she is familiar with one of the classic versions) that it will start on an A flat (equivalent to the note that would sound around the middle of a keyboard – see Figure I.1), and jump to another that has the same name, though it sounds higher.

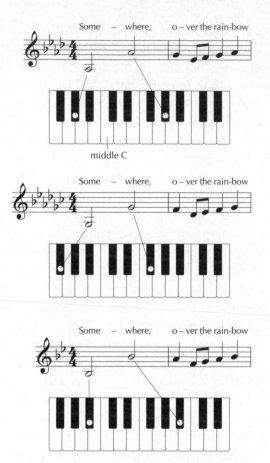

Figure I.1 'Over the Rainbow' beginning on three
possible notes: most people would not notice, but
for people with AP they sound quite different

For 40 per cent of blind children, then, music – in fact, all sound
– has an added aesthetic dimension, offering an experience that is
neither better nor worse than for most of us, but *different*. However,
the possession of AP can have a significant impact on other areas
of musical development. Playing by ear – that is, playing just by
listening, without needing to read music, or being told or shown
which notes to press (in the case of a keyboard) – becomes a relatively
straightforward matter, since rather than trying to work out how the
relationships between notes translate into different distances between

the keys, children with AP know, even before they have pushed a note down, what it's going to sound like. So learning to play an instrument is relatively straightforward: it's just a question of finding out which key is associated with each of the pitches they can hear in their head, and many young blind children do indeed teach themselves in the early stages.

EXCEPTIONAL EARLY COGNITIVE ENVIRONMENTS

Why do so many blind children process sound in such a different way from most of us? No one knows for sure, but blindness causes what I call an 'Exceptional Early Cognitive Environment' (EECE), in which musical skills are particularly likely to flourish. Human brains evolved to work in a certain way, with a wide range of perceptual input (sight, hearing, touch, taste, smell, balance, and so on). Deny the brain its principal source of information about the world (vision), and its focus of attention will be driven elsewhere – particularly to sound – and, in the first years of life, it will literally wire itself up differently to ensure optimum performance with the limited data that it has available.

For some years now, there has been a debate among academics and educators about the relationship between blindness and autism. Clearly, there are some people who are autistic but not blind, there are others who are blind who do not have autism spectrum condition, and there are a number who are both blind and autistic (see Dale and Salt 2008; Hobson and Lee 2010; Pring 2005). But the issue is that blind children are quite likely to exhibit behaviours that are generally considered to be characteristic of autism, potentially calling into question how autism is defined and recognised, and making the assessment of severely visually impaired children in the early years particularly challenging. Suffice it to say that most of the examples given above of autistic-like behaviours, such as a fascination with the sounds of certain household appliances, computers and phones, an obsessive interest in particular fragments or features of music, and the tendency to echolalia, are commonplace among blind children. And, like children born with little or no sight, autistic children too have a markedly higher probability of having AP than those with neurotypical development – perhaps around 1 in 20 – and music is often among their special areas of interest and achievement.

So, could it be that young children with autism are also affected by an Exceptional Early Cognitive Environment, similar to that experienced by blind children, and with the same potential to promote high levels of musical interest and development? Although at the first blush this may seem unlikely (since blindness and autism are manifestly so very different), that is exactly the theory that I will be advancing in this book. That is *not* to say that I believe a significant number of severely autistic children are likely to become publicly recognised musicians, performing or composing at a high level within their culture (although some may). However, I do contend that where exceptional musical interests or abilities are to be found (and I believe that these are far more widespread than is generally recognised among the population of autistic children, hidden in behaviours such as those described above), they should be nurtured, potentially offering both a source of enormous pleasure and fulfilment in its own right, as well as having the capacity to promote wider learning and development, and well-being.

FINDING YOUR WAY AROUND THIS BOOK

Music, Language and Autism comprises seven chapters that are to an extent self-contained, although most readers will probably be best served by working systematically through the book, depending on the knowledge they bring to bear (particular expertise in any of the three areas – music, language or autism – is not required).

Chapter 1 reflects briefly on the nature of autism, how it is identified and the main theories that have been developed to account for it. While some of those on the spectrum who are higher functioning may flourish with little or no specialist pedagogical intervention (though they may need support in relation to their social and emotional needs), others with greater cognitive challenges, for example, who find language problematic or who are unwilling to move beyond a few narrow behavioural routines, may derive most benefit from one or more of the targeted educational interventions that have been developed in recent years. However, music plays little or no part in any of these, which I believe to be a serious omission.

Chapter 2 examines how (verbal) language works in some detail, and identifies the features that many of those on the autism spectrum are likely to find challenging. Chapter 3 investigates how music functions, how it is that abstract patterns of sound intuitively make sense, and why these are likely to be particularly appealing to many children with autism.

Chapter 4 explores the nature of musical development, and sets out a framework of six stages across three domains of engagement (reactivity, proactivity and interactivity) that have proved to be of value in gauging the levels at which children are functioning, and in planning and delivering music curricula appropriate to their needs and interests. A case study of a profoundly autistic but deeply musical boy and is presented to show the framework (termed *Sounds of Intent*) in action.

Chapter 5 looks more broadly at the development of communication and considers how the model of evolving musicality set out in Chapter 4 corresponds with this, and how, with some children with autism, there may be markedly uneven profiles of development in different areas of auditory processing. It considers how music may be used as an augmentative strategy to bolster communication in other domains, and explores its potential value in supporting social development.

Chapter 6 analyses the impact of the Exceptional Early Cognitive Environments that are caused by autism in the context of growing up and learning in spaces that are likely to be suffused with music. It seems that the self-referencing and highly repetitive nature of music is a perfect match for a number of traits of those on the autism spectrum: little wonder then that so many young autistic minds latch onto music as a source of predictability, interest and comfort in a generally confusing world. EECEs are seen as an explanation for the development of exceptional musical abilities in around 5 per cent of autistic children, and also provide the grounds for believing that music can be of particular value in supporting the development of language and socialisation. Examples are provided of how this may work.

Chapter 7 considers the 1 in 20 children who are likely to have AP: how to recognise them, and the strategies that teachers may adopt, in some cases to coax individual musicality out and into an interpersonal forum, and in others, to persuade autonomous and idiosyncratic learners of the value of benefiting from the knowledge, experience and technical expertise developed by musicians and handed down over many generations.

CHAPTER 1

Reflections on Autism

INTRODUCTION

Autism is a lifelong, neurological condition that manifests itself early on – typically within the first two or three years of childhood (for helpful summaries, see Boucher 2009; Frith 2003; Happé 1995; Hobson 1993; Wing 2003). Its effects can be profound, pervading the whole of a child's development. Yet in medical terms, autism is elusive. It is not *one* condition with a single physiological source: researchers have not been able to isolate a particular part of the brain that is wired up anomalously and say 'this is the cause'. Rather, autism is identified only on the basis of observed behaviours, which can vary widely both between and within individuals in different contexts and at varying stages of their maturation. Diagnostically, the best that clinicians can currently do is to offer a list of attributes, and say that if a child exhibits certain combinations of these (as a minimum), he or she can be described as having an 'autism spectrum condition'. Hence one wonders, as our understanding of brain function improves, whether the notion of 'autism' will ultimately be resolved into many, more specific conditions.

This notion feels intuitively right: visit any school, centre or unit for children or young people on the autism spectrum, and it is likely that you will be struck by the diversity of the pupils or students present. For example, one child (typically a boy) may come up to you, and start to address you animatedly and eloquently, as though in mid-conversation, about a topic that bears no relation to the immediate environment, the people in it, or any activities that may be underway. Another child, in contrast, may completely ignore you, his whole attention apparently taken up with the pattern of parallel light and dark stripes made by the window blind, in front of which he is flicking his fingers. Looking round, you may notice one of his classmates sitting at a desk, concentrating intently on a drawing comprising nothing but tiny geometric shapes that fit together to form intricate patterns, which are well on the way to filling a large sheet of paper. And you may see a fourth child, sitting in the corner of the room, hands over his ears, eyes closed, rocking, and making high-pitched, repetitive vocal sounds.

Pending the development of more sensitive diagnostic tools, all these children are likely to be classed as 'autistic' according to the criteria published by the World Health Organization (WHO 1993) and the American Psychiatric Association (APA 2013), which are internationally accepted and the most widely used. Certainly they are sufficient for the purposes of this book. The important thing is that the thinking and ideas set out in the chapters that follow will, I hope, have relevance for a broad range of children and young people, including not only those with 'classic' autism, Asperger syndrome and pervasive developmental disorder not otherwise specified (PDD-NOS), but also those with learning difficulties more generally.

DESCRIBING AUTISM

The WHO and the APA define autism in terms of three broad characteristics: (a) qualitative impairment in social interaction, (b) qualitative impairment in communication, and (c) restricted, repetitive and stereotyped patterns of behaviour, interests and activities. These descriptors are broken down further as follows:

(a) Impairment in social interaction…

- lack of eye contact, facial expressions, postures or gestures
- failure to develop peer relationships appropriate to developmental level
- lack of spontaneous seeking to share enjoyment, interests or achievements with other people
- lack of social or emotional reciprocity.

(b) Impairment in communication...

- delay in or lack of spoken language

- in individuals with adequate speech, marked impairment in the ability to initiate or sustain a conversation

- stereotyped and repetitive use of language or idiosyncratic language

- lack of varied, spontaneous make-believe play or social imitative play appropriate to developmental level.

(c) Restricted, repetitive and stereotyped patterns of behaviour, interests and activities...

- encompassing preoccupation with one or more stereotyped patterns of interest that is abnormal either in intensity or focus

- stereotyped and repetitive motor mannerisms

- persistent preoccupation with parts of object.

EXPLAINING AUTISM

In the 1990s three theories dominated academic thinking about the causes of autism, each of which has been associated with one of the main characteristics of the WHO/APA definition. Specifically, defective 'theory of mind' – the ability to attribute mental states to oneself and others, and to understand that others may have ideas that differ from one's own (see Baron-Cohen 1995, 2000, 2009; Baron-Cohen, Leslie and Frith 1985; Frith 2001; Tager-Flusberg 2001) – was held to be responsible for 'impairment in social interaction'. 'Weak central coherence' – the tendency to think about things in terms of their parts rather than as a whole (see e.g. Frith and Happé 1994; Happé 1996; Happé and Booth 2008) – has been linked to communication difficulties (as well, more positively, as accounting for enhanced perception of detail and some 'savant-like' abilities). 'Executive dysfunction' – a problem with the domain of processing that regulates and controls other cognitive functions (see e.g. Hill 2004; South, Ozonoff and McMahon 2007; Turner 1997) – was thought to lead to rigid and repetitive behaviours.

This swathe of thinking has proved to be enormously helpful for those seeking to educate or care for children on the autism spectrum, though they are more *descriptive* than *explanatory*, which can yield a certain circularity of thought. For example, while impaired social interaction may be presented as evidence of a weak 'theory of mind', it is equally possible to assert that mentally being unable to put oneself in another's shoes is testimony to poor social interaction. More recently, psychologists have turned to more 'general purpose' (rather than domain specific) cognitive mechanisms, such as those relating to 'primary intersubjectivity' (a basic sense of self in relation to other, which develops very early on), to see whether impairments in these fundamental areas of processing may offer a more coherent explanation of the 'autistic mind' (see e.g. Boucher 2011). However, this is still very much work in progress, and it may be that, if autism, as the term is commonly used, is indeed not 'one thing', but an umbrella term for many different types of cognitive impairment (with potential areas of overlap), then the search for a single neurological cause is in any case likely to be frustrating.

What is clear, though, is that autism, in all its manifestations, is for life. There is no 'cure'. Indeed, many adults with Asperger syndrome regard the notion of being 'cured' as pertaining to an old-fashioned medical model based on the notion of deficit (see e.g. Waltz 2005), which they find highly offensive. Rather, as a society, we should be celebrating difference. They point to a range of figures from science and mathematics, including Isaac Newton, Albert Einstein and Alan Turing, and cite examples of musicians, including the composers Wolfgang Amadeus Mozart and Eric Satie and the Canadian pianist Glenn Gould, as evidence that an exclusively 'neurotypical' human race would be far less rich than one with a smattering of exceptional (if eccentric) minds.

Nonetheless, there are many children on the autism spectrum, perhaps with little or no language, who resist social contact, and who may be locked into narrow routines for many of their waking moments. Here the instinctive adult reaction is to try to remediate things, to enhance children's quality of life, by encouraging them to communicate, to form reciprocally warm relationships with other people, and to broaden their range of experiences.

Here there is one thing – and only one thing – that has consistently been shown to have a positive effect, and that is sustained and systematic programmes of education. Some of these use 'applied behaviour analysis' – ABA (see e.g. Fox 2008; Kearney 2007) – while others, such as 'PECS' (see e.g. Bondy and Frost 2011; Charlop-Christy *et al.* 2002), focus on communication; 'TEACCH' aims to improve skills by modifying the environment to mitigate the impact of what are deemed to be cognitive deficits (see e.g. Mesibov, Shea and Schopler 2004; Panerai, Ferrante and Zingale 2002). None, however, has much if anything to say about the potential role of organised sound and music in teaching and learning. In the Introduction, I asserted that this is in my view a serious omission, and the remainder of this book seeks to explain why music may benefit the learning and development of many children with autism, and, for some, may even constitute a central feature of their educational curriculum. I am not, of course, claiming that music has the answer to all the diversity of challenges faced by children on the autism spectrum, but I contend that it may be an important piece of the jigsaw for a large proportion, and for some – maybe as many as 1 in 20 – music may quite simply be the most important piece in the puzzle, into which all the others fit.

There is a secondary focus on *language*, since getting to grips with verbal interaction is such an important issue for many children with autism, and music – a close (though distinctly characterful) cousin in the domain of auditory communication – is particularly well placed to support words or even, in some cases, to replace them. Also, by understanding how language works, we are able to get a better idea of how it is that music makes sense and is able to convey thoughts and feelings. Hence it is to the construction of meaning through words that we first turn our attention.

CHAPTER 2

The Challenge of Language

INTRODUCTION

Just how language and music work, and the nature of the similarities and differences that exist between them, are issues that lie at the very heart of what it is to be human: little surprise, then, that they have engaged philosophers since the time of the ancient Greeks. More recently, linguists, music psychologists and neuroscientists (among others) have entered the fray too, and the ever-expanding literature in both academic journals and the popular press is testament to the amount of thinking and research now devoted to these topics, and the high level of public interest they engender. Although there are different views as to how language and music function, there is broad agreement that they are uniquely human forms of communication, which appear to have featured in all societies from time immemorial.

While aspects of language and music can be *taught* (and usually are, in schools), in the majority of cases, children acquire skills in both domains from a very early age, without any instruction: most babies and toddlers learn to understand what people are saying just by interacting with others in day-to-day situations, and develop the ability to speak with little or no conscious effort. In some societies, as they get older, children are instructed how to write and to read: to encode and decode what they hear using visual symbols. In a similar way, as infants, we intuitively come to understand and enjoy the music of our culture, effortlessly absorbing the patterns of sound that bombard us, and instinctively joining in by singing and dancing and clapping. Formal education is usually needed to enable children to take the further step of acquiring the skills needed to play instruments at an advanced level, or to read and write music. But for the great majority, speaking and listening and making music are as natural a part of growing up as learning to walk and run and climb.

What about children with autism, though? As we saw in Chapter 1, one of the main challenges they face is trying to fathom the vagaries of other human behaviour in general and the arcane intricacies of verbal language in particular. Interestingly, there is no evidence that autistic children's understanding of *music* is impaired – in fact, quite the reverse: a disproportionately large number of young people on the autism spectrum appear to be very musical.[1] Why should this be? What can it tell us about the way the autistic mind works? And ultimately, can an understanding of what is going on neurologically help educators and therapists find better ways of supporting the children and young people on the autism spectrum with whom they work? These are topics for later chapters. For now, we return to our opening questions, and consider first how language operates.

THE ELEMENTS OF LANGUAGE

For something that seems to come so easily to most of us, language is highly complex, as the ongoing challenge of the 'Turing Test' – to design a computer that can understand and persuasively emulate human speech – shows. One reason why a solution to this problem is so elusive is that linguistic competence requires a number of different, advanced cognitive (or, in the case of a computer, pseudo-cognitive) processes to function together in an integrated fashion (Pinker 1994). And what makes linguistic emulation particularly difficult is the fact

---

1 Rimland and Fein (1988) found that, in a sample of 5400 people with autism and related conditions, 531 had 'savant-like' abilities (approximately 10%). In a follow-up study of 119 of those with the special abilities, 63 (around 50%) had a focus on music. Based on these figures, we can estimate that around 5 per cent of children with autism may have special musical abilities. In my experience of working with thousands of children with autism, the proportion may well be higher than this, though it is difficult to be more precise, since children's potential musicality need not be immediately apparent.

that a message between two humans is not just about *content* but *context* too: language can fully be understood only if the receiver is able to appreciate the point of view of the sender – to be empathetic. 'Yes' can mean 'certainly', 'maybe' or even 'no!', depending upon the manner and the circumstances in which it is said.

But let us for the moment take a step back from ambiguities such as these, and consider what lies at the core of language: the cognitive acknowledgement that a chunk of vocal sound can stand for – *symbolise* – something else, whether an object, a person, an action, a concept, a feeling…or a characteristic of any of these (see Ballard 2007). That is, a verbal utterance has a *meaning*, which, in the case of successful communication, is shared between two people or more. This will have been learnt through exposure (starting in the first few months of life) or conscious intervention on the part of others, and stored as an associative memory (in this case a bond between sound and concept). Irrespective of this input, though, the human brain seems to have an innate tendency to label objects and people in the environment that are particularly salient with abstract sounds: as those experienced in caring for young children know, they delight in making up their own words for things, and adults cannot resist copying them!

Although some words are 'onomatopoeic' in nature, in that there is a more or less literal connection between the sound they make and the sound of the thing they represent (such as 'cuckoo', 'splash' and 'zip'), the connection between the signifier and the thing signified tends to be arbitrary. Hence the very different phonetic patterns 'bird', 'oiseau', 'Vogel' and 'uccello', for instance, can all mean the same thing in English, French, German and Italian respectively. Moreover, different words can share the same meaning (synonyms), while words with the same sound can have different meanings (homophones).[2] So even in the simplest of linguistic contexts – a single noun or verb – there is not necessarily a regular, one-to-one mapping between a word and a concept (see Figure 2.1).

---

2   And words with the same spelling can have different meanings (and sometimes different sounds). For the challenge this can pose children with autism, in which an appreciation of context is essential to understanding, see Happé (1997).

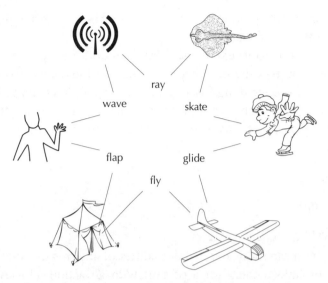

Figure 2.1 There is often not a one-to-one correspondence between words and the concepts to which they pertain

A key feature of the English language is its sheer size, in 2012 estimated to comprise something over one million words (Global Language Monitor 2012), of which the 'average' person may recognise around 50,000 and regularly use about 10,000.[3] Even these lower figures represent years of learning, and, given that people generally speak at around 150 words per minute (National Center for Voice and Speech 2005), it means that linguistic comprehension demands rapid, random access to a sizeable store of associative memories (notwithstanding the fact that, in speech, many words are primed by their preceding context).

Meaning is rarely conveyed by words used in isolation: most of the time, it seems, humans want to share information about a *plurality* of concepts and how they relate to one another, and so it is that *combinations* of words are the norm. In principle, this sounds straightforward enough, but in reality, it is a situation that is fraught with complexity, since, while our experiences and ideas are multidimensional, with events and thoughts occurring in all conceivable temporal arrangements (including in parallel), words are

---

3 According to David Crystal: see Gall (2009).

almost invariably produced and received in series – one at a time – in a single stream of sound.

How is this achieved? The simplest method, which young children usually acquire in the second year of life, is to juxtapose words that pertain to the same thing (see e.g. Starr 1975). Toddlers typically talk about people and objects: what they are like, what they are doing or wish them to do, or what they want to find out about them.

crayon red

mummy sit

me up

where Sam?

Here, the meaning of one word qualifies or interrogates that of the other, or links a thing (or a person) with an action. However, the relationship between two more or less equal entities, such as relative location or ownership, may also be implied by verbal juxtaposition

cup table

daddy car

As any parent knows, the magical thing about early linguistic utterances like these is that they are not just copied or adapted from what is heard, but may well be created anew. I still remember the day when my two-year-old son, Tom, as we were about to go out for a drive, slapped the front tyre of our Ford Galaxy and said

car shoe

Humans are not just great imitators: they – we – are all programmed to think, speak and act independently.

Whatever their provenance, short utterances such as these make considerable cognitive demands, including, in the case of the listener, the capacity to recognise the import of two words, to hold the concepts they evoke in working memory, and to juggle these mentally in order to determine their intended relationship, which will necessarily be based on previous experience. Hence symbolic meaning in language derives from two sources: the words themselves and the connection or connections between them. If, in the case of a two-word utterance, no meaningful relationship between the concepts that are represented can be discerned, then, despite the words potentially making sense individually, a coherent linguistic narrative will not be formed. That is, logic in language is contingent upon what are perceived to be rational linkages between the ideas that are symbolised.

This principle of verbal juxtaposition being used to denote a relationship between the concepts that are represented, first found in two-word utterances, extends to more complex language too. But here, given the multiplicity of related ideas that can be expressed, merely concatenating words is not enough to express their networks of potential connections, and other linguistic devices – the province of *syntax* – have evolved. These include the acknowledgement and differential treatment of words that signify different types of concept. Inevitably this reflects human experience and understanding of the world, and what a given culture holds to be important. Hence, as one would expect, some word classes and the types of relationships that can exist between them are more or less universal, while others are language-specific. Here is one view of how it works in English.

1. Things

A *thing*, represented in language by a noun (or substitute), is that which is or could be – an entity or an idea distinct from others: an object or a person; a perception, such as a colour; a feeling, such as love; or even an abstract value, such as integrity.[4] The representation of *things* lies at the heart of language; most other words that are used ultimately relate to a noun or its proxy – including, in English, pronouns such as I, you, it, another, someone, that, this, these and those. Pronouns exist because although things are often referred to repeatedly in a given chunk of prose, written or spoken, enabling a picture of something to emerge gradually or changes to be described sequentially, there is a tendency *to avoid repetition* in everyday language. Instead of 'Jane went to the shops and Jane bought some celery', we would be more likely to say 'Jane went to the shops and *she* bought some celery.'

This is an example of 'anaphora', where one word replaces or refers to another that was used earlier. Cognitively, anaphora involves a noun initially evoking an image or idea, which is held in working memory and then triggered afresh by a pronoun. The interval between

---

4 Over half the words in English are nouns, according to Oxford Dictionaries (see http://oxforddictionaries.com).

the two may be short, with little or no intervening material (as in the account of Jane's purchase of the celery). Here we can surmise that the demands on mental processing are modest. However, there may be a more substantial gap between the two references that are made to something, and other information may intervene. Indeed, several noun-pronoun correspondences may be in play at the same time. For example: '*Jane* went to the shops on the high street and bought some *celery* for the *rabbit* living in a hutch at the end of the garden. *She* watched, amused, as *he* ate *it* with alacrity.' Here, assuming a moderate speaking pace, there is an interval of around five seconds – 25 words – between 'Jane' and 'she'. Moreover, this connection overlaps with the pronominal links between 'celery' and 'it', and 'rabbit' and 'he', which themselves cross over in time. We can identify which nouns and pronouns are related since the latter are grammatically (and, in this case, exclusively) gendered: feminine, neuter and masculine. Hence, although the ideas presented about Jane, the rabbit and the celery are simple enough, their linguistic mode of presentation evidently affords a number of cognitive challenges.

It is worth noting too that, on occasion, the meaning of a pronoun may be ambiguous, only becoming clear in retrospect (if at all). Consider, for example: 'Jane gave her daughter the celery. She smiled.' We may never know who was smiling, Jane or her daughter – or this may subsequently become clear. Consider how your understanding of 'she' changes according to whether the second sentence takes the form: 'She smiled and ate it.' or 'She smiled, knowing it was a good source of riboflavin.' Here, determining which noun (Jane or her daughter) the pronoun (she) refers to demands contextual understanding that can be gleaned only by thinking beyond the information that is immediately conveyed and comparing this with knowledge gained previously. The message itself is incomplete.

This is an example of how *nebulous* language can be. In fact, words can communicate ideas only as precisely as the commonality of the mental images they are able to evoke in different people. And since everybody's experiences necessarily differ, so the same word will denote slightly different things to anyone who hears it. *Connotations* (ideas or feelings that are invoked in addition to primary, denotative meanings) are likely to vary even more. For example, if I say the word 'tree', while a similar archetypal notion will be elicited in those who hear and understand me, there will nonetheless be differences. For instance, one person's image may be coloured by the plane trees outside their London office (maybe connoting a sense of 'work'), while someone else's mental picture may be influenced by the oak that stands in their garden, and on which their children have a swing (with connotations of 'family'). The complex relationship between individual things and categorical concepts is considered below. Irrespective of this, though, the important thing, from a linguistic point of view, is that there is sufficient overlap between one person's mental imagery and another's to enable successful communication to take place.

The greatest degree of intersection is likely to occur when people have a shared, direct experience (that maybe extends over a long period), when a noun merely serves as a cursory label for a rich, common knowledge of something. For example, if any of my three children hear the word 'dad' (meaning me), although their notions of the man who always seems to be in his study writing will no doubt be subtly different, they are sure to have a great deal in common. Here, a single noun brings to mind a good deal of specific information. However, if they were to read the opening of a (somewhat pedestrian) book, 'Dad got in the car', their picture of the person concerned would inevitably be far more limited; imagination would necessarily have to play a far greater role.

But it is this very fuzziness that is core to the richness of literature: sentences are not mathematical equations, complete and unambiguous; they are kicking off points for mental peregrinations. As we read about people in books, we create imaginary personalities whom we get to know and love or despise – and all this based on what can only ever be partial information: authors can never describe anything comprehensively, and neither would they want to. They rely on the human capacity and propensity actively to create a world of meaning from the ineluctable economy of verbal messages.

2. The qualities of things

Things have *qualities*, expressed through adjectives,[5] which necessarily vary as much as the nouns they qualify. In English, when adjectives

---

5 Around a quarter of the words in English are adjectives, according to Oxford Dictionaries (see http://oxforddictionaries.com).

are juxtaposed with the nouns to which they refer, they generally precede them (while in other languages, different sequential rules can apply). Moreover, in languages other than English, adjectives often 'decline': changing form according to the number (single or plural), gender and case of the noun to which they relate – grammatically strengthening the bond between them. From the point of view of people seeking to speak and to understand what others say, the important thing is not which (arbitrary) approach is adopted, but that it is used systematically. Hence when an English listener hears an adjective, we may surmise that an initial, partial meaning is brought to mind, and held in working memory until a noun appears, which similarly initially stimulates a further, incomplete meaning. The full, blended sense of what has been said emerges shortly afterwards as the relationship between the two is formulated.

The implication here is that, like pronouns, the meaning of an adjective will be contingent on the meaning of another word or words – in particular, the noun to which it relates. Consider, for example, that someone starts to ask you a question (but is interrupted): 'Have you seen the big…' What meaning do you ascribe to 'big'? An abstract sense of relative size, presumably. Were the person to continue, 'Have you seen the big spider?', then clearly 'big' in this context would mean something very different from its use in the question 'Have you seen the big tree?' Or how about, 'Have you seen the big tree in the photo?' It may be that this visual representation of the tree is smaller than the spider! Hence the meaning of 'big' becomes fully apparent only in retrospect; and, as we discovered in relation to two-word utterances, and nouns and pronouns, even the simplest of linguistic expressions can make significant demands on cognition.

Moreover, things typically have *multiple* qualities, which, in English, can be captured in *chains* of adjectives. Consider what this means cognitively. Let us assume we hear the words 'The beautiful…' Leaving aside for the moment the function of the definite article 'the' (of which more later), the mind prepares itself for a noun to follow: what is it that is beautiful? The answer to this question is deferred, however, and we hear a further adjective, 'blue'. At this stage, in the absence of a noun, the mind does not know precisely how the notions of 'beautiful' and 'blue' fit together, and so we can surmise that a *preliminary* blended meaning is held in working memory, pending further information. Another deferral occurs with the addition of a third adjective, 'Italian'. Now we have an initial blend of three abstract qualities, waiting to be reified. Consider how the meaning of this adjectival fusion changes according to the noun that follows, for example, 'car', 'shoes' or 'porcelain' (see Figure 2.2).

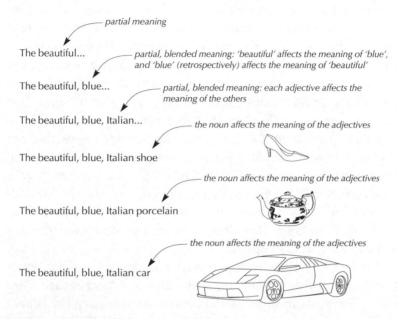

Figure 2.2 The meaning of individual words is contingent on those around

To aid understanding, we grow used to the fact that different adjectival types invariably occur in the same order (though even most native English speakers would be hard pushed to say why, for instance, the phrase 'the beautiful, blue, Italian shoes' is immediately comprehensible, whereas 'the Italian, blue, beautiful shoes' takes a moment or two to decode and sounds unnatural). That is, just by being exposed to successions of adjectives in speech (rarely more than three in a series), we learn the following order in which descriptive concepts tend to appear: opinion, size, age, shape, colour, origin, material and purpose. This means that young minds not only have to learn the *meanings* of adjectives, but also develop a deeper, abstract understanding of the *types* of qualities to which they refer, in order to be able to use them according to syntactic convention.

Structurally, then, we have identified two rules in relation to adjectives and nouns in English that tackle the fundamental linguistic challenge of expressing simultaneous experiences and thoughts sequentially: descriptions of *qualities* should precede the names of the *things* to which they refer, and adjectival chains should present concepts in a certain sequence. Although we can surmise that rules such as these must exist cognitively in abstract form (since we can create original utterances that use them), they cannot be instantiated in a content-free bubble, as the words that are used to reify them will have meanings, and it is these meanings that dictate the category to which a word belongs (here, a noun or an adjective), which in turn defines its function. That is, the *structure* of speech is defined by its *content.*

This is particularly evident in phrases that use words that can serve either as nouns or adjectives. Imagine, for example, that someone starts speaking, and says 'The crisp'. The structure here is of the definite article followed by a noun. But then the speaker adds the word 'air'. Now we have a three-word phrase – 'The crisp air' – article, adjective, noun. Hence the structure depends on the meaning ascribed to the word 'crisp'.

Yet at the same time, as we have seen, rules governing the structure of language regulate how its content is conveyed. Meaning arises *as a fusion of the two*: both structure and content are necessary, but neither is sufficient, for a string of words to make sense. The phrase 'Air crisp the' brings the concepts of the atmosphere and nippiness to mind, but the listener is likely to be confused as to how the speaker intended them to be related. And one can conceive of phrases that are 'well formed' – that conform to syntactical conventions – but are incoherent, because the relationships between the concepts they elicit are unimaginable: even in the most fantastical of worlds, 'The beautiful, blue, Italian empathy' is not a plausible notion.

3. Relationships between things

Fundamental to human understanding is how one thing relates to another: cognitive processes such as learning and memory, problem solving and anticipation, could never get off the ground if the millions of separate experiences that assail us every day remained as isolated phenomena. Inevitably, then, a great deal of language is devoted to comparison – explicitly or, as we shall see, implicitly.

As we observed in relation to adjectives, things typically vary along a number of dimensions (such as size, age, shape and colour), and many relationships between objects are defined in terms of similarities or differences pertaining to their qualities: 'The mouse is smaller than the cat', 'The water is colder than the milk', 'Dad is older than Mum', 'This car is cleaner than that one'. Some connections are made not through qualities but through relative location, using prepositions: 'the tree is *behind* the fence', 'the beaker is *on* the table', 'the key is *in* the box', 'my car is *next to* yours'. Note that although such relationships refer to physical states that exist concurrently, the sequential nature of language compels speakers to impose a directionality on their thinking, and therefore to emphasise one aspect of a two-way relationship at the expense of the other. 'The mouse is smaller than the cat' has a subtly different meaning from 'The cat is bigger than the mouse', even though, logically, they are equivalent. Inevitably, listeners will pick up on the conceptual asymmetricality that is present. Whichever way the relationship is expressed, though, meaning evolves in stages as the three concepts are revealed (through noun, comparative adjective and noun) and the connections between them gauged. Our perception of each concept is affected by the context provided by the others. Consider how your perception of a mouse's size varies if it is said be smaller than (a) a piece of cheese, (b) a cat, and (c) an elephant. One has to 'zoom out' mentally from the mouse with the cheese or the cat in order to accommodate it in the same conceptual frame as the elephant.

Differences between things may be important to our understanding of the world, but it is the recognition of *similarities* that has really enabled human thinking to get off the ground. If one thing is more or less like another, they can both be imagined to exist in the same conceptual category: they are, in an abstract sense, the 'same thing'. While this principle is straightforward enough, it has resulted in conceptual edifices of huge complexity (just consider, for example, the taxonomy of living things), and it represents one of the great achievements of the human mind.

Conceiving of things in the universe in a categorical way has had profound ramifications for the way that language has developed (see Lakoff 1990); conversely, there seems little doubt that the capacity to represent increasingly complex ideas in words has facilitated the development of abstract categorical thought. The impact is evident in even the simplest of linguistic constructions: nouns can denote a specific thing (or things) that is (or are) a member (or members) of (a) a category – 'the cat' or 'the cats'; (b) a category of things – 'cats'; or (c) a non-specified member of a category – 'a cat'. In English, these fundamental differences in meaning are indicated by the subtle use of definite or indefinite articles and the singular or plural form of the noun concerned.

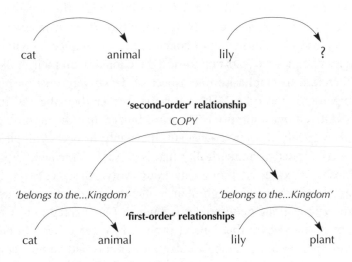

Figure 2.3 Completing the analogy involves using a 'second-order' conceptual relationship

Relationships between categories are abstract, existing outside time and space, and are necessarily bidirectional (though usually asymmetrical). However, the sequential nature of language once more means that a bias is inevitable, and, by convention, in English, the lower category (the subset) precedes the higher (the superset): for example, 'cats are mammals' (however, mammals are not necessarily cats). Categories can form hierarchies since subsets are able to function simultaneously as supersets: 'cats are mammals, and mammals are animals'. The nature of the categorical hierarchy must, again, be inferred from the order in which the concepts are presented. And because here we have a chain of two relationships that function transitively, a third link between the first concept ('cats') and the third ('animals') is implied: as 'felidae' (cats) is a member of the class 'mammalia' (mammals), and mammalia is a member of the kingdom 'animalia' (animals), it follows that felidae is a member of animalia. Other forms of relationship *between* the connections that link categories are possible too: for example, to be able to answer the questions of analogy that are the stock-in-trade of intelligence testers, such as 'a cat is an animal; a lily is a ——', requires (a) an understanding of the four concepts involved (three given and one implied), (b) a grasp of the 'first-order' relationships between 'cat' and 'animal', and 'lily' and 'plant'; and an appreciation (through a 'second-order' relationship, that can be imagined to exist between two first-order relationships) that these connections are analogous (see Figure 2.3).

Moreover, things can be members of many different categories, which can overlap in myriad different ways: consider how a cat, an owl and a hamster can be related on a conceptual level. For instance, a cat may be a mouse-catcher, a pet, and, barring mishap, a quadruped; an owl may be a mouse-catcher but is unlikely to be a pet and definitely not a quadruped; a hamster is not a mouse-catcher but may well be a pet and almost certainly a quadruped. Categories may, for example, reflect physical attributes (quadrupeds), functions (mouse-catchers) or ownership (pets), or they may be purely subjective or humanly constructed: 'things I like', 'fruit beginning with "P"'. The key thing is that language will make sense only to the extent that the conditions for category membership, and the assumptions underlying relationships between categories – and, very often, the connections between these – are understood.

A key component of our identity as people is how we relate to others of our species, particularly through familial connections, and, in many languages, special sets of words have evolved to define such associations precisely. These seem to be deeply embedded in the human psyche: 'Dad' and 'Mum' (or variants) are often among the first words that children use. A challenge is that although such terms start out as 'absolutes' (there is only one mother in a baby's life),[6] in conventional adult usage they are relative and, generally speaking, express a polarity that may be gender specific. Hence your mum and my mum are most likely to be different people, and the inverse of motherhood may be sonhood or daughterhood. However, you may be my cousin, and, if so, I am yours. And at his first extended family gathering, a toddler

---

6   Although words such as 'Mum' may initially be subject to overextension – in referring to any adult female, for example.

may have to come to terms with the fact that the man he calls 'Dad' is classed by others as their 'uncle', 'son', 'brother' or 'nephew'.

Finally, we should note that human conceptual thought allows one thing to *possess* another, and in English this special ('genitive') relationship is marked through 's at the end of the noun of ownership ('John's ball') or by reversing the two nouns' order of appearance and using the preposition 'of' (as in 'the heat of the sun'). Pronouns take special possessive forms: 'my ball', 'your ball', 'his ball', 'her ball' and so on.

4. The actions of things

Things *exist* (or used to exist or may yet exist) and many of them *act* (now, in the past or in the future). Existence and action are the territory of verbs.[7] Very often, these are 'conjugated': modified so that they agree with the subject to which they refer, linguistically strengthening the perceived relationship between them. In English, I *am*, you *are* but she *is*; a cat *purrs* yet cats *purr*. However, I *may be* walking, just as you *may be* and she *may be*: here there is no difference, and verbal adjacency is all that a listener has to go on to link person and action.

By convention, in English, verbs follow the nouns to which they refer: boats yaw, dogs bark and men perspire. This rule means that understanding is facilitated when adjectives are also involved, since they will be separated from the verb by the noun to which they pertain (which is therefore adjacent to both). For example, in the sentence 'The wet pebbles glisten', both 'wet' and 'glisten' are at once set apart yet proximate to 'pebbles'. Consider how a blended meaning evolves as the four words are heard; the order in which they occur is important since a concept, once introduced, will tend to have primacy over those that follow. That is, blends are directional. It is the *wet* pebbles that are glistening. Moreover, there is a sense of causality here, reflected in the order of presentation: the pebbles are glistening *because they are wet*. The sequence in which the concepts appear can be reversed, and the meaning subtly changed, by using the present participle: 'The glistening pebbles are wet'. In the absence of the speaker putting particular stress on 'pebbles' or 'wet' (something

---

7   About a seventh of the words in English are verbs, according to Oxford Dictionaries (see http://oxforddictionaries.com).

that is discussed below), there is greater emphasis on the sparkling reflection of the stones rather than their moist state.

Verbs like 'glisten' are intransitive, in that they do not involve or act upon anything else; many others, however, have a grammatical 'object' to which they refer. Here the order in which words appear can be crucial to understanding. In English, for example, convention dictates the sequence should be 'subject–verb–object', and a sentence such as 'The dog spotted the cat' has a different meaning from 'The cat spotted the dog'. Some verbs additionally take an 'indirect' object and, again, the order in which ideas are presented needs to follow the custom of the indirect object appearing first. 'Tom fed the cat the fish' conjures up quite a different image to 'Tom fed the fish the cat' (perhaps he had a pet shark). Observe, however, that the use of prepositions can reverse the effect of word order. For example, 'Tom fed the fish *to* the cat' returns us to more expected domestic territory.

English makes little use of inflection to reinforce function: that is, to indicate which thing (or person) is doing the acting and which (or who) is being acted upon, directly or indirectly. *I* (nominative) love *you* (accusative), though perhaps *you* do not love *me*. However, *the* man gives *the* boy *the* ball, whereas in German, *Der* Mann gibt *dem* Jungen *den* ball. Here, all the definite articles are masculine, but each appears in a different case. Moreover, 'Junge' ('boy') takes an additional 'n' ('Jungen') in the dative. These morphological changes reinforce the meaning of the message by indicating precisely the nature of the relationships between the three nouns.

Actions have characteristics, described in English by adverbs, which are often marked with the suffix 'ly', and are thus clearly identifiable. This clarity may be one reason why, generally speaking, the placement of adverbs in relation to the verbs to which they pertain has more flexibility than the positioning of adjectives relative to their associated nouns. Consider, for instance, the following ways of expressing what is essentially the same action:

Slowly he came into the room.

He slowly came into the room.

He came slowly into the room.

He came into the room slowly.

To a fluent English speaker, the changing location of the adverb yields subtle differences in meaning, however, which I suspect may vary between listeners (or readers). Placing the adverb first seems to give it particular emphasis: the most important thing about his entry was evidently its lack of pace. Putting 'slowly' second gives the impression that there is more of the sentence to come, for example, 'He slowly came into the room...and sat down'. Placing the adverb third sounds slightly unusual; perhaps even potentially poetic. Positioning 'slowly' at the end of the sentence means it has least significance: here, the main thing appears to have been that a male came into the room, and that this action took place unhurriedly. One suspects that codifying semantic nuances such as these in a general way would be difficult. The important thing in the current context, though, is to appreciate how changing the order of words – altering the sequence in which semantic blends are formed – can introduce fine shades of meaning that experienced users of a language can detect and use.

❊ ❊ ❊

One of the great riches of human thinking is our capacity to move beyond the world as we immediately perceive it and, using language, draw parallels between things where none physically exists, in the process lending fresh insights to our perception of one phenomenon or both. For example, by saying the earth was 'dry as a bone', we are hinting at a level of desiccation incapable of supporting life. Here, one concept is juxtaposed with another through the use of simile. A further step is to *fuse* concepts through metaphor, whereby two unrelated things become one. Take, for example, 'All the world's a stage', upon which, Shakespeare tells us, men and women are merely players. In other words, while we may like to think of ourselves as important, self-directed individuals, all we can do in reality is to act out, with others, a preordained script; our fates are sealed from the time of our mewling, puking infanthood. To grasp complex notions such as this demands a higher level of symbolic understanding than is required for day-to-day language (although this makes far greater use of metaphor than most people realise: see Fauconnier and Turner 2002), where abstract patterns of sounds – words – represent ideas and feelings: here, one *concept* symbolises another.

Traditionally, a great deal of linguistic analysis has taken words on the page – the visual representation of verbal sounds – as its starting point (rather as the analysis of most music has tended to be undertaken by people viewing scores). However, the visual symbols we use to capture language do so incompletely and imperfectly (just as printed musical notes convey only partial information about their intended sounds). In either case, readers have to bring a good deal of their own experience and understanding to make the written word (or music score) come alive. As any actor knows, the *way* that words are expressed in sound is crucial to their meaning, and there are a number of different vocal mechanisms that are used to impart or enhance the sense of what is said. One is *emphasis*, as we discovered above in relation to the wet pebbles glistening. For example, an ostensibly neutral statement such as 'He can open the front door' can have quite different implications if one word is emphasised at the expense of the others. For instance, '*He* can open the front door' gives the impression that there is someone else who cannot. 'He *can* open the front door' suggests that he may previously have tried and failed. 'He can *open* the front door' implies that he may not be able to shut it. 'He can open the *front* door' indicates that he may be unable to open the one at the back. 'He can open the front *door*' hints at the possibility that opening the front windows may be problematic. So, just by using different emphases, one short sentence can have five different meanings.

Another element is the *emotional quality* of the vocal sound that is produced. As babies, before speech evolves, we express and communicate feelings with affective whoops and glides and giggles and cries. As we shall see, it is thought that these non-verbal expressive vocalisations have been assimilated into music, whose melodies borrow their pitch contours to convey comparable emotions. But they are a vital element in speech too, whether standing alone, semi-formalised as interjections ('wow!', 'argh!', 'yippee!'), or fully integrated into more formal language, where, classed as 'intonation', they add immediacy and intensity to the symbolic meaning of words. Intonation also serves a more prosaic but nonetheless important function in differentiating questions from statements. Really? Really! Hear how the pitch of your voice goes up and then down to convey quite different things. Emotional quality also depends on the tone colour (or 'timbre') of the voice as well as its pitch, and any additional sighs, sharp intakes of breath, sobs or laughs. These non-verbal elements of language fuse with the verbal to create rich blends of meaning.

Take, for example, the sentence 'You fell off the chair', spoken in a neutral voice. Maybe we experience a certain vicarious regret, but probably little more. Now consider the following scenarios.

Giggling, Wendy turned to her best friend, Alice. 'You fell off the chair!'

Maybe Alice had imbibed a little too much the night before, but in any case, Wendy's tone has nothing in it to suggest that her friend had hurt herself.

His voice thick with sadness and guilt, Alan leant over his son, still sedated, lying in the hospital bed. 'You fell off the chair.'

Perhaps the boy's back was broken.

The sergeant major's incredulity and anger were evident as, red-faced, he yelled at Private Klutz: 'You fell off the chair?'

How could he have been so stupid to do such a thing in front of the colonel?

Danny could not resist taunting his little brother, chanting 'You fell off the chair!'

The joys of being a younger sibling!

Hearing her father coming up the stairs, Julie glared at her twin sister, who was still sobbing, and, in a conspiratorial whisper, tried to impose once again her revisionist account of what had happened. 'You fell off the chair.'

That would explain the bruise then!

The doctor examined Samuel's arm carefully, and with a hint of irony repeated the assertion that the young man had just made to him. 'You fell off the chair?'

In the last two examples, the implication of what is conveyed is the *opposite* of the words' face value: it seems that Julia's twin got hurt other than by falling off the chair, and the doctor clearly suspects that Samuel's injuries were sustained in some other way too.

Everything we think and do happens in a given *context*, and all our thoughts and actions are coloured with emotions that derive from the circumstances in which things occur. In language, the context of a communication may be known at the outset, or it may become apparent as the message is conveyed. In these cases, it is particularly evident how the full meanings of words only become apparent retrospectively, as more information about what they signify becomes known.

Take, for example, a novel that opens in the following way:

'Slowly she ate her breakfast: a simple meal of boiled eggs, toast and orange juice.'

Now consider how one's understanding of the scene conveyed by these words and, in particular, one's emotional response to them, changes according to the sentence that follows.

'And then came the knock on the door of her cell. It was time.'

'She remained, sitting upright in the hotel bed for a while with the tray on her lap, but then the temptation to return to the arms of her still-sleeping lover proved irresistible.'

'She'd been waiting for this most undemanding of luxuries during all her three years as a hostage.'

'Such a straightforward task, and yet so difficult on this first occasion since she had been blinded in the explosion.'

And just as vocal tone can reverse meaning through irony, so can context.

'I love you', she said, kissing him once more, and toying with the sparkling new engagement ring on her finger.

'I love you', she said, kissing him once more, knowing that the honey trap was set, and that his every word, every action, were being recorded.

The more one scrutinises language, the more it becomes apparent that words are so much more than regular symbols that function rather like computer code, where the same input consistently produces identical output; rather, words are vexatious, fickle things – at least as capricious as the humans who use them. Little wonder that the Turing Test is proving so difficult to solve! And little wonder that so many children with autism, with their somewhat literal view of the world, and who crave consistency and predictability, find language so challenging.

Parrots and voice synthesisers notwithstanding, all language ultimately has a human source, even if we do not know who that person is (or was). And all that is said or written emanates from a particular perspective: the action can be seen through the eyes of the narrator ('first person'), or from the point of view of someone the narrator is addressing ('second person'), or from the position of an imaginary spectator, looking in on the thoughts, feelings and actions of others ('third person'). Conceptually, these three possibilities may appear to be straightforward enough, but their use in many potential combinations is a recipe for boundless syntactic complexity, resulting in shades of meaning that are infinitely subtle. Again, the cognitive demands are likely to be substantial.

To illustrate this, consider a simple scenario: a woman is observing her son (Ed) and his interaction with a cat.

His mum watched as Ed stroked the cat.

Here the action is described in the third person: the narrator is remote from what is going on, and the account has a neutral quality. But how do we, the reader of the text, and the receiver of the information encoded in it, relate to that position of neutral observation? There is an assumption that we are situated in the same place as the sender of the message – adopting a similar third-party vantage point. But is this necessarily the case? Clearly not. Consider the differing impact of an ostensibly neutral statement such as 'In 1966 England won the World Cup' on English and German audiences. Opposing views of the infamous ball-crossing-the-line (or failing-to-cross-the-line) incident are likely to flash into mind, and to be emotionally tagged in contrasting ways (particularly for fans who followed the match at the time). Moreover, thanks to 'theory of mind' – the uniquely human capacity to put ourselves in other people's shoes – we have the capacity to step back and imagine how the message will be interpreted by different parties.

First-person narratives can be even more demanding from a cognitive-linguistic point of view. Let us return to the cat, Ed and his mum, and view the action through her eyes.

I watched as Ed stroked the cat.

The interesting thing here is the ontological status of 'I': who does it refer to? Counterintuitive though it may seem, there are a number of possibilities. First, imagine it was Mum herself recounting something (to her husband, perhaps) that had happened recently. Here, we can assume that there is no ambiguity: the man listening grasps that the narrator and the person who watched the action are one and the same, and in his mind, he can put himself in the shoes of the woman who is talking to him and imagine what happened as though he were there.

But now let us move forward in time some 20 or 30 years. 'Mum' is now a grandmother, and is reading an extract from her diary to her grandson. Here it is as though there are *two* narrators: the mother in the past who witnessed Ed stroking the cat and wrote about it, and the older woman, reliving the episode for the next generation. The present 'I' and the past 'I', although referring to the same person, are situated differently (see Fauconnier 1994), and for the grandchild to understand this requires a leap of the imagination, including an understanding of how people and their relationships to others evolve over time. This becomes even more apparent if the grandmother changes the original text, to make it easier (ostensibly) for the child to understand:

I watched as your dad stroked the cat.

But Ed wasn't a father when the incident took place – he was himself a child!

The issue of dual identity becomes even more strongly pronounced if a third party is conveying a message written in the first person. For instance, if an actor were to speak the line 'I watched as Ed stroked the cat', this would make sense only if we understood that one person can *pretend* to be another. The necessary capacity to suspend disbelief, which is linked to linguistic development, occurs early in childhood – though watching wide-eyed three- and four-year-olds at the children's theatre suggests that they regard what is happening on stage as having a high level of verisimilitude. And while parents may smile fondly at the naivety of their offspring's powerful reaction to a man dressed up rather ridiculously as a wolf, they should perhaps remember feeling the need to turn off the radio before the ghost story came on the previous night for fear of the images conjured up permeating their dreams. Once learnt, we cannot 'switch off' the symbolic or associative meanings of the words that we hear: we simply can't help language evoking thoughts and feelings, whether they be trivial ('pink elephants'), worrisome ('cancer'), funny ('Monty Python') or profound ('altruism').

Returning to Ed's dealings with the cat, similar cognitive-linguistic issues are invoked if the action is viewed from his perspective (rather than his mother's).

Mum watched as I stroked the cat.

There is a further possibility, though, which demands a further leap of the imagination: that the cat is treated as the entity through which the encounter is seen.

His mum watched as Ed stroked me.

But how can this be? As far as we know, cats do not have the capacity for such reflection nor the wherewithal to use the language needed to capture and communicate it to others (feline or otherwise). Such statements are conceivable because of our capacity – tendency, even – for personification: the attribution of human qualities to nonhuman entities, even inanimate ones, that seems to be steeped deep in our evolutionary past (phylogenetically) and occurs early in childhood (ontogenetically); hence, Tom's notion of 'car shoes' (see p.32).

We have now dealt with just 3 of 12 possible personal perspectives from which the interaction between Ed, his mum and the cat can be reported. Others involve the 'second person' too:

You watched as Ed stroked the cat.

Your mum watched as you stroked the cat.

His mum watched as Ed stroked you.

I watched as you stroked the cat.

You watched as I stroked the cat.

I watched as Ed stroked you.

Mum watched as I stroked you.

You watched as Ed stroked me.

Your mum watched as you stroked me.

It is hard to read these accounts through quickly and make the necessary mental adjustments in time: it takes a moment to come to terms with the different viewpoints that are implied. Each is subtly different, and imbues a single, everyday event with a slightly different meaning.

As well as enabling a narrative to be recounted from different personal perspectives, languages permit – to varying degrees and in different ways – a narrator to be situated in different *temporal* orientations in relation to the action they are reporting. Each relates to a syntactic category known as a 'tense', of which there are numerous possibilities, and, given the abstract nature of time, it is amazing to think that mere exposure to language is usually sufficient for the brain to grasp the manifold intricacies of linguistic temporal representation. Moreover, the same words can sometimes indicate different temporal perspectives, which are discernible only from the context in which they occur. For example, the phrase 'I am going home' could mean that I am currently on my way there, or that I will be at some point in the future. Similarly, 'I was going home' could be referring to an action that happened in the past, or it could allude to something that *was* going to happen (potentially even in the future) but no longer is: 'I was going home next year, but I can't afford the air fare'. 'I go home' can signify an undertaking that is temporally non-specific ('I go home...on the train'), or belong to a series of times that straddle the past and the future ('I go home...at weekends'), or a specific time that is yet to occur ('I go home...next Wednesday'). It can also signal the 'subjunctive' mood, which is used to express uncertainty, implication, desire, opinion or necessity. For example, 'He insisted that...I go home'.

A narrative can be situated in the present but look back in time to a previous occasion or occasions ('I went home...last Friday', 'I went home...at weekends'), or it could be located in the past and report on an event that happened even earlier ('I had gone home...'), or an event that was to have happened in the future, but would nonetheless still have occurred before the present time ('I would have gone home...'). Such expressions are said to be 'conditional' in tone, since an event that may have happened or may yet occur was or is contingent on something else. For example: 'I would go home (if)...' Again, the cognitive challenge of linguistic acquisition merely by experience is immense.

We began this discussion of language by noting that a key challenge is how to convey multidimensional ideas through a one-dimensional narrative that flows through time and can be registered piecemeal only as a series of auditory sensations in the perceived present: that is, even the most complex linguistic information has to be sent and received one 'frame' at a time. We are able to make sense of serpentine sentences such as this, comprising 61 discrete terms (and so well beyond the compass of working memory), because words have the capacity to form more or less self-sufficient groups constituting discrete 'chunks' of meaning. These can be signalled and linked in different ways. For example, pronouns such as 'that', 'which' and 'who' indicate that more information will follow (in the form of a phrase or clause) about something that has already been identified. The precise nature of the relationship between the phrase or clause and the object or person it qualifies may depend on syntax, context, or just on the way it is articulated, with pauses and emphases on different words. For example, if someone declaims in even tones 'The ball that had red spots on it rolled slowly down the hill', we are likely to understand that (a) there were two balls or more, (b) one was distinguishable by red spots, and (c) only the red-spotted ball rolled down the hill. Now imagine hearing the following sentence: 'The ball, which had red spots on it, rolled slowly down the hill'. The pauses either side of the clause (marked with commas), and the use of 'which' rather than 'that', tells the listener that here the clause is *descriptive* rather than *prescriptive*. As far as we are aware, (a) there is only one ball, (b) it has red spots and (c) it rolled down the hill.

Conjunctions work in a different way, affirming the end of one chunk of information and indicating that another is to follow, and apprising the listener (or reader) of the nature of the connection that exists between the two. These small connectors can have a huge impact on meaning. For example, 'Tim is happy *and* Tammy is sad' expresses the idea that both emotional states are existing independently at the same time. 'Tim is happy *but* Tammy is sad', emphasises the contrast between the two, though there is still no sense of contingency between them: we do not get the sense that Tammy's sadness arises from Tim's happiness. With 'Tim is happy *because* Tammy is sad', the position is quite different, however: here, we can attribute Tammy's negative feelings to Tim's positive ones. Conversely, 'Tim is happy *unless* Tammy is sad', indicates an inverse correlation, in that he will not be cheery if she is miserable, while 'Tim is happy *whenever* Tammy is sad' suggests a direct association between the two.

Although, as we have seen, there are conventions as to the order in which individual words in a sentence appear, there is more flexibility with the sequencing of chunks. While in broad terms, these are likely to follow the temporal order of the events they describe, or the contingencies that may exist between them, their presentation can be reversed so as to give greater emphasis to one element or another:

Tom ran inside, turned the television on and watched a cartoon.

Tom turned the television on, having run inside, and watched a cartoon.

Tom watched a cartoon, having run inside and turned the television on.

Since the one million or so words in English are made up from a limited bank of phonemes (around 40 – the precise number varying according to the speaker's accent), inevitably, there is a good deal of overlap in the way words sound. These similarities have found service in a number of different contexts, from the humour of Cockney rhyming slang to formal literary genres such as poetry. Here, word sounds are juxtaposed to create particular effects, affording the primary meaning of the text a further, aesthetic tenor. Because the sounding qualities of words have little or no symbolic meaning, any perceived connections between them cannot derive through semantic or syntactical logic, but must rely on a purely auditory rationale. As we shall see in Chapter 3, in our discussion of *musical* meaning, the ultimate source of syntax in abstract sequences of sounds is sameness or similarity, and techniques such as sibilance (as in the preceding part of this sentence), assonance (where vowels are echoed), consonance (the repetition of consonants) and rhyme (in which the ends of words correspond) all take advantage of this.

'Metre' refers to regular patterns of accented and unaccented syllables that may be formed by series of words, and so pertains to relative loudness and timing. Again, repetition lies at the heart of things: 'To *be* or *not* to *be*', for example, comprises three successive 'iambic' feet, each comprising an unstressed syllable followed by one that is stressed. The speed (or 'tempo') with which words are (or can be) enunciated is a further variable that can be used to enhance meaning, as Alexander Pope (1711) famously illustrates:

When Ajax strives some rock's vast weight to throw,

The line too labours, and the words move slow:

Not so when swift Camilla scours the plain,

Flies o'er th' unbending corn, and skims along the main.

We noted above how intonation (or 'pitch') can clarify or even alter meaning. Usually, though, the conventions of how pitch contour relates to meaning are distinct from semantic content. Hence, in English, questions, whatever they refer to, are often indicated in speech with a 'high rising terminal'. Occasionally, however, there can be a direct cross-modal connection. For example, try saying 'The balloon went up, up, up in the air' *without* your voice ascending in pitch. Again, repetition is in play here: the *repetition of difference*. The *difference* in pitch between the first 'up' and the second is echoed in that between the second 'up' and the third through a 'second-order' relationship (see Figure 2.4).

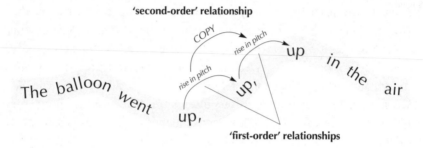

Figure 2.4 Example of 'second-order' relationship
of pitch in a rising vocal contour

LANGUAGE IN ACTION: 'TWINKLE, TWINKLE, LITTLE STAR'

It is incredible to think that, just through exposure and supportive interaction, children typically unthinkingly acquire all the knowledge and skills to use the language or, in many cases, languages of their culture, and rapidly become expert in expressing their thoughts and understanding the thinking of others. This acquisition seems all the more miraculous when one considers that, while adults intuitively adapt some of their speech for infants' ears (using limited vocabulary that refers directly to contemporaneous experiences, speaking slowly, and exaggerating intonation, for example), a good deal of the language to which children are exposed is highly intricate. Surprisingly, this is nowhere more in evidence than in many nursery rhymes.

Take, for example, the well-known lullaby, 'Twinkle, Twinkle, Little Star', strains of which seem to greet me whenever I visit a children's centre or nursery school, and ask what songs the children know. 'Twinkle, Twinkle' is a firm favourite (of the staff – and, by extension, their young pupils, since familiarity and preference are particularly strongly associated at this age). The lyrics constitute the first verse of an early-nineteenth-century poem, *The Star*, written by the English poet and novelist Jane Taylor, published in 1806.

> Twinkle, twinkle, little star,
>
> How I wonder what you are!
>
> Up above the world so high,
>
> Like a diamond in the sky.

It is traditionally sung to the French melody 'Ah! Vous dirai-je, Maman', which first appeared in print in 1761. This combination of music and words involves repeating the opening lines of the text at the end.

Let us consider how the poem 'Twinkle, Twinkle' 'works' as language, how it conveys meaning, and what that is likely to constitute for different audiences. In Chapter 3, we will undertake a comparable analysis of the music. Subsequently, we will explore how language and music can function together to create a blended meaning.

Although it is difficult, we will try to imagine what it is like for a child, with a receptive vocabulary of a few hundred words, hearing the poem for the first time.

From the outset, things are unusual. 'Twinkle' rarely appears in spoken English (apart from its appearance in 'Twinkle, Twinkle, Little Star'!) – with an estimated frequency of around two in one million words (Corpus of Contemporary American English 2012). (Compare this with the incidence of the next word 'little', which is thought to be approximately one in a thousand.) So it would be unsurprising if a young child had not encountered 'twinkle' before in a context that would have made its meaning evident. The rarity of the word is compounded by a relatively uncommon syntactic context: the 'imperative' form of the verb, through which the speaker is commanding (something as yet unknown) to twinkle. Of course the child concerned would not know this, and while he or she would doubtless have experienced a good many instances of verbs in the imperative mood ('Sit down!', 'Stand up!' or 'Stop that!'), it would be highly unlikely that 'Twinkle!' would have figured among them, since it is not something that children are generally asked to do. As a consequence, it may be that our young listener would not recognise 'twinkle' as a verb at all, given its unusual position at the beginning of a sentence. Moreover, unless the recitation of the rhyme were accompanied by a picture or a direct view of the night sky, the child would have to rely entirely on his or her imagination to work out what was being said. Indeed, we could speculate that 'Twinkle' would be just as likely to be construed as a noun: in particular, since it is not preceded by an article, someone's name ('Twinkle' ranked around 5000th among girls born in 2012 in the USA: see US Government Social Security Administration 2012).

If the first 'twinkle' was unusual, its immediate repetition, were this everyday speech, would have been truly exceptional, since, as we observed above, the same word (used with the same syntactic function) rarely occurs twice in succession. Such a construction (called 'epizeuxis') is almost entirely rhetorical. However, in children's rhymes, repetition of the opening word (or short group of words) is comparatively common, as is the imperative mood: 'Row, row, row your boat', 'Pat-a-cake, pat-a-cake, baker's man', 'Baa, baa, black sheep'. Add this to the fact that the adult enunciating the rhyme may well be intoning the words rhythmically; like much children's poetry, 'Twinkle, Twinkle' is in trochaic metre, comprising pairs of stressed-unstressed syllables. Hence the child may quickly become aware (at some level) that here is something other than day-to-day language: rather, here is a sequence of words that one can just listen to and enjoy learning, perform actions to, and chant with others. The cognitive processing this implies is surprisingly complex, as the thinking shown in Figure 2.5 indicates.

For the adult (and, perhaps, children familiar with the poem) the repetition of 'twinkle' may be suggestive of the twinkling continuing, quasi-onomatopoeically, in time, a view that may be supported by the 'twinkling' finger movements that often accompany the rhyme.

The next word is 'little', which the child hearing the poem for the first time is likely to recognise as describing a quality of something whose identity is about to follow. At this stage, then, the child will have three words held in working memory with preliminary meanings, whose full import is waiting to be 'released'.

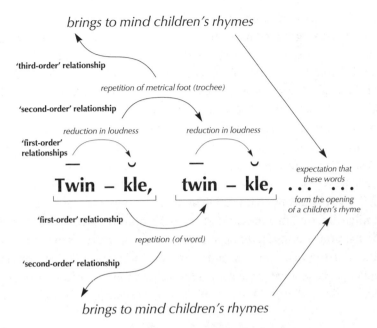

Figure 2.5 Some of the cognitive processing that may occur as a child hears the opening of 'Twinkle, Twinkle' for the first time

This release occurs with the fourth word – 'star' – which the child will probably understand as one of those minute points of light that appears in the night sky when it is clear, though there is a chance, of course, that 'star' will be taken to be someone who appears on television! For the time being, though, let us assume that it is an imagined or remembered shining dot in the sky whose image is conjured up. Syntactically, 'star' has a 'vocative' function; it is the thing being addressed. Hence there is the implication that someone or something (as yet unidentified) is doing the addressing. This uncertainty notwithstanding, the word 'star' completes the first main idea of the poem: we now know that there is a star, that it is little, and that we are telling it to twinkle.

But this is not as straightforward as it may seem. Whose idea is it (or was it) to tell the star to twinkle? While, as we have seen, children are great personifiers, experience suggests that the focus of their attention tends to be with tangible objects that form part of their immediate environment. Stars hardly fall into that category. It seems that, in 'Twinkle, Twinkle', words are being put in children's mouths and thoughts attributed to them that are not necessarily theirs. This notion is strengthened in the next line when the ostensibly first-person perspective is stated explicitly: 'How *I* wonder what you are'. Who is the 'I' here? Is the child intended to function like an actor, reading a third party's script? Or is it in reality a (Georgian) adult's fantasy view of what children think? That is, are the children more or less unwitting conveyors of a message that is largely for adult consumption?

In any case, the second line has an intricate syntactic structure, which is by no means straightforward to decode. It takes the form of an 'exclamative' sentence – one that is used to express emphasis or strong feeling. This means that the initial adverb ('how') is not used with its familiar interrogative intent, but to stress the strength of thought that the narrator is bringing to bear on the nature of the star's existence. The object of the main verb 'wonder' is a further clause ('what you are'). Hence in generative grammatical terms, this implies a further (second) level of dependency on the main subject, the star (see Figure 2.6).

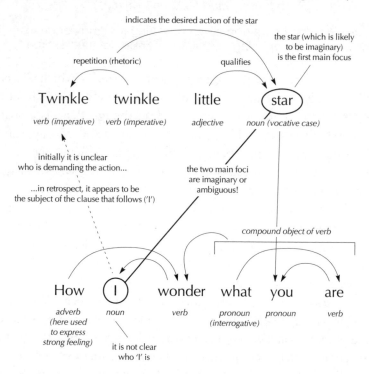

Figure 2.6 The complex web of syntactical and semantic relationships functioning in the first two lines of 'Twinkle, Twinkle'

The third line, 'Up above the world so high', is characterised by a sequence of words that is not characteristic of colloquial English, which may therefore present challenges to a young child whose linguistic capacity is still developing. Clarity of meaning has been sacrificed to maintain the trochaic metre of the first two lines (comprising stressed followed by unstressed syllables) and the rhyming pattern of paired lines (whose resolution is still to come in the fourth line). This is achieved by transposing the words 'so high' from where they would naturally occur at the beginning of the sentence ('So high up above the world') to the end. The result is that the naive listener may hear 'so high' as referring to the world rather than the sky (and, anecdotally, several people have reported to me that this was what they understood the line to mean as children).

In the fourth line, 'Like a diamond in the sky', the use of figurative language, first employed in relation to the personification of the star, is extended through its comparison with a precious stone. For the 'neurotypical' adult listener, the imaginative leap from attributing a human sense of self to an inanimate astral object, to likening it to a precious stone, is likely to cause few problems. Moreover, the simile involving the diamond is multilayered: here is something that not only glistens, but also connotes value and eternity, that can evoke a sense of awe. However, such analogies are likely to be beyond the comprehension of young children, particularly those on the autism spectrum, with their somewhat literal take on language.

CONCLUSION

In summary, then, linguistic communication is highly complex, and comprises ten main elements that work together to form meaning:

- *semantics* – through which experiences (and the relationships we perceive between them) are represented, more or less precisely, by distinct but largely arbitrary chunks of sound ('words')

- *syntax* – the rules, determined by convention, through which words can be juxtaposed

- *simile and metaphor* – through which humanly imagined comparisons between two things are drawn, offering fresh insights to one or both

- *standpoint* – the position in time ('tense') from which existence or action is described

- *source* – the personal perspective (first, second or third person) of a narrative

- *sequence* – the order in which words, and groups of words, are presented in time

- *sound* – the auditory quality of words and combinations of words (such as rhyme, alliteration, metre)

- *spoken quality* – the tone of voice with which words are enunciated

- *shared knowledge* – the commonality of experience between the sender and receiver of information to enable communication to function

- *social context* – an understanding of the relative status and linguistic competence of the participants in a conversation.

These result in a system of communication through sound (perceived, remembered or imagined):

- whose principal function is to share everyday information about oneself, others and the wider world, where it is usually improvised and ephemeral – although language can be elevated to function as art, where it is typically planned, recorded, learnt and reproduced, and valued for its aesthetic qualities

- whose principal method of conveying meaning is through symbolic representation, though with powerful (and sometimes contradictory) secondary meanings arising from context and manner of expression

- that relies on a shared experience and understanding of what is being represented – hence there will always be differences in the message as sent and received, though there is generally sufficient conceptual overlap for language to be regarded as an accurate and reliable mode of communication

- that contains very little immediate repetition, but is nonetheless tightly structured, based on the capacity of words to fulfil a limited number of discrete functions in relation to one another – functions that are ultimately determined by the way we perceive and represent the world

- that is largely learnt informally, and never completely, in a process that can potentially continue all our lives – in English, people generally understand around 1 in 20 of the words that exist and regularly use only about 1 in 100

- that is used by all people functioning 'neurotypically' both as generators and receivers of linguistic messages

- that is universal but varies from culture to culture.

CHAPTER 3
Making Sense of Music

INTRODUCTION

Music has been called a language, though whether it actually is or not has been the subject of sometimes heated philosophical debate. It depends (of course) on the definition that is used. If one takes 'language' to mean a medium through which *concepts* can be symbolised and conveyed, then, for sure, music fails the test. Music cannot express the thought that 'The house on the hill has three bedrooms' or instruct someone to 'Go to the shops and buy a pint of milk'. However, it can evoke a more or less consistent emotional response in those who compose, perform and listen to it. Hence there is, broadly speaking, common ground in the sense that both language and music are human forms of communication that occur through streams of sound (heard or imagined). And in both instances, these streams are 'chunked' in cognition: in the case of language, into distinct events at different hierarchical levels (phonemes, words, phrases and sentences); while in music, the sonic continuum is heard as notes, 'motifs' (short patterns of notes such as the openings of 'Yesterday' by Lennon and McCartney, and Beethoven's Fifth Symphony), longer phrases (the first line of any national anthem, for example) and complete melodies (see Figure 3.1).

So where do the differences lie? To answer this question, let us return to the ten characteristics of language that were identified in Chapter 2 and examine their relevance to music. The way in which the ten features work together to create meaning is shown in Figure 3.2.

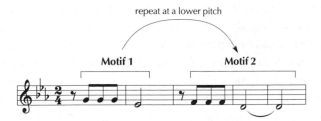

'motifs' – short, characteristic patterns of notes that are the building blocks of music

Figure 3.1 The musical 'language' of the opening
of Beethoven's Fifth Symphony

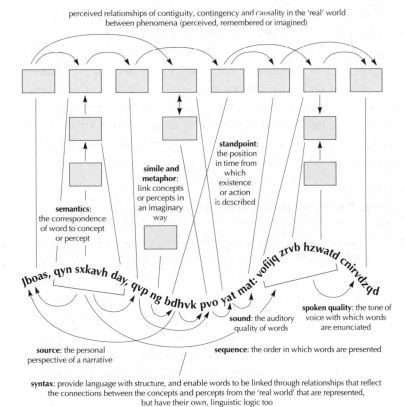

Figure 3.2 The ten elements of language
interact to create meaning

But in music, the position is rather different. Musical events (notes, chords and so on) do not usually *symbolise* other phenomena in the way that words do (though there are occasional exceptions, as we shall see). Rather, they have the capacity to *evoke* an emotional response directly, depending on their perceived attributes (such as high, low; loud, soft; coarse, mellow; major, minor) – something that is discussed further on p.67. As we saw in Chapter 2, words can also evoke emotional responses, partly in the way that they are enunciated, but largely through their powers of representation: it is not the sounds of the phonemes in the word 'cancer' that tend to produce a powerful negative response (after all, you *can sur*vive it), but the notion of serious, potentially fatal, illness.

The fact that notes are generally 'asemantic' – they do not stand for anything – means that a number of the other features of language cannot apply to music. Syntax, for instance, that gives language its structure, depends ultimately on content: as we saw in Chapter 2, what a word means determines its function. Then, in the absence of meaning, a narrative cannot have a standpoint in time (past, present or future) or be understood as stemming from a particular source (first, second or third person). And simile, metaphor and comparable figures of speech are not available. So what does this leave?

Read the following sentence aloud (approximate pronunciation will suffice to make the point! – or recordings are available online):

'Hwæt! We Gardena in geardagum, þeodcyninga, þrym gefrunon, hu ða æþelingas ellen fremedon.'

Assuming that you are not a scholar of Beowulf, you will not have the option of processing these words meaningfully as language: you can assimilate them only as a series of pure sounds, which have (a) auditory qualities and (b) occur in a particular sequence. These are the two core characteristics of music (see Figure 3.3). But with only the sound and order in which notes occur as factors, how does music make sense? How is it structured, and how does it convey meaning?

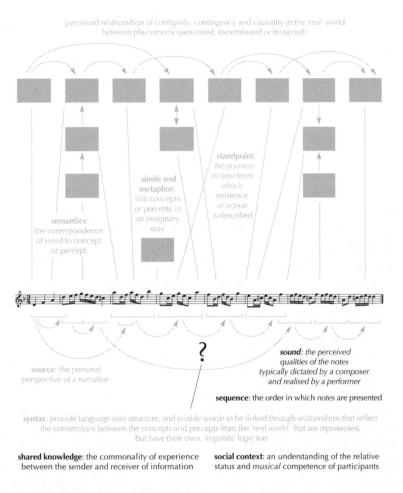

Figure 3.3 The impact of music's non-representational nature on the creation of meaning

EXPLAINING MUSIC

In the 1980s, I first started to formulate a theory that sought to answer these questions. I called it 'zygonic' theory, for reasons that will become apparent on the next page. Although originally conceived as a system through which musicologists could analyse the structure of pieces in an academic way, it has proved valuable too in trying to understand how music makes sense to all of us, and, as we shall see, is particularly good at explaining how some children with autism may process music: indeed, the theory could have been constructed with them in mind!

Zygonic theory sets out from the position that every note or chord, in the minds of those who hear it, potentially bears a tiny emotional 'charge' that can be evoked in listeners. I speculate that it is from series of such emotional flecks that the meaning of music derives. It is worth stressing that the feelings we may sense are not inherent in the sounds themselves: they are just one of the ways that we, as humans, respond to them.

Some responses are more powerful and so easier to appreciate than others. Take, for example, the hushed, sustained, spine-tingling low Cs played on double basses, contrabassoon, bass drum and organ that open the introduction to Richard Strauss's *Also Sprach Zarathustra* (popularised in Stanley Kubrick's *2001: A Space Odyssey*). Or bask in the warm, radiant beauty of the D major harmony that ushers in Bach's *Air on a G String*. Or be awe-struck by the pellucid top C of choirboy Roy Goodman's 1963 recording of Allegri's *Miserere* with the choir of King's College Cambridge.

Our reactions to these musical sounds may be particularly strong, but they are not unique. And while we can take time out (as we are doing here) to reflect on how different notes and chords affect us, such responses are typically unthinking and, research has shown, very rapid – usually occurring within a fraction of a second (see e.g. Koelsch and Friederici 2003). What is their origin? It seems that they have two main roots: (a) what psychologists have called 'expressive non-verbal vocalisations' (Juslin, Friberg and Bresin 2001/2002), and (b) 'music-specific' qualities of sound (see Ockelford 2012).

'Expressive non-verbal vocalisations' are the cues that we use to express emotions vocally in non-verbal communication and speech. They are present across cultures and first surface in 'motherese', the special vocalising that serves both as proto-speech and proto-music, which adults (particularly mothers) instinctively make to their babies (Scherer 1991). These cries of joy, fear, frustration, sadness and sheer excitement are there to communicate *feelings* between carers and infants (Malloch 1999/2000); it is believed that they are the forerunners of the emotional qualities associated with musical fragments such as those used by Strauss, Bach and Allegri that were described above. It is even possible that some of the responses we make to musical sounds originate in the womb. As our mothers listened to music, they will have reacted in different ways to different pieces, resulting in changes in certain hormone levels. Inevitably, these will have been transferred to us, babies, waiting to emerge, and so the potential connection between certain features of music and our response to them may have been established even before we were born (Welch 2005).

Whatever the mechanism through which the links between sounds and feelings develop within us, psychological research since the 1930s or so has shown that features such as *register* (how 'high' or 'low' the music is: Scherer and Oshinsky 1977; Watson 1942), *tempo* (its speed: Balkwill and Thompson 1999; Gundlach 1935; Thompson and Robitaille 1992) and *dynamic level* (louds and softs: Juslin 1997; Nielzén and Cesarec 1982) relate consistently to particular emotional states. For example, passages in a high register can feel exciting or powerful, whereas series of low notes are more likely to be perceived as serious. A fast tempo will tend to induce feelings of excitement, in contrast to slow tempi that may connote tranquility or even peace. Loud dynamic levels are held to be exciting, triumphant or to represent gaiety, while quiet sounds have been found to express fear, tenderness or grief. Conversely, as the influential American musicologist Leonard Meyer observed, 'one cannot imagine sadness being portrayed by a fast forte tune played in a high register, or a playful child being depicted by a solemnity of trombones' (Meyer 2001, p.342).

'Music-specific' qualities of sound, just like those identified above in relation to early vocalisation, have the capacity to induce consistent emotional responses, *within* and sometimes *between* cultures. For example, composers do not start with a sonic 'tabula rasa', but typically take advantage of predetermined 'frameworks' of pitch. These are modelled subconsciously merely through frequent exposure to pieces that use them, and they can be heard in the scales and arpeggios – which are nothing more than particular selections of notes – that musicians perform up and down countless times when they practise. These pitch frameworks are closely related to certain patterns of sound that occur naturally. For example, whenever a string vibrates, or the column of air in a pipe oscillates, it may seem as though only one note is present, but actually there are many different pitches occurring at the same time, which usually blend to form a single sensation: the 'tone colour' or 'timbre' of the sound. This pattern of notes is known as the *harmonic series*. You can hear this for yourself by trying out the experiment shown in Figure 3.4 on a piano (it won't work on an electronic keyboard).

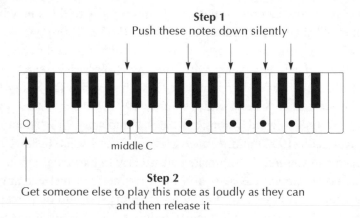

Step 1
Push these notes down silently

middle C

Step 2
Get someone else to play this note as loudly as they can
and then release it

Step 3
Listen carefully – how many notes can you hear?

Figure 3.4 Hearing the harmonics present in a musical note

The lowest note is called the 'fundamental', and when it resonates, many other notes sound too. These are known as 'harmonics'. By pressing these notes down silently, you freed their strings to oscillate, and they picked up on the harmonics that were sounding in the air, and began vibrating sympathetically.

Do the experiment once more, and this time just listen to the overall effect without trying to hear individual notes. You should become aware of a rather pleasant sounding chord (it's called a 'major' harmony). This harmony is used over and over again in virtually all the music that you hear.

Combinations of notes can be extracted in different ways from the harmonic series, and these are used in idiosyncratic permutations, with some sequences of pitches occurring more frequently than others. Each pattern, or 'mode', potentially bears distinct emotional connotations. These are learnt through habitually being associated with events or circumstances that have particular emotional tags (see e.g. Crowder 1985; Hevner 1936). Reinforcement occurs since it is key to our sense of identity that, as members of a social group, we all get the same message from what we experience; something that is bolstered by the phenomenon that psychologists call 'emotional contagion', where the feelings of one person are 'caught' by others (see e.g. Hatfield, Cacioppo and Rapson 1994).

In traditional Indian music, for example, modes are known as 'ragas', and each is typically prescribed for a particular time of day or season (Jairazbhoy 1971/1995). In the Western tradition of the last four centuries or so, the 'major mode' is typically associated with happiness (consider, for instance, Mendelssohn's *Wedding March*) and the 'minor mode' with sadness (as in Chopin's *Funeral March*, for example), perceived differences that have recently been shown to have neurological correlates – they are wired deep in our psyche.

On their own, however, separate emotional responses to a series of individual sounds or clusters, no matter how powerful, do not add up to a coherent musical message; a unified aesthetic response that evolves over time. So what is it that binds these discrete, abstract experiences (see Figure 3.3) together to form a cogent musical narrative?

As we have seen, the meaning of words resides in their capacity to point the mind to things beyond themselves – to people, places, events, activities, thoughts and feelings – and *strings* of words make sense because they evoke series of ideas that are themselves logically connected through contiguity, contingency or causation (see Figure 3.2). However, in 'pure' music (which consciously makes no reference to the outside world), there is no signified thing to which sounds refer. So how is meaning over time constructed? How do the emotional 'charges' associated with individual notes come to constitute a coherent message? The only things notes have for composers to use are their sounding qualities, so it is in these that the syntax of music – its logic – must reside.

In fact, the most important thing for most listeners (as we shall see, for some children on the autism spectrum the position is rather different) is not the 'absolute' qualities of particular notes, but *the differences between them*. Whenever we hear one note and then another, the mind cannot help comparing them, and an imaginary connection is formed between the two. It is upon such mental relationships that *all music is founded*.

To hear this in action, try singing a very simple song (say, 'Frère Jacques' – see Figure 3.5).

Figure 3.5 The first two notes of 'Frère Jacques'

Did you catch yourself comparing the two notes? In fact, you knew what the second one was only because you had a memory of how the difference between them should sound. Now do the same with the first four notes (see Figure 3.6). Each note is related to the one preceding by a particular difference in *pitch* (how high or low the note sounds).

Figure 3.6 The first four notes of 'Frère Jacques'

But there were other relationships being formulated too. The time between the beginning of one note and the onset of the next should have been the same each time, and these intervals probably matched the note-lengths, or *durations*.[1] And, if you hummed or lah-ed the notes in an unexceptional way, they were probably all of similar *loudness* and sound quality (or *timbre*) as well.

These four qualities, *pitch, loudness, timbre* and *duration*, which can all vary in the way they sound, supply the brain with all the information that it needs to understand music. *Every* note in *every* piece that has ever been performed has these four characteristics and, insofar as a listener can isolate them from those around, notes are mentally gauged in relation to their neighbours along each of these dimensions. (Other characteristics, such as 'tempo', the speed of a

---

1   The time between the start of one note and the next can of course be different from the length of the first note (imagine tapping a wood block once a second – the sound of each tap has disappeared before the next appears). However, to make the ensuing discussion easier to follow we will for now assume that the two are the same, as they are in most music.

passage, harmony and texture are all based on compounds of these four basic qualities.)

Not all of the four qualities (pitch, loudness, timbre and duration) are equally important to musical structure and meaning, however. For example, think again about your recent rendition of the opening of 'Frère Jacques'. How did you know which note to start on? You probably just chose one that felt about right (cf. p.17) (as we shall see, this may be very different for a fair proportion of children with autism). This is because your memory of 'Frère Jacques' is not stored as exact, 'absolute' values of pitch, loudness, timbre and duration but 'relative' values, which are the *differences* (or, in the case of durations, the *ratios*) between them.

In fact, you can change pitch level and speed at which you sing the piece as much as you like, but provided the relationships between notes remain the same, 'Frère Jacques' will remain 'Frère Jacques'. Admittedly, the degree of urgency with which the singer is trying to rouse him may vary!

What about loudness and timbre? These were more or less uniform originally, and singing or playing the opening of the song with different loudness and timbres will, again, have no impact on its identity. However, one can go further and *change* loudness or timbre in the course of the phrase, and although, once more, there will be an aesthetic effect, the essence of the tune will not be compromised. That is to say, the relationships *between* notes' dynamic levels and tone colours are not critical to a tune's substance.

So, to sum up, the identity of a melody (and, by extension, virtually any piece of music) is bound up in two things that remain invariant between different renditions:

(a) the perceived differences between the pitches – which may be higher, lower or the same – and

(b) the perceived ratios between durations (assuming the end of one note coincides with the beginning of the next) – which may be longer, shorter or the same.

To show this in action, hum or lah the first phrase of 'Frère Jacques' again at the same speed (and with the same loudness and timbre), but starting on a higher note.

The only thing to have changed is the absolute values of the pitches; you will instinctively adjust your voice to make the perceived differences between them the same as before. What do you hear? Is it still recognisably the 'same tune'? It should be! So what has changed? Something of the aesthetic quality, perhaps – the higher notes may give a sense of greater intensity.

Now try singing the four notes more quickly (so each has a shorter duration). Again, the identity of the opening phrase should have remained intact (maybe it just feels a bit more energised).

Higher, lower, faster or slower, 'Frère Jacques' is still recognisably and distinctively 'Frère Jacques' (see Figure 3.7).

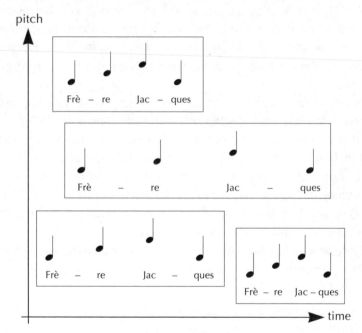

Figure 3.7 The opening of 'Frère Jacques' at different pitches and speeds

Compare this with language. People can enunciate the two words 'Frère' 'Jacques' at different levels of pitch and loudness and at a wide range of speeds without affecting the symbolic meaning. Changing the pitch contour (the pattern of ups and downs) – for example by saying 'Jacques' higher than 'Frère' – may put a different gloss on things (seeming to ask a question), but the underlying representation will remain intact. It's the *sequence* of absolute sound qualities (timbres) – vowels and consonants – that makes the words what they are and gives them their identities.

So much for the 'content' of music – absolute values of pitch, loudness, timbre and duration, and, to a greater extent, the relationships between pitches and durations. But what of structure? We can surmise that, just as language requires syntax to make sense, music must possess an equivalent structural mechanism (otherwise it would comprise nothing more than a succession of random sounds). But, as we have seen, syntax depends on words fulfilling distinct roles in relation to one another (as nouns, verbs, adjectives, and so on) – functions that arise from their symbolic meanings. These are absent in music, though. So how does musical structure work?

Let us think reflect on just what structure means in the context of language. One interpretation is to regard it as a set of *rules* or *constraints* through which one element in a linguistic system *controls* (or is perceived to control) another.

Zygonic theory applies a similar definition to music: that musical events are somehow perceived to influence or control one another, and I believe that this process works through special types of (imaginary) relationship through which one note, or a feature of that note, is heard as imitating another. That is: when the ear hears a sound in a musical context that is the same as or similar to one that it has just heard, the listener may get the impression that the second note *derives* from the first. Or, to put it another way, the first seems to *generate* the second.

Now you may, of course, object to this theory on the grounds that you have enjoyed listening to music for many years and never thought of hearing it in this way. However, I would argue that you *have*, it is just that you have been unaware of it. But, rather like acquiring the ability to see the three-dimensional nature of a 'magic eye' picture, it is relatively easy to learn to recognise the processes that I believe that your mind is going through when you make sense of music.

Let us return to 'Twinkle, Twinkle' – to the tune this time – and hear how the music works. This will be compared with the linguistic analysis that we undertook in Chapter 2.

MUSIC IN ACTION: 'TWINKLE, TWINKLE, LITTLE STAR'

> Hum the first note to yourself (at whatever pitch feels comfortable) and then stop. Now just *think about* the second note. In your imagination, what does it sound like? It should be the same as the note that you just hummed.

In fact, according to zygonic theory, your brain calculated what the second note should be by recalling the first and issuing a 'copy' instruction. That is how the opening of 'Twinkle, Twinkle' is stored in most people's memories – as a rule saying: 'whatever the first note is, imitate it to produce the second'. The second note is heard as *deriving from* the first. Or to put it another way, the first is heard as *generating* the second (see Figure 3.8).

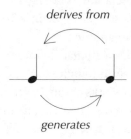

Figure 3.8 Imitation of musical sounds gives the sense of one deriving from (or, conversely, generating) the other

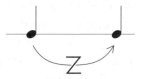

Figure 3.9 Representation of a 'zygonic' relationship, through which one note is heard as generating another through imitation

This mental connection between the two notes I call a 'zygonic relationship' (see Ockelford 2005b). 'Zygonic' comes from the Greek word 'zygon', meaning 'yoke', or a bond between two similar things. It is useful to be able to represent zygonic relationships visually, to illustrate how musical structure is created or heard, and to do that, a 'Z' is placed in the 'generates' arrow (see Figure 3.9).

It is worth stressing that zygonic relationships are *purely imaginary*. There is no *physical* connection between the notes that causes the second to be the same as the first. As we shall see, this distinction is very important: typically, our brains process pattern in music and other, non-musical patterns in sound differently. For example, we hear a regular drumbeat and a clock ticking as two distinct types of experience (even though, physically, they have a lot in common). But the contextual filter that determines how these different streams of sound are processed may not work in quite the same way for some children with autism.

The important thing to grasp for now is that all musical structure ultimately depends on relationships like the one shown in Figure 3.9. And in this case, *all* the qualities of the first note were imitated: pitch, loudness, timbre and duration.

So much for the way the music is initially *structured*. But how is musical *meaning* conveyed? Unlike the word 'twinkle' (which denotes a star emitting fluctuating amounts of light and, for adults, as we have seen, may well have connotative meanings too, perhaps bringing to mind the childhood awe of gazing up at the infinite beauty of the night-time sky), the notes actually convey rather little. You will probably have chosen to start on a pitch that is in the lower half of your normal vocal range (in subconscious anticipation of the leap that is about to come), with rather a gentle dynamic. This means that the note's capacity to evoke an affective response will be limited: if anything, it is likely to evoke a sense of emotional neutrality. In this context, the repetition that follows sounds like an introductory statement of a more extensive musical narrative that is about to unfold, rather than having any particular rhetorical significance of its own.

While exact imitation (which results in repetition) is the source of musical logic, a message, if it is to convey information and so engage the interest of fellow humans, has to be more than the same thing heard over and over again. Indeed, we are programmed to ignore most unchanging, moderate stimuli in the environment, since, ultimately, they are unlikely to be of importance for our survival. On the whole, it is loud sounds and sounds that change that we need to be worried about. (As I write this, I have to make a conscious effort to bring the humming of my computer's cooling fan into the foreground of my attention.) As the composer Arnold Schoenberg (1967) observed, repetition is not enough: music has to contain difference – variation – too. But if similarity equates to musical coherence through imitation, surely difference amounts to chaos? How can difference be incorporated into a musical narrative in a way that makes sense? How does the ear connect one note to another that is different?

Hum the first two notes of the tune 'Twinkle, Twinkle' and *think about* the third (Figure 3.10). As you thought about the next note, did you feel a slight physical rise in tension in your throat as your vocal cords prepared to sing at the higher pitch? You may have sensed an accompanying elevation – albeit a very small one – in emotional arousal too.

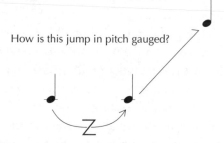

How is this jump in pitch gauged?

Figure 3.10 The first three notes of 'Twinkle, Twinkle, Little Star'

The anonymous composer of the tune to 'Twinkle, Twinkle' intuitively knew one way of squaring this circle. (Actually, from a very early age, almost all of us can spontaneously make up little tunes that use a range of different notes, which nonetheless make musical sense.) Let us return to our musical mind experiment to see how he or she did it.

Just as individual notes have the capacity to evoke responses, so do the relationships that we perceive between them, and a rise in pitch is likely to evoke a positive increase in arousal, a reaction that goes right back to those early mother–baby interactions. (For example, think of a baby's ascending 'whoop', and the effect it has on you.) But why was the jump up to Note 3 of that particular size? (Indeed, how did you know how big to make it?) Would different sized leaps ('intervals' in musical parlance) have done just as well?

It turns out that the interval in question derives from the harmonic series (it is the difference between harmonics one and two – see Figure 3.4). And when the Western-enculturated musical ear hears that interval, it automatically brings to mind one of the imaginary frameworks of pitches (the 'modes' mentioned above), also with close relationships to the harmonic series, on which the notes of melodies are invariably hung. Early exposure to countless hundreds of pieces of music heard time and again is enough to prime one of the brain's auditory pattern detectors, so that whenever fragments of melody are heard, the *whole framework* on which it is based is subconsciously activated.

We can think of these frameworks as imaginary ladders in sound, where the notes are the rungs on which the ear can climb up or down. Moreover, the rungs are spaced unevenly, so that your brain usually knows, at any point in a piece of music, where you are on the ladder.

To hear the first six rungs of the 'major' mode (Figure 3.11), which 'Twinkle, Twinkle' and, indeed, most other Western music uses, sing the beginning of the theme tune to *EastEnders* to yourself. Can you hear which is the smaller step? It's between the third and fourth notes. If you're not sure, try playing it on the keyboard or piano. The smaller step comes between the two white notes that are adjacent.

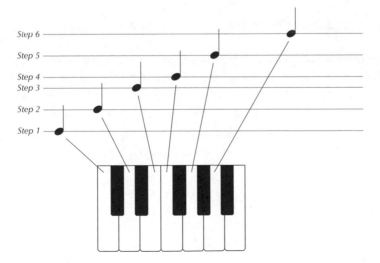

Figure 3.11 The framework outlined by the first six pitches of the 'major' mode

As you hummed the first two notes of 'Twinkle, Twinkle', your mind's ear was setting up the pitch framework ready for you to use for the rest of the tune; and, although you probably didn't know you knew it, your brain had remembered the instruction 'go to Step 5 on the ladder' in order to produce the third note (Figure 3.12).

To summarise: we can assume that the composer of 'Twinkle, Twinkle' chose the leap between Steps 1 and 5 because of the sense of positive arousal that it evokes, intuitively affirming the harmonic series, and giving a feeling of movement, of progression – of setting off on a musical journey. (Stopping the song after Note 3, even if 'Twinkle, Twinkle' were not familiar, would give a distinct sense of more to come.)

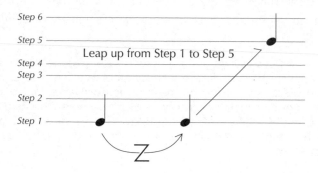

Figure 3.12 The initial melodic leap in 'Twinkle, Twinkle'

Let us now consider from the listener's perspective how Note 3 is likely to be heard as being tied in to the musical narrative. This is achieved by a reiteration of the *pattern* that linked Notes 1 and 2. That is, the sense of derivation through imitation is itself copied. This involves a 'second-order' relationship – equivalent to that in language seen in Figure 2.3 in relation to analogy (see Figure 3.13).

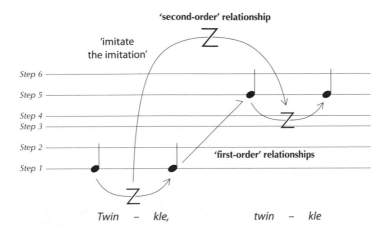

Figure 3.13 Copying the pattern of imitation
ensures musical coherence

As it happens, this repetition of repetition is reinforced in the words, as 'twinkle' is repeated. We have already discussed the significance of the verbal restatement, and one interpretation is that the two 'twinkles' themselves function in an imitative way – rather like a visual onomatopoeia that is suggestive of the *ongoing* nature of the star's scintillations. As we have seen, the tune incorporates both repetition and change in the same gesture (as only music can). Hence the *blended* meaning of the words and music together suggest that, while the twinkling of the star is unchanging, the way we view it is nonetheless shortly to evolve. Since words and music were written separately, this blended meaning was not part of original thinking of either the composer or author. The fact that this new, compound meaning came about by chance is irrelevant to the listener's experience, however.

So far, we have discussed how content and structure pertaining to pitch combine to create meaning in the first four notes of 'Twinkle, Twinkle' – but what about the other qualities of sound? All four durations are equal, and this means that a steady beat is set up in the minds of listeners, enabling them to predict the *when* of the music, which greatly assists their perception and understanding of the *what*. This happens through further zygonic relationships, functioning as follows (see Figure 3.14).

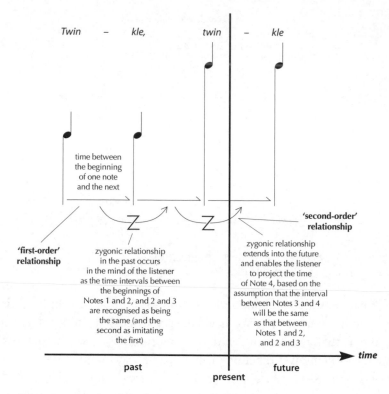

Figure 3.14 A regular beat in music is perceived and predicted through second-order zygonic relationships

Hence, 'Twinkle, Twinkle' appears both *to create* in the mind of those who hear it (and who are familiar with Western mainstream music) and subsequently *to be governed by* an imaginary framework in the domains of pitch and time. As we have seen, in terms of pitch, listeners know how to 'locate' what they hear on the framework since not all steps are equal. With respect to time, things necessarily function rather differently, since, as we learn from an early age, tempus fugit, and one can never return to a moment that has past. However, that doesn't mean that all the points (or 'beats' in musicians' parlance) on the musical framework of time are equally important. As one listens to a piece – or, even more noticeably, dances to it – there are usually distinct points of reference every two, three or four beats (that musicians call 'downbeats') that have a greater emphasis than their neighbours. Whether it's a cha-cha, a samba, rock, reggae or hip-hop, dancers instinctively know when to kick-off and then are able to synchronise their more or less regular patterns of movement with the music.

One way of modelling this phenomenon is to think of the musical framework of time as wrapped around a rotating cylinder (see Figure 3.15). A regular point of reference is provided by an added emphasis being applied (physically or perceptually or both) to one or more of the beats.

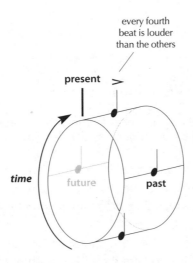

Figure 3.15 The framework of time in music can be likened to a rotating cylinder

Unfurling this imaginary cylinder yields a notional 'two-dimensional' framework (Figure 3.16), upon which notes can be positioned in pitch and time, such that every location is at once *distinct* yet *replicable*. Frameworks with this dual characteristic are fundamental to music, since, as we have seen, pieces rely on repetition for structure and, ultimately, meaning. From a cognitive perspective, the music psychologist John Sloboda (1985) contends that such frameworks are a *necessary* feature of music, since they enable musical understanding to get off the ground. As we would expect, then, frameworks are a universal feature of all styles and genres.

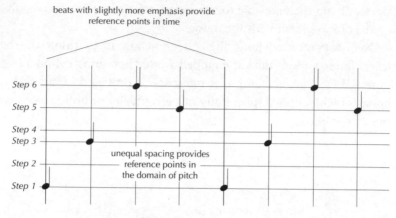

Figure 3.16 Example of an imaginary framework of pitch and time that forms the background structure of music

As we shall see, children typically grasp pitch-time frameworks pertinent to their culture from the age of four or so, enabling them to sing short songs with which they are familiar from beginning to end, in time and in tune (see Chapter 4).

In Chapter 2, we noted that actors and speechmakers have a certain flexibility in the way they declaim their lines, with potential variation in pitch, loudness, timbre or duration clarifying, enhancing or even transforming the core semantic meaning of what they are saying. The conventions through which language is modified to make it sound expressive are something that most people grasp intuitively, through hearing and imitating others speak in the context of shared thoughts and emotions. However, the mental processing involved is highly complex, as the difficulty of making even very simple synthesised speech messages sound 'natural' shows: merely having a computer produce successive syllables precisely is not enough for it to emulate human communication persuasively.

Similarly, gauging the affective content of speech can represent a particular challenge for those on the autism spectrum – something, I suspect, that is less due to problems in processing the auditory content of what is heard than a lack of understanding of the underlying affect. We can surmise that what are perceived to be unimportant features of a message (the expressive nuances) come, over time, to have diminished perceptual salience: hence it seems that something of a vicious circle is established whereby, in young autistic children, early signs of emotional intent in language are missed and then (inevitably) not reinforced in subsequent interactions; accordingly, the foundations of future insights into the feelings of others, which are conveyed in the way that people speak, consistently fail to be laid. This may explain why the speech of some young people with autism is held to be inexpressive, and why some prefer dealing with the written word rather than language in auditory form, since the representation of words as visual signs strips out the affective connotations that most speakers unthinkingly incorporate, and provides the reader only with the raw semantic gist.

Even in the absence of literacy, though, we all have the capacity (and, unlike autistic children, the choice) to slough away the non-verbal affective components of speech, leaving the denotative core. For example, in a drama class, one could ask a student to listen to the following sentence declaimed tragically 'I'm leaving now, and I'll never be back again!' and restate it (for example) ecstatically.

Surprisingly, perhaps, the position is similar with music. Just as the printed word on the page conveys only the skeleton of a particular verbal message, so music notation provides only the bare bones of what performers are intended to do: pieces would sound oddly mechanical, and wholly unmusical, if players and singers were to reproduce literally, and only, what was written – if they were to conform strictly to the framework of pitch and time implied in the score. For music to 'live' requires that the framework be flexed in at least one dimension (time). However, marks of expression notwithstanding, most subtleties of performance are not captured in print – and they do not need to be: as music psychologists such as Eric Clarke (1999) have shown, musicians intuitively vary the intervals between the onsets of notes (see Figure 3.14) to signal the ends of phrases and to mark events that are held to be particularly important, by delaying their arrival ('rubato'). Singers, and players who are able to vary pitch, including violinists, introduce features such as 'vibrato' (whereby notes wobble up and down) to add intensity to sounds and make the music come alive. In addition, levels of loudness and even timbre are varied to reinforce the changes that are made in the domains of pitch and time and to contribute additional nuances to the expressive mix.

Just as one experienced in a given language can strip away the affective elements of speech and access the nub of what is said, so the knowledgeable musical ear (with or without the benefit of notation) can hear beyond the expressive additions of a particular performer to the melodic, harmonic and rhythmic essence that lies beneath. Indeed, one could argue that, without an awareness of the musical 'core', one could not appreciate the expressive deviations of performance; for example, a note that forms the climax of a phrase to which a singer gives prominence by delaying its arrival can be heard as being 'late' only against an imaginary temporal framework that is 'in time'. Having rediscovered the invariant nucleus of a piece of music, players can interpret the music afresh. In so doing, they are likely to 'borrow' some of the interpretative gestures of previous performances and, if they are to be anything other than pastiche, will introduce new ideas too.

As Figure 3.17 shows, the borrowing can be understood as imitation (and therefore deemed to function through zygonic relationships). And, just as with verbal language, of all the features of music, it is these expressive elements that appear to be most likely to elude listeners (and therefore performers) with autism. One can speculate whether this stems from a failure to pick up on the emotional content of the early pre-verbal vocalisations of their caregivers. Whatever the cause, though, as we shall see, it does not preclude them subsequently coming to appreciate expressivity in musical performance and being able to emulate it.

For now, though, let us return to our analysis of 'Twinkle, Twinkle'. As you hummed or lah-ed the first four notes, tiny expressive inflections notwithstanding, it is likely that loudness and timbre would have stayed much the same too, implying that an intuitive imitation of these sound qualities took place. Generally speaking, though, similarity of this kind tends to go by unnoticed (though the position may be somewhat different for children with autism, as we shall see). It is as though these characteristics, which exist in the 'background' of most Western music, form the 'carrier wave' of the primary message, which is conveyed in the domains of pitch and time.

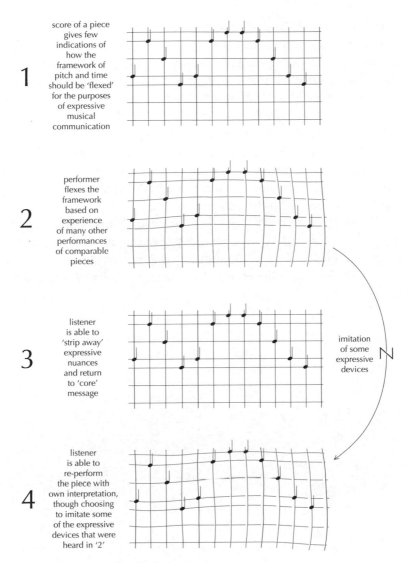

Figure 3.17 The process of hearing a performance
and creating a new interpretation

The reason for this seems to be to prevent cognitive overload: trying to attend to and calculate the significance of changes happening in four auditory dimensions at once appears to be just too much for the ('neurotypical') brain to manage. However, some composers in the middle of the twentieth century tried to do this in what was called 'integral serial' music, in which complex forms of control extended to every aspect of the musical texture at the same time. (An example is Olivier Messiaen's *Mode de valeurs et d'intensités*.) Paradoxically, listening to music composed in this way often gives the impression of randomness, since the brain apparently gives up trying find patterns it can comprehend, and the music flows by as a series of seemingly unrelated sounds. Words and music *can* work together though, without overwhelming perception and cognition. In fact, singing and chanting are among the most natural and universal of human activities. Perhaps it is because, as we are discovering, the syntax of language and the structure of music work in different ways so that one does not interfere with the other.

Turning now to notes 5 and 6 of 'Twinkle, Twinkle': these extend the principle set out by notes 3 and 4, moving another step up the imaginary pitch ladder, while utilising the 'repeat the note' pattern once again. So both coherence and change are simultaneously assured (Figure 3.18).

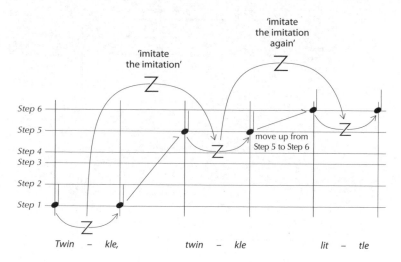

Figure 3.18 Imitation of imitation means that Notes 5 and 6 evolve coherently from those that precede in 'Twinkle, Twinkle'

Again, there is consistency of duration, and loudness and timbre are likely to remain more or less constant too, though there is a distinct sense of a two beat pattern in which the first of each pair of notes is emphasised slightly at the expense of the second.

In terms of the *meaning* of the musical narrative, at this point, the ascent in pitch raises the tension a fraction more. Partly this is due to the increased 'height' of the note, and partly because it occupies a rung on the imaginary pitch ladder that is acoustically further away from the one that is perceived to be the musical 'home' of the piece. To understand what this means, it is important to appreciate that, in almost all music, some rungs in the pitch ladder feel more 'settled' than others. How settled a particular pitch sounds depends on a number of factors, including how the rung in question relates to the harmonic series (in very broad terms, lower harmonics sound more settled than higher ones) and how it has been used in the past.

Different composers have availed themselves of the pitch ladder in different ways. In Western music of the last four centuries or so, pieces have usually ended on Step 1, and so, to modern listeners' ears, this makes the most satisfactory conclusion to a piece (rather like the word 'Amen' in Jewish, Christian and some Islamic prayers). Other conventions (again rooted in the harmonic series) evolved over the centuries too. Among the most important of these is a movement to Step 5, the 'next-best-thing-to-home', which often offers the main staging post en route to the final goal.

'Twinkle, Twinkle' accords with this convention: as we have heard, it starts on the 'home pitch' (Step 1) before moving up to Step 5. In our thinking, we left the tune at Step 6, which feels moderately unsettled (it is sixth in the harmonic series). With the end of the first line of words approaching ('star'), the music needs a point of temporary repose (rather than a sense of complete closure) and, as we shall see, Step 5 has the necessary qualities.

> To hear this in action, sing the first six notes ('Twinkle, twinkle, little...') and *imagine* the seventh.
> Could you feel the sense of physical and emotional relaxation as you prepared to sing 'star'?

Here, the rhythm is necessarily different too, since 'star' has only one syllable. This means that the repetition that was responsible for the music's logic up to this point is not an option. However, coherence is assured since the new appearance of Step 5 echoes those that occurred earlier. And the longer note at this point reinforces the intuitive pause in the words (Figure 3.19).

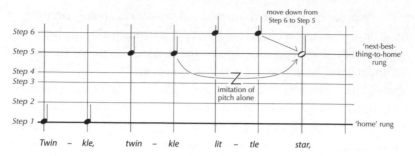

Figure 3.19 Note 7 gives a feeling of temporary repose

In summary, the first line of the music of 'Twinkle, Twinkle' takes the listener on a miniature musical journey: the changes in sound give the illusion of movement up and down an imaginary ladder of pitch, and lead to a moment of provisional stasis. This is engendered through familiarity with many other pieces of music that use the same pitch scheme in idiosyncratic ways, and is ultimately rooted in the harmonic series. The abstract narrative in sound is coherent because we hear individual notes as deriving from one another through imitation, a structural feature that is itself imitated.

Notice that although there are seven different musical events, there are only four different pitches and two different note-lengths. This high degree of 'redundancy' (to borrow a term from information theory: see e.g. Cohen 1962) is a consequence of musical events having to refer to themselves to make sense. As we have seen, the position with words, however, is very different: because their meaning resides in things beyond themselves, the amount of repetition they engender – even in poems, such as 'Twinkle, Twinkle, Little Star', where reiteration is used to add another, rhetorical layer of meaning – is generally much less. This is one reason why, as we shall see, music is easier for children to remember (and reproduce) than words, and why it can be of such assistance in early language development – particularly for children with autism. I think of the shape of the melody (its 'contour') rather like a clothesline: the notes are pegs, and the words 'clip on' to these in the mind.

In music, the ends of lines are of particular interest and importance, since they are potential turning points in the abstract narrative in sound, where melodies could head off in a number of different directions, according to the shape of the piece that the composer wishes to create. For example, should we have the same thing again, or something different? If so, how different should it be? If it is *very* different, how will the music be made to sound coherent? Children typically (and intuitively) start to experiment with these notions of connectivity when they are about three years old: without thinking, they combine snatches of this tune and that in original combinations, as though it were the most natural thing in the world to create new, 'potpourri' songs (see Figure 3.20; see also Hargreaves 1986).

Ma – ry,   Ma – ry,   quite   con – tra – ry,   Couldn't put Hump-ty to – ge–ther a – gain.

Figure 3.20 Example of 'potpourri' song

While these may come across to adults as the charming consequences of an as yet immature musicality, the capacity of one phrase to join logically with another is in fact fundamental to the process of composition, and a vital element in our understanding of how musical structure works and how it is processed cognitively. And because tunes like 'Twinkle, Twinkle' are so familiar – their design so firmly fixed in our minds – it can be hard to imagine that, following the first phrase, there are actually many different directions the melody could take that would be perfectly satisfactory in musical terms.

To convince yourself that things don't need to be the way that you are accustomed to hearing them, try another experiment.

Hum the first line of 'Twinkle, Twinkle' followed immediately by the last line of 'Frère Jacques' (the words to which would have been 'Din, dan, don; din, dan, don').

How does it sound?

A little disconcerting, perhaps.

Now try something similar by humming the first line of 'Twinkle, Twinkle' followed by the last line of 'Mary, Mary, Quite Contrary' (whose words would have been 'And pretty maids all in a row').

How does this new combination strike you?

More or less convincing than the 'Frère Jacques' ending?

To my ear, Mary pips Jacques to the post, though even she is still some way behind the original in the race to be more aesthetically satisfying.

Why should this be? All three versions take us back to the repose of Step 1, though the ways in which they do it are different. Let us examine the routes and ascertain what is happening in each case.

First, consider Jacques's trajectory: here the music drops immediately back to Step 1, then down to a *lower version* of Step 5.

How can there be a 'lower version' of a scale-step?

Because, although there are only seven steps in the major mode, these repeat at higher and lower pitches – rather like a series of staircases in a tall building, where Step 3, Staircase 1 has certain equivalence to Step 3, Staircase 2, for example. To see (and hear) this in action musically, look at a keyboard. Can you see how the pattern of keys repeats every seven white notes? Play some notes that occupy the same step on different 'staircases' ('octaves' in musical terminology). Can you hear their special auditory affinity? Again, this is due to the way that our ears process the harmonic series (see Figure 3.21).

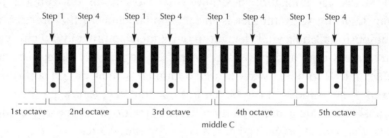

Figure 3.21 Equivalent scale-steps can exist at different 'octaves'

To return to Jacques's last line: from lower Step 5, he moves back to Step 1; then the 1, 5, 1 pattern is immediately repeated (Figure 3.22).

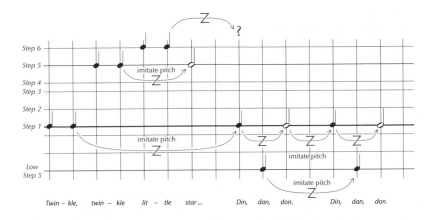

Figure 3.22 A musical chimera comprising the first line of
'Twinkle, Twinkle' and the last line of 'Frère Jacques'

So Jacques's version fulfils the urge of the music to return 'home' – to
Step 1 – and the need for musical elements to be derived through
imitation of at least one other in order to make sense is fulfilled.
Hence one cannot object to the continuation that Jacques offers on
logical grounds. However, ending with 'Twinkle, Twinkle' with 'Din,
dan, don' does leave Step 6 from the first line 'hanging in the air'.
While the other pitch steps appear on three or four separate occasions
(even ignoring their immediate repetitions), Step 6 does not.

> Hum the 'Twinkle–Jacques' combination through again. Can you
> hear how Step 6 is introduced and then abandoned?

Mary, on the other hand (her contrary reputation notwithstanding), is
metaphorically more considerate of all three opening pitches.

> Hum the 'Twinkle–Mary' aggregation. Can you hear what is going
> on? Mary's version goes from Step 4 ('And'), down to Step 3
> ('pretty maids'), then Step 2 ('all in a') and finally Step 1 ('row').

So, in terms of movement *between* steps, Mary takes over from where
Twinkle left off (with a descent from Step 6 to Step 5).

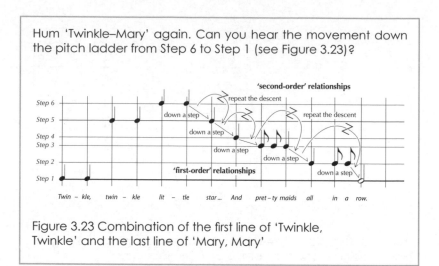

Figure 3.23 Combination of the first line of 'Twinkle, Twinkle' and the last line of 'Mary, Mary'

This illustrates another form of perceived derivation that occurs in music: through imitation of the *differences between notes*. Repetition of this kind – reiteration of the way that notes are related to each other rather than the way they sound individually – is a fundamental principle of all musical construction. It is the reason that tunes can be performed and heard starting on different pitches, yet still considered to be the 'same thing' (see Figure 3.7). As most 'neurotypical' people don't have a memory for how particular pitches sound, this relative (rather than absolute) way of hearing is a prerequisite of music perception. And, as we shall see, musical relativity remains important even for those with 'absolute pitch' (AP), including, as we shall see, around 1 in 20 people with autism, for whom each pitch sounds distinct, although their perception of music has an added dimension.

Although the logic of Mary's ending to Twinkle in the domain of pitch is impeccable, *rhythmically*, her version leaves something to be desired.

There is little sense that the second is derived from the first. However, in the original version of 'Twinkle, Twinkle', the situation is quite different: here, the second line is an exact rhythmic copy of the opening seven notes. Hence two different kinds of musical logic – repeated steps of pitch and repeated note lengths – work together across and between the two phrases to create a narrative that is both coherent and aesthetically satisfying (Figure 3.24).

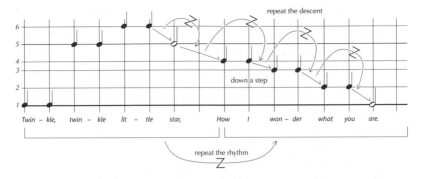

Figure 3.24 The first two phrases of 'Twinkle, Twinkle' create
a self-contained musical narrative, with overlapping
patterns of imitation of pitch and rhythm

We have now arrived at the end of the first section of 'Twinkle, Twinkle'. It is a self-contained musical miniature that has all the elements to form an aesthetically complete narrative in sound: there is sufficient variation in pitch to give a sense of setting out from a particular point, moving away from it and returning, while, at the same time, every note is coherently related to at least one other through imitation. This repetition of one form or another locks the diversity together, giving the fourteen separate notes – discrete auditory events with no concrete causal links – a powerful sense of perceptual unity.

However, as we know, this is not the end of the musical journey. The music starts up again in what listeners familiar with the music will recognise as the 'middle section'. Aesthetically this demands to be something different, yet also belong to the same whole. Let us remind ourselves how the text, which has reached the same point in its structure, achieves this need for variety within unity. The first two lines identify a star as the object of the poem, describe it briefly, and speak of the subject's contemplation of it. The third and fourth lines proceed with the same topic, also continuing the first person perspective. Hence they cohere with the first and second lines. However, they move on to cast the subject's perception of the star in a new light, through comparing it with a diamond, a simile rich in connotations: here is something that not only glistens, but also is prized – even awe-inspiring.

What does the music do to achieve a comparable aesthetic end? How does the composer indicate to the listener that what he or she is listening to belongs to the same narrative while telling a different part of the story? Is it possible for the second section of the music to 'comment' on what went before in the same way that the words do, throwing new light on what was said before?

Although, as well shall see, a form of metaphor is possible in music through external imitation ('musical onomatopoeia', as found, for example, in the cuckoo calls in Beethoven's 'Pastoral' Symphony), this is not a technique used in 'Twinkle, Twinkle'. Hence, the only method available to the composer to link ideas is through imitation that functions *within* the music.

We have already observed how repetition of the differences between successive notes can underpin logical change (the regular pattern of descending scale-steps that links the first two lines). Now we will see how the same principle be used to connect more substantial musical ideas, whereby one is perceived to be a transformation of another.

'Twinkle, Twinkle' achieves this in a way that is at once straightforward yet subtle. With the word 'up', the tune returns to Step 5, the goal of the first line, thereby taking the listener to a place that is at once familiar and yet indicative of more to come. What will happen this time? As the end of the second line provided a sense of completion, the ear demands something else, and this is achieved by replicating the whole of the previous line of music, but taken up one pitch step (Figure 3.25).

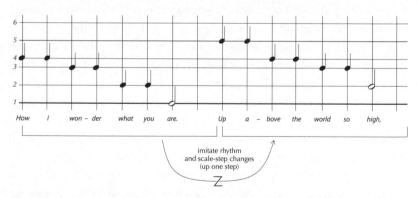

Figure 3.25 Lines 3 and 4 of 'Twinkle, Twinkle'

This works since, while the notes themselves are different, the relationships between them are the same, following the pattern 'repeat the note, move down a step; repeat the note, move down a step'. Aesthetically, the effect is also similar in some respects, yet with a fundamental difference, since the music ends not on Step 1 but on Step 2. This means that the line ends with the feeling of being close to home, but not there yet.

However, our expectations are to be frustrated, since the fourth line ('Like a diamond in the sky') begins not with Step 1, but by jumping back to Step 5, and then doing what music does best – repeating what has gone before! The notes of the fourth line are identical to those of the third, but in terms of *meaning*, listeners may interpret this repetition in different ways. For example, I usually hear the fourth line as an affirmation of the third in musical terms, as though the performer were declaring: 'Did I mean what I just said? Yes I did – and I'll say it again!' I find I can emphasise this way of understanding the music by singing the fourth line slightly louder than the third, rather as people sometimes speak more loudly to underline a point whose significance you suspect may have been missed the first time round (pity foreigners, deaf people, and young autistic children). But I can also hear the fourth line of 'Twinkle, Twinkle' as an *echo* of the third, particularly if I sing the repeat more quietly than the original. Here, it is as though one is *reflecting* on the musical meaning of the third line: 'Did I mean what I just said? I *think* so. Let me listen carefully one more time' (see Figure 3.26).

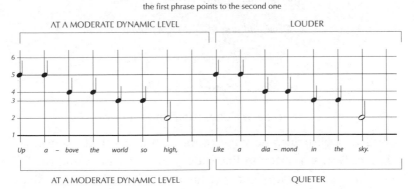

Figure 3.26 The aesthestic consequence of performing lines 3 and 4 of 'Twinkle, Twinkle' with different dynamics

Whichever interpretation one adopts will spill over into one's understanding of the text: Interpretation 1 stressing the diamond-like nature of the star, Interpretation 2 putting more weight on its position above the world. Either way of reading the connection is reinforced by the repetition that occurs at the end of the lines in the form of 'sky' rhyming with 'high'. Because the two series of words are in any case linked semantically, this correspondence in sound is not necessary to ensure coherence: contrary to the position in music, where repetition is essential for things to make sense, in poetry it is an optional extra.

By the end of the fourth line ('Like a diamond in the sky'), with its repeated move down to Step 2, the urge for musical closure is stronger than ever, and what follows is one of those magical moments, in the form of a double meaning, which can only occur in music. The closest that language comes to it is in a figure of speech called 'anadiplosis', where the word or words used at the end of a phrase (or clause or sentence) are used to start the next.

Here is an example of anadiplosis in the text of a song I wrote for children with autism and learning difficulties, where the repetition was intended to facilitate learning (by addressing the problem of memory normally breaking down *between* phrases rather than within them) – see Figure 5.19 (p.191):

Music: time to *sing and play.*

Sing and play along, *come and join us.*

Come and join us in the circle now.

In the circle, now it's *music time.*

Music: time to *sing and play.*

Sing and play along, come and join us.

Consider, in particular, how the connection between the fourth and fifth lines works. The fourth line ends with 'music time' and the fifth line (which is a repeat of the first line) uses the same words 'Music: time', but with a subtly different meaning, which is reinforced by a change in punctuation. In music, however, the same effect can be achieved *without repeating the note or notes concerned,* since sounds can perform more than one function – have more than one meaning – at the same time (see Figure 3.27).

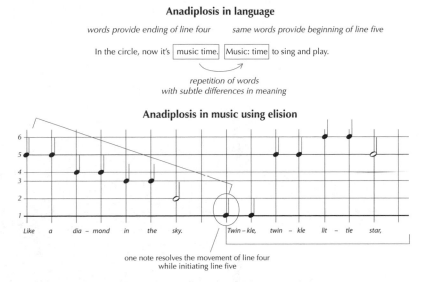

Figure 3.27 A single note can fulfil two different functions

And so 'Twinkle, Twinkle' comes to an end as it began, with a repetition of the first two lines. The corresponding text is repeated too (we have already noted this came about through an adaptation to the original poem so that it would fit the structure of the music). The coherence of the music – the sense of derivation through imitation – is clearly audible. But what narrative meaning can possibly be engendered through repeating half the material of the song? What new information can be added by saying so much of the same thing again?

The metaphor of a journey, which starts from home, moves away and then returns, which was invoked to explain the sense of the first two lines (with their movement from Step 1 to Step 5 and back again) seems appropriate again, though here it is writ on a larger scale. It is as though the first two lines ('Twinkle, twinkle, little star, How I wonder what you are') represent 'home' (Step 1) at a deeper structural level, while the second two lines ('Up above the world so high, Like a diamond in the sky') personify 'being away' (Step 5), and the last two lines (a repeat of 'Twinkle, twinkle') depict 'home' again (Step 1). Hence the design of the song as a whole can be heard as an extension of the narrative set out in the opening lines. But as the action takes place over a longer period of time, the sense of return is stronger, and the final descent to Step 1 feels more complete (see Figure 3.28).

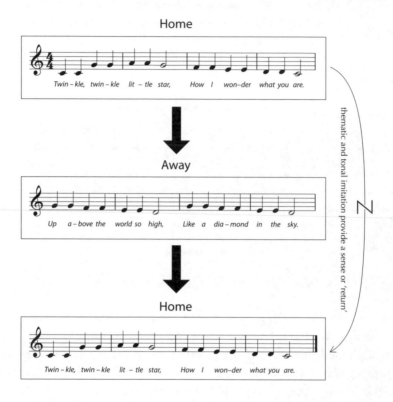

Figure 3.28 The overall structure of 'Twinkle, Twinkle', as a narrative in sound, is determined by thematic and tonal imitation

So, within a short and unremarkable children's song, then, lies an intricate and enduring musical message – enduring because it is at once so simple and yet so subtle. Although most music is far more complex than this, the underlying principles are essentially the same. What a stroke of human genius – at some stage in the prehistoric past – to realise that coherent narratives in sound could be formed through imitation. Why? Perhaps it occurred as an initially unintended (and almost certainly unrecognised) consequence of the wider importance of similarity processing in cognition. As the American musicologist Eugene Narmour once said:

One concludes that humans are similarity automatons regardless of domain, level, or operation. Such cognitive dependence of so much on so little stems directly from evolution, where the ubiquitous complexity found in life is comprehensible only because the high-level abstract rules governing our unconscious processing are so very simple – and for that reason so very powerful. (Narmour 2000, p.395)

We know from our discussion in Chapter 1 that, for many people with autism, similarity and sameness, in the form of predictability and a love of routine, are particularly important. It is as though music, with its reliance on repetition, could have been especially devised for those on the autism spectrum! But what about the subtleties of meaning described above and the metaphorical emotional journey that even a simple tune can delineate in the minds of listeners?

At one level, music is pure pattern in sound, and it can be understood and appreciated just as this and nothing more. As far as children with autism are concerned, it is my belief that this potential for functioning perfectly satisfactorily on different levels constitutes an important difference between music and language. With language, as one moves beyond simple two- or three-word constructions, as we have seen, things rapidly become complex and the extraction of meaning exponentially more difficult. For example, there is no easy way of interpreting what is expressed in this sentence unless one grasps the symbolic meaning of each of the words, as well as the plethora of relationships that exists between them, and the wider context in which the concepts are couched. There is no 'half-way house'; language tends to be an 'all or nothing' experience; half-understood messages are unsatisfactory and potentially dangerous. With music, the position is very different, however. Here, it *is* possible to understand on different levels the series of sounds that are presented. The patterns of similarity and difference formed by 'Twinkle, Twinkle' can be regarded fascinating in their own right, and one does not need to understand the metaphor of movement, or the notion of rising tension and repose to have a perfectly satisfactory musical experience.

As we saw in relation to the first line of 'Twinkle, Twinkle', music is easy on the brain, thanks to the amount of repetition that it incorporates (the whole piece comprises 42 different notes but only six different pitches and two different durations). These ratios mean that pattern is both *inevitable* and *ubiquitous*. The structures described above are merely the ones that I hear when I listen to 'Twinkle, Twinkle', and reflect my experiences as a music theorist with a particular take on how music works. However, there are plenty of alternative interpretations that are equally valid, and other musicians approaching the piece with contrasting analytical mind-sets may hear different forms of structure (and, therefore, meaning). The ubiquity of patterning in music also means that the gist of it can be understood even if the message is heard incompletely or with errors (for example, through a child's poor attention to or a carer's imperfect rendition of a nursery rhyme). In summary, music may lack language's capacity for imparting information with a high level of precision, but a trade-off is that it is a more 'forgiving' form of communication, tolerant of higher levels of 'noise' in the system. The chances of a message getting through – meaningful at some level – are much higher with notes than with words: food for thought for those working with children and young people on the autism spectrum for some of whom language can be so problematic.

MUSICAL MEANING THROUGH ASSOCIATION

While zygonic theory maintains that the main form of musical meaning is stimulated by the fabric of music itself – abstract patterns of sound – it is important to acknowledge that there is another type of meaning too, and this may be as important for people on the autism spectrum as it is for the 'neurotypical' population. This form of meaning often has little or nothing to do with the intrinsic properties of a piece, though is frequently what people are referring to when they talk about their emotional response to music. It is called *meaning by association*.

Maybe because music is both non-representational yet has the capacity to evoke an emotional response, it seems particularly prone to 'catching' the emotions that are stimulated in listeners by other features of the environment in which it is heard. This leads to 'pure' musical meaning being overlaid (or even confounded) by the vicissitudes of personal experience: in particular, through the association of certain pieces with key events in our lives.

For example, after she was widowed, my mother would experience terrible emotional anguish upon hearing the Hornpipe from Handel's

Water Music, since it was the music to which she and my father had elatedly walked down the aisle following their marriage some thirty years earlier. Yet the piece, particularly the opening, could hardly be more cheerful: that, of course, is why it was originally chosen as a wedding march! And had I asked my mother, she would doubtless have acknowledged that the music was intrinsically joyous in tone (she knew that others still found it so); it was *she* who had changed. The musical code had not altered, nor her ability to interpret it. What had happened was that the effect of this particular musical narrative had become overwhelmed by personal circumstance.

Similarly, think once more of 'Twinkle, Twinkle', which normally has broadly happy associations of childhood. However, I once worked with a blind, autistic boy for whom even the first three or four notes of the song played on the piano were overwhelmingly distressing. This was apparently because of a traumatic early experience that had occurred while a musical box played the tune.

On a lighter note, the jazzer and music psychologist John Booth Davies (1978) gives the following wry account of what he terms the 'DTPOT' phenomenon ('Darling, they're playing our tune').

> The lady from whose mouth this apocryphal saying is supposed to have emanated has acquired a specific emotional response to a specific tune simply because she heard it at a time when some other pleasurable business was taking place, at some time in the past.... Even the most unmusical people usually have an associative response of this type to at least one or two tunes. (A man might therefore justifiably feel some alarm if his unmusical wife suddenly develops an apparently spontaneous liking for a new tune.) (Davies 1978, p.69)

MUSIC AS SYMBOL

Although, as we have seen, a fundamental difference between language and music is that the former largely functions symbolically (with its primary meaning arising from the capacity of words to point to things beyond themselves and secondary meanings accruing to sounding qualities such as rhyme, assonance and metre) while music's meaning stems largely from the capacity of individual sounds and the relationships that are perceived between them to evoke emotional responses in their own right, with additional meanings deriving from connections to events in the 'real world'. The 'meanings through association' described above are examples of this.

However, other, more down-to-earth, connections are possible too. Consider, for instance, the power of even a short snatch of a familiar theme tune to bring to mind a television or radio series, and the capacity of clock chimes to given precise information about the time. As we shall see, this notion can be extended to enhance communication with children on the autism spectrum.

MUSIC: A DEFINITION

We are now in a position to define music. Zygonic theory proposes the following:

1. The essence of music is that one sound or group of sounds should be heard as deriving as a whole or in part from another or others through imitation.

2. Hence music is a *purely cognitive phenomenon* (existing only in the mind), and while there may (but need not) be physical correlates of our internal audition, these do not constitute 'music'.

3. A sense of derivation through imitation enables us to hear a series of discrete sonic events as a coherent stream of abstract sounds, as 'music': and just as each event has the capacity to induce an emotional reaction, so the contingencies we hear in a series of musical sounds can evoke an emotional narrative that unfolds in time. (This is distinct from musical meanings that derive through association.)

4. Almost without exception, it appears that mature, 'neurotypical' humans have the capacity to hear sounds and the relationships between them as being derived from one another through imitation; this requires no formal education, and typically occurs non-consciously.

5. A sense of derivation through imitation is a necessary feature of all structures that we perceive as musical; a consequence of this is that all music is infused with repetition in all domains and at all levels.

6. Hence music is typically supersaturated with far more repetition than is required for it to be coherent, and this has two consequences: (a) listeners do not need to hear all the available structure for a given musical message to make sense, and (b) different listeners

(or even the same listener on different occasions) can apprehend different structural elements, yet each can still have a coherent musical experience. Moreover, it is possible that a sense of derivation through imitation that was conceived by a composer need not be detected by listeners, and *vice versa*. Nonetheless, there is normally enough common perceptual ground for pieces of music to exist as shared and meaningful cognitive enterprises.

7. Music can and may well be associated with other social and communicative activity (such as dance and verbal language), which may interact with the cognition of purely musical structures and contribute additional layers of meaning. In some cultures, the notion of 'music' embraces more than just abstract patterns of sound. Nonetheless, streams of sound, structured through a sense of derivation through imitation, are a feature of all musical experience.

WHERE DO THE BOUNDARIES OF MUSIC LIE?

Although it may seem a strange thing to do, having arrived at a definition of what music *is*, it is important for us to consider what music is *not*: in particular, where the boundaries between everyday sounds, language and music lie. This is because one of theories set out later is that some children on the autism spectrum may *hear non-musical sounds in a musical way*. Clearly, a prerequisite for the existence of this theory is to have an agreed sense of what 'non-musical' sounds are.

So what do people commonly regard as 'music'? There is generally no argument that the pieces people download onto their iPods, listen to on the radio or go to hear at concerts, from Bach to Count Basie, Ravel to Radiohead, constitute 'music'. The debate is around the 'edges'. For instance, some people hold that certain everyday sounds – thinking particularly of sounds of nature – such as Tennyson's 'babbling brook', should be classed as music. Now, this may be regarded by some as 'music to the poet's ears', but zygonic theory would contend that it can be so only in a metaphorical sense, since there is no imitation present; no coherent narrative in which sounds are deemed to derive from one another through imitation. Hence rushing water (or similar features of a naturally occurring soundscape, such as pattering rain and the wind sighing through the trees) fail the 'musical' test (see Figure 3.29).

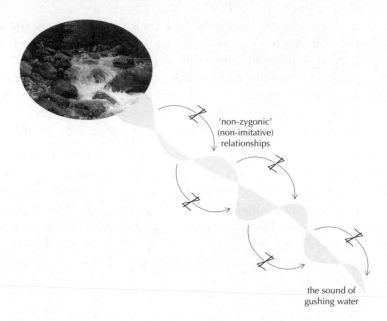

Figure 3.29 Since the sound of the babbling brook does not create patterns that can be considered to be derived through imitation, it does not constitute music

With another natural sound – birdsong – the position is more complex. Birds typically use short, distinct motifs that are well defined in terms of pitch, time and timbre, and which as youngsters they have usually learnt from an adult of the same species. They often repeat their calls to form chains of avian melody. But do such concatenations constitute music? Consider, for example, a series of four 'cuckoo' calls recorded in a natural setting (Figure 3.30).

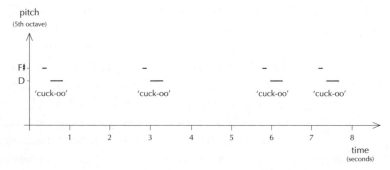

Figure 3.30 Representation of four 'cuckoo' calls recorded in a natural setting: do they constitute music?

It is, of course, impossible to say for sure whether the bird acted with any sense of self-imitation as he sang to defend his territory, or whether the repetition that occurred was merely a by-product of his communicative instincts. There is evidence that cuckoos have some awareness of their vocal products, since they can distinguish their own songs from those of other species. However, since the development of their singing need not have been influenced by an adult of the same species, and as their calls are very similar across a wide geographic range, it appears that they are innate rather than learned, and therefore *not* deliberately imitative. However, it is perfectly conceivable that humans may hear the successive 'cuckoos' illustrated in Figure 3.30 as being derived through imitation, implying that the series of calls constitutes, in their minds, music (see Figure 3.31).

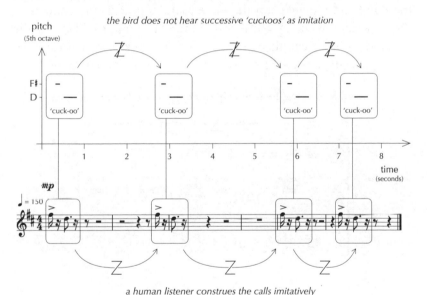

Figure 3.31 A listener hears cuckoo calls as music, despite imitation not being part of the bird's thinking

So is the sequence music or not? The repetitive structure of the succession of calls means that they *have the capacity to be heard as music*, even though they were produced (we assume) with other-than-musical intent. Hence, the classification of the sequence as music will depend on the knowledge and beliefs of the listener. If this appears to be unacceptably open-ended, a further scenario will show that a certain fuzziness is inevitable. Consider another set of four 'cuckoos', similar to those shown above, but somewhat lower in pitch, more equal in duration, and with shorter time periods between each pair of sounds. These differences should not in themselves produce phenomenological change of any substance, so the arguments set out in relation to the sounds' classification as music still apply. But now consider that the tone-colour is that of a B flat clarinet. For those familiar with the timbre, it is unequivocally indicative of a musical instrument and therefore, very likely, a sense of human agency. For 'neurotypical' listeners, the chances of the motifs being heard as deriving through imitation – of the passage being heard as music – increase markedly. Finally, imagine a context in which the cuckoo calls are heard in combination with a nightingale's song (played on the flute) and a quail's (on the oboe), and appear in the context of the slow movement of a classical symphony (Figure 3.32). To the culturally attuned ear, the implication of imitation is now irresistible, and representations of the sounds of nature are definitely 'music'.

Beethoven: Symphony No. 6; 2nd Movement, 'Scene am Bach'

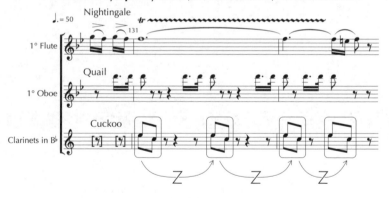

Figure 3.32 Cuckoo calls used in the context of a symphony ensure that they are heard as music (although the original avian associations are maintained)

We now move on to consider music and language. Since it is driven by semantics rather than the imitation of the sounding qualities of words, language generally fails the 'musical' test. However, exceptions do exist: rhyme, assonance and alliteration, for instance, provide examples where musical logic has arguably encroached upon the realm of verbal language. The regularity of metre in poetry can also be interpreted as imitation in sound and therefore construed musically. Whether or not listeners *do* hear phonetic and metric repetition in a musical way is not yet clear. Some indirect evidence does exist, however. For example, according to the neuroscientist Aniruddh Patel (2012), elements of linguistic and musical structural processing may share resources in the brain, and empirical work has suggested that in songs, music and language may be encoded together (see Morrongiello and Roes 1990; Serafine, Crowder and Repp 1984), although expert singers may have the capacity to decouple the two forms of auditory communication in neurological terms (see Wilson *et al.* 2011). Then, the presence of a melody can increase phonetic recognition, and a tune can facilitate the learning and recall of attendant words, *provided that the music repeats* (see e.g. Wallace 1994).

Given this, if aspects of language alone were being processed musically, we could reasonably assume that those verbal strings that were structured partly in a musical way (for example, through the imitation of words' sounding qualities, as in poetry) would be learnt and recalled more easily than in prose that lacked these features. And the psychologist David Rubin (1995) has indeed found evidence that poetic forms support memory. Furthermore, it appears that the cognitive advantages of 'word-music' are not confined to learning and recall: alliteration has been shown to aid verbal comprehension, for example (see Lea *et al.* 2008). The implications for children on the autism spectrum are considered in Chapter 5.

Finally, consider Morse code, a specialised manifestation of language in which the poetic niceties of rhyme, assonance, alliteration and metre are eliminated, and with them, any phonetic and metric similarities that could potentially have been heard in a musical way. However, as the system uses only one pitch and two different durations, there is an immense amount of repetition. Could this be construed as music? To those using Morse code as a form of communication, the answer is usually 'no', since any replication is driven either by the design of the code (for example, the three dots or 'dits' that make up the letter 'S' and the three dashes or 'dahs' that make up the letter 'O') or by semantics (as in the repeated 'S' – 'dit-dit-dit' – in 'SOS', for instance); see Figure 3.33.

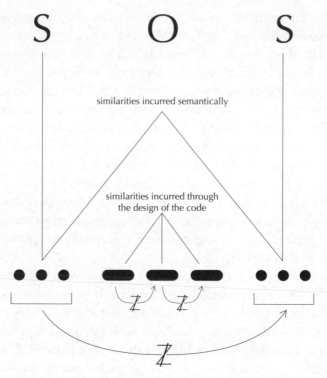

Figure 3.33 Morse code heard purely as a means of communication does not constitute music

For those who do *not* recognise the code as a representation of verbal language, it is conceivable that it may be interpreted in a musical way, though the irregular additive nature of the temporal structure (in which the duration of a 'dah' is three 'dits', the interval between sounds that make up the same letter is equivalent to one 'dit', and the time *between* letters is three 'dits') makes it difficult to parse events other than at the surface level, and the rapid speed at which individual sounds pass by militates against this.

However, the fact that Morse uses materials that resemble the notes that are the building blocks of much music means that it has been relatively easy for composers to incorporate the code – or, at least, readily recognisable transformations of it – into pieces. Such modifications enable the syntactic demands of music for repetition and the semantic requirements of Morse to correspond to a series of letters that make up a word to be reconciled. Take, for example, the theme from a UK television series (1987–2000) featuring the Oxfordshire detective Inspector Morse. The composer, Barrington Pheloung, captured something of the enigma of the central character by incorporating his name into the music. This was achieved by playing the code around a quarter speed, changing some durations to permit metrical regularity, and sounding the entire M-O-R-S-E sequence repeatedly as an ostinato. These strategies mean that, while enough of the identity of code was retained for it to be interpreted semantically, it could also be heard as pure sound, structured through imitation that occurred both within the M-O-R-S-E sequence and between its many appearances.

Hence the full meaning arises from a 'conceptual blend' (Zbikowksi 2002), created by the composer, and which can be appreciated only by those listeners who are able to process the structures of both the Morse code and the music. A reverse example, of a conceptual blend that was *not* planned by the composer, but that was subsequently foisted upon the music by listeners, occurs in the opening four notes of Beethoven's Fifth Symphony. These correspond to 'V' in Morse code ('di-di-dit-dah') and, in 1941, the BBC started to use the opening of the symphony as a theme for radio shows beamed across Europe, in the hope of reminding people of Winston Churchill's famous two-fingered salute, and so boost morale during the Second World War. Here, what was originally pure music, subsequently acquired a semantic overlay.

CONCLUSION

In conclusion, and before moving on to consider language and music in relation to children and young people on the autism spectrum, it is helpful to summarise what the key similarities and differences between language and music are (in Western cultures): see Table 3.1.

Table 3.1 The key similarities and differences between language and music

Function	Language	Music
Universal characteristics	Highly evolved and complex communication through sound.	
	A feature of all societies.	
	Understanding acquired implicitly through exposure and interaction.	
Engagement	Most people engage with language reactively, proactively and interactively as children and adults.	In the West, most people engage with music reactively, proactively and interactively as children, but only reactively as adults.
	Primarily improvised by everyone in day-to-day contexts to express feelings and communicate.	In the West, primarily produced by a small handful of performers as recordings in re-creating the work of a tiny number of composers for large audiences (who generally aren't present at the performance).
Elements	Largely comprises words, whose core meanings are symbolic, representing different aspects of human experience; refers to things 'beyond itself' – hence cross-modal relationships are essential.	Largely comprises notes, which exist in their own right as non-symbolic perceptual entities; refers primarily to itself – hence unimodal relationships (existing only in the domain of sound) are sufficient.

Elements	There are a large number of basic units of meaning (one million or so words available in English, typical reactive vocabulary of 50,000 words and proactive vocabulary of 10,000 words).	There are a small number of basic units of meaning: for the majority of listeners, most music comprises melodies made up of 12 potential small intervals of pitch, and six low whole-number ratios of duration (taken as the gap between the onsets of notes).
	Words tend to have *strong* 'absolute' meanings, which can be qualified through relationships with other words.	For most people, notes tend to have *weak* 'absolute' meanings: it is the relationships between them that bear the burden of the message.
Structure	Words (in English) can be categorised as fulfilling one of eight different basic 'functions' (parts of speech), with many subcategories, that work together in ten different ways to form meaning: through semantics, syntax, simile and metaphor, slandpoint, source, sequence, sound, spoken quality, shared knowledge and social context (see pp.59–60).	In tonal music, notes can fulfil one of 12 functions with regard to pitch and usually up to one of four different functions in relation to metre (the pattern of accented and unaccented beats).
	Structure (syntax) depends on the function of words, which rely on semantics; hence many forms of structural relationship are possible.	All musical structure ultimately depends on one type of (zygonic) relationship – through which imitation is perceived between any features of notes.

Table continues

Table 3.1 The key similarities and differences between language and music *cont.*

Function	Language	Music
Structure	Repetition is the exception.	Repetition is the rule.
	50 per cent redundant.	90 per cent redundant.
	Maximum level of semantic abstraction is relationships between relationships (second-order relationships) – as in analogies.	Maximum level of abstraction is relationships between relationships *between relationships* (third-order) – as in a beat that regularly speeds up.
	The sequence of words is important, though there can be some flexibility, which can lead to different shades of emphasis.	Sequence is of primary importance in the identity of a melody: change the order of events and you will have a different tune.
Meaning	Tends to convey specific information.	Tends to convey general feelings.
	Demands shared understanding of concepts that are conveyed symbolically; understanding of everyday language tends to be 'all (or virtually all) or nothing' – though with literature there is more room for the imagination.	Only limited shared understanding is required: pieces of music can be understood satisfactorily at different levels, from complex emotional narrative in sounds, to series of simple patterns.
	Meaning often arises over time through concatenations of ideas that are abstracted; omissions and errors can cause difficulties in understanding.	For most listeners, music exists 'in the moment'; errors or gaps in transmission or reception tend not to be critical for basic levels of engagement.
	Meaning is highly contextually dependent.	*Associative* meaning is contextually dependent; intrinsic musical meaning is much less so.

Consequences	'Real-life' consequences often follow from what is said (although language can convey imaginary ideas).	Music exists outside 'real life', conveying ideas that exist only in the realm of the imagination.
Development	Language follows early musical development.	At its simplest, engagement with music occurs early in development – as a primary means of communicating with others.

CHAPTER 4

How Musicality Develops

INTRODUCTION

If we really *do* make sense of music in the way described in Chapter 3, it must be the case that this capacity *develops* as we grow up. Since 2002 I have been involved in a research project called *Sounds of Intent*, with colleagues Graham Welch and Evangelos Himonides from the Institute of Education, University of London, and Sally Zimmermann, from the Royal National Institute of Blind People (RNIB), which set out to show how musicality develops in children with a range of special needs, including autism.

We worked with a group of teachers, music therapists, parents and others to analyse video recordings of children and young people engaging with music. We were interested in trying to find out what colleagues would describe as 'typical', what they thought was 'exceptional', and what activities and behaviour seemed to be necessary precursors or possible successors to others. In other words, were there certain things that children had to learn to do before they could move on to achieve others?

Over a period of three years or so, we ended up with many hundreds of examples of young people in action. Their responses, actions and interactions were carefully noted and encapsulated in short descriptions such as those that follow.

EXAMPLES OF CHILDREN WITH LEARNING DIFFICULTIES, INCLUDING AUTISM, ENGAGING WITH MUSIC

1. Anna sits in her wheelchair making no voluntary movement. Her teacher approaches and plays a cymbal with a soft beater, gently at first, and then more loudly, in front of her and then near to each ear. Anna makes no reaction that the teacher can observe.

2. Radwan is lying in the 'Little Room',[1] vocalising in an almost constant drone. Occasionally a sudden movement of his right arm knocks his wrist against some windchimes, which glint in the light. Each time, he smiles and his vocalising briefly turns into a laugh (Figure 4.1).

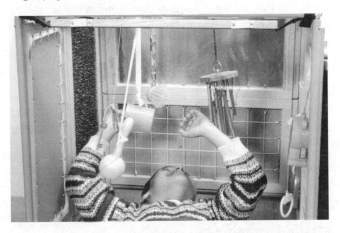

Figure 4.1 The 'Little Room' minimises auditory clutter from outside and maximises acoustic feedback from within

3. Mark's music therapy session begins – as ever – with the 'Hello!' song, during which he is given a rainstick adorned with reflective paper – a multisensory sound-maker – which he is encouraged to

---

1   A 'Little Room' is a small, largely enclosed area, originally designed by the Danish psychologist Lilli Nielsen, which may be placed over a prone child's head and upper torso, and in which potentially sound-making objects and toys are suspended, so that movements the child makes (whether accidentally or deliberately) are likely to create a range of sounds with a good deal of acoustic feedback. At the same time, auditory clutter from the outside is minimised. For further information, see www.lilliworks.com/products.htm.

use as a personal symbol. And, as ever, he makes no discernible response.

4. Ben startles and then smiles when someone drops a tray of cutlery in the dining room.

5. Taybah brushes her left hand against the strings of a guitar that someone is holding near to her. There is a pause and then she raises her hand and brushes the strings again, and then for a third time.

6. Yakov usually makes a rasping sound as he breathes. He seems to be unaware of what he is doing, and the rasping persists, irrespective of external stimulation. His class teacher has tried to see whether Yakov can be made aware of his sounds by increasing their intensity (using a microphone, amplifier and speakers), but so far this approach has met with no response.

7. Grant's teacher notices that he often turns his head towards her when she sings to him, but she has never noticed him turn towards other sounds.

8. Wendy giggles when people repeat patterns of syllables to her such as 'ma ma ma ma ma', 'da da da da da ', or 'ba ba ba ba ba'.

9. Jamie's short, sharp vocalisations, which vary in quality according to his mood, are interpreted by his teachers and carers to mean that he wants someone to vocalise back to him.

10. Khira gets very excited when she hears the regular beat on the school's drum machine.

11. Ubanwa enjoys 'call and response' games and joins in by making his own, distinctive sounds.

12. Carol copies simple patterns of vocalisation – imitating the ups and downs of her speech and language therapist's voice.

13. Samantha waves her hand more and more vigorously through an ultrasonic beam, creating an ever wider range of swirling sounds.

14. Nathan often vocalises in response to vocal sounds that are made close to him, although he doesn't seem to copy what he hears.

15. Zabrina loves the sight and sound of the bell-tree and when it stops she rocks in her chair which staff interpret as a gesture for 'more'.

16. Damario has been able to make a wide range of vocal sounds ever since he started school, but recently he has begun to make more melodious vowel sounds, which he repeats in short sequences.

17. Lottie hums distinct patterns of notes and repeats them. Her favourite sound is rather like a playground chant, and she repeats it from one day to the next, though not always starting on the same note, her music teacher notices (see Figure 4.2).

Figure 4.2 Lottie's song

18. Freya cries whenever she hears the 'Goodbye' song. It takes only the first two or three notes to be played on the keyboard, and she experiences a strong emotional reaction.

19. Hirsch enjoys copying simple rhythms on a non-tuned percussion instrument. Now he's started making his own rhythms up too, and he flaps his hands with delight when someone else copies what he's doing.

20. Ellen just laughs and laughs when people imitate her vocalisations.

21. Vaughan vocalises to get his therapist to make a sound – it docsn't matter what, he just seems to relish having a vocal response.

22. Imogen always gets excited in the middle of the 'Slowly/Quickly' song – to which she has recently learnt to tap the beat – anticipating the sudden change of pace.

23. Oliver scratches the tambourine, making a range of sounds. Whenever he plays near the rim and the bells jingle, he smiles.

24. Qiang's eye movements intensify when he hears the big band play loudly; *what* they are playing seems unimportant.

25. Xavier distinctly tries to copy high notes and low notes in vocal interaction sessions.

26. Peter has learnt to associate his teacher's jangly bracelet, which she always wears, with *her*; for him, it is an important part of her identity.

27. William's rocking increases markedly as the Japanese taiko drumming gets faster and faster.

28. Milán is the lead singer in a pop group at school, whose members all have learning difficulties. With the help of their music teacher, the group are getting better at following him as he slows down before the return of each chorus for expressive effect.

29. Ashley's parents have tried playing her just about every kind of music, and have taken her to all sorts of performances, from traditional church choirs to big band jazz, but as yet she has shown no reaction.

30. Hackett gets a buzz out of playing the drum, starting with a slow beat and getting faster and faster.

31. Yuma likes it when her teaching assistants play 'catch' with short vocal phrases, each person picking up from where the other left off.

32. Dennis will respond to musical sounds that are made near to him by vocalising next to his right ear, so he can feel the adult's breath on his skin, and he is now sustaining his concentration on this listening task for longer periods of time.

33. Vic can choose which activity he would like to do next by shaking the bells (for music) or squeezing a horn (for 'ride the bike').

34. Faisal has severe learning difficulties and hemiplegia. He has AP and plays the keyboard with his left hand only, learning material by ear quite quickly. He has recently joined the school's band, and has found a role for himself playing the bass parts. Now he not only picks up on what the left hand of the other keyboard player is doing, but also has started improvising around the harmonies too.

35. Penny has come to realise that the gong in her classroom means 'lunchtime' when it is sounded.

36. Gabrielle does not appear to relate to others' sound-making and, in an effort to gain her attention, her co-workers react positively to sounds that she makes, apparently by chance, and they model interactions for her, one taking her part vocally in the 'good morning' routine, for example.

37. Emily makes up songs with short phrases that sound connected – and when her teacher listened carefully to a recording that she

had made of Emily's singing, she noticed that one phrase often started more or less where the one before left off.

38. Jamil has severe learning difficulties and is on the autism spectrum but he has sophisticated musical tastes. He likes the vocal music of the Baroque period – especially Bach and Handel – but much prefers a purity and lightness of vocal tone with little vibrato.

39. Tanya likes improvising responses on the keyboard to the melodic openings that her teacher makes up – and she's now learnt to 'hear' the same structures in many themes by Haydn and Mozart.

40. Quincy knows that when his music teacher plays the last verse of 'Molly Malone' in the minor key, it signifies sadness.

41. Noriko loves the little runs on the panpipes in Papageno's 'Birdcatcher's Song' from *The Magic Flute*.

42. Sabina plays her cello with a Suzuki group, and is much better now at performing in time and in tune with the other children.

43. Osman enjoys singing the bass line in his school choir, and has memorised around 50 pieces that they have sung over the last few years.

44. Brett went to an African performing arts workshop, and he was really engaged as the short bursts of music were echoed back and forth between groups.

45. Ruth is a good singer, used to performing in public, although she has severe learning difficulties and autism. She can learn new songs just by listening to her teacher (who is not a singer) run through them, and as she gets to know a piece, she intuitively adds expression as she feels appropriate, showing that she has an underlying sense of the structure and content of the music. Later, when she listens to other people singing the songs she knows, she clearly prefers some performances to others. Her teacher believes this shows that she has a mature engagement with pieces in mid-to-late twentieth-century popular style.

46. Lacey uses a switch to operate a drum synthesiser, and she is showing an increasing ability to control the sounds that are made. Originally, she would concentrate on the task only in the relatively constrained auditory environment of her classroom, but now she enjoys making music in the school hall too.

47. Ursula, who is blind and has learning difficulties, improvises pentatonic tunes on the recorder using the notes (D, E, G, A, B). Initially, it didn't seem to matter to Ursula which note they ended with, but more recently, they have tended to conclude with 'G'.

48. Liz can tap out a regular beat at different speeds on a range of handheld percussion instruments.

49. Zachary, who has moderate learning difficulties and is on the autism spectrum, loves to compose using the computer, which he can do with someone to help him control the software. He has been creating pieces to accompany the school play, and has now put together a dozen excerpts that convey a range of different moods.

50. Tabitha can't speak, but she can hum short phrases to communicate her preference for certain activities (see, for example, Figure 4.3).

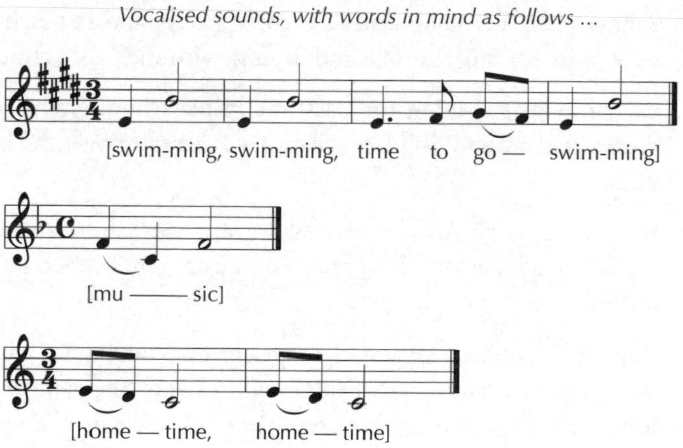

Vocalised sounds, with words in mind as follows ...

[swim-ming, swim-ming,   time   to   go —   swim-ming]

[mu ——— sic]

[home — time,   home — time]

Figure 4.3 Tabitha hums short melodic contours to communicate

51. Ude, with profound and multiple learning difficulties, is fascinated with the ever-changing sonorities produced by the didgeridoo.

52. Ciara, who is a good vocalist despite having severe learning difficulties, is learning how to convey a range of different emotions in her singing through using techniques such as *rubato*, consciously employing a wider range of dynamics, and producing darker and lighter sounds.

53. Aletia, who is severely autistic, experiences a strong emotional reaction when she hears 'This Little Light of Mine' ever since it was played at her classmate's funeral.

54. Xiang, who has profound pervasive developmental delay, has at last started to respond to her teacher singing as well as her mother, and this occurs in an increasing range of contexts, including her classroom and the multisensory room.

55. Valerie has a good deal of involuntary movement in her arms, and her music therapist has tried to give her a sense of cause and effect by using an ultrasonic beam, which she links to a variety of electronic sounds. To date, Valerie has shown no signs of awareness that she is controlling the sounds, however.

56. Diane makes short melodic patterns – usually going up three or four notes – using single syllables such as 'dah' or 'me'.

57. Heidi's speech and language therapist tries to interpret her vocalisations and facial expressions in the context of early communication, producing similar sounds in return.

58. Chas really enjoys playing the bongos in his college band – maintaining a regular beat even when the music gets quite syncopated, and not afraid to add his own ideas too.

59. Eamon, with moderate learning difficulties and autism, is always listening to pop music, but he has his clear favourites to which he returns time and again.

60. Iona appears to have no voluntary movement, and her therapist lifts her arm up and down in the ultrasonic beam to generate flute-like sounds from the computer.

61. Faith, who has severe learning difficulties, used to be able to play only a few nursery rhymes on the keyboard, mostly with her right hand, but now she can manage whole pop songs, with a simple bass line all the way through.

62. Oscar has learnt to sing much more in time and in tune over the last year, his music teacher notices, and he improvises simple melodies, typically comprising several short phrases, that are always in the major key, the first phrase beginning, and the last ending, on the tonic.

63. Xena waits for the tick-tocks in 'My Grandfather's Clock' and grins with excitement when the moment comes. Very occasionally she joins in.

64. George loves it when his one-to-one support worker claps short rhythmic patterns to him.

65. Imran's piano technique has improved dramatically over the past year since his new teacher taught him scales and arpeggios in every key, and he can now perform his repertoire of early jazz much more fluently.

66. Janet, with severe learning difficulties, has developed the confidence to introduce new material on her saxophone in the school's jazz quartet, and is thrilled when the other players pick up on what she is doing.

67. Yolanda can sing most of 'Twinkle, Twinkle Little Star' when prompted at the beginning of each phrase, though her sense of key tends to drift.

68. Keith can improvise over a number of pop songs in a simple style on the keyboard.

69. Stephen plays the clarinet in the local wind band, and intuitively picks up on the changes in dynamics and tempi that they make.

70. Mehul performs expressively on his guitar, whether he's playing folk music, blues, or country and western. He's happy playing on his own or with others, and he enjoys going to concerts to hear music in these different styles played live too. If he had to choose, his preference would always be for folk music, though.

71. Zeeshan laughs and rocks when he hears his teacher imitating Tom's vocal sounds.

72. Neha copies elements of the short phrases her music therapist sings, particularly picking up vocally on the highest or lowest notes, or the first or last in a group.

73. Patrick's music therapist tries interacting with him in a number of different environments – the music room, the multisensory room and the hall – to see if the different acoustics will encourage him to engage with her and respond.

74. Rachel enjoys 'give and take' sessions with her piano teacher using two keyboards. She can copy the short rhythms that her teacher makes up and gets most of the pitches right too.

75. Wallace is getting better at holding a steady tonal centre when he sings, and has recently started making up pieces that have a distinct 'beginning', 'middle' and 'end'.

76. Brian always plays the bell-tree in music sessions (he becomes distressed if attempts are made to encourage him to play other instruments) – for him, at this stage, it is an integral part of the experience.

77. Karen thinks it's great fun when her music therapist copies the number of beats that she makes on the tambourine.

78. Qabil's day at school is organised so that key activities have sounds that precede them as auditory cues – shaking the bell-tree means 'it's time for music', for example, banging the gong means 'lunchtime', and a horn means 'ride the bike'. Similarly, his key worker, Anna, always wears the same jangly bracelet (see Figure 4.4), and his classroom is identifiable by the windchimes at the door. Currently, Qabil does not react to any of the sounds, and there's no evidence that he understands the connections that are being presented to him – but staff persist in the hope that offering Qabil a structured learning environment will eventually pay off.

Figure 4.4 Anna can be identified by her jangly bracelet, although Qabil has yet to make this connection

MAKING SENSE OF THE EXAMPLES: DOMAINS
AND LEVELS OF MUSICAL ENGAGEMENT

In the light of examples such as these, it was evident that musical development was occurring in at least two different dimensions: 'listening and responding', for which the single term '*reactive*' was adopted, and 'causing, creating and controlling', for which the label '*proactive*' was used. In relation to the examples given above, Scenarios 1, 2, 4, 7, 8, 10, 15, 18, 22, 23, 24, 26, 27, 29, 31, 35, 38, 39, 40, 41, 44, 45, 51, 53, 54, 59, 63, 64, 70, 71 and 78 could be considered to be entirely or predominantly 'reactive' and Scenarios 2, 5, 6, 13, 16, 17, 23, 30, 33, 37, 39, 42, 45, 46, 47, 48, 49, 50, 52, 55, 56, 60, 61, 62, 63, 65, 67, 68, 70, 75 and 76, 'proactive'. (Some observations, such as Scenarios 2 and 23, pertained more or less equally to two or even three dimensions.) However, that left a further group of observations (as in Scenarios 3, 9, 11, 12, 14, 19, 20, 21, 25, 28, 32, 34, 36, 42, 43, 54, 57, 58, 66, 69, 70, 72, 73, 74 and 77 above) in which listening to sounds and making them occurred with other people, and it was decided that this concept too should have the status of a separate dimension, which was labelled '*interactive*'.

The types of musical engagement that were observed covered a huge developmental range, from the very beginnings of musicality (or even, in some cases, stages of development in which musicality was yet to evolve) to highly sophisticated levels of participation in musical activity. We defined this range in terms of six levels of music-cognitive development as shown in Table 4.1.

Table 4.1 The six levels underpinning the *Sounds of Intent* framework (acronym 'CIRCLE')

Level	Description	Core cognitive abilities
1	Blooming, buzzing **C**onfusion*	No awareness of sound as a distinct perceptual entity.
2	Awareness and **I**ntentionality	An emerging awareness of sound as a distinct perceptual entity and of the variety that is possible within the domain of sound.
3	Relationships, repetition, **R**egularity	A growing awareness of the possibility and significance of *relationships* between sonic *events* and the basic aspects of sounds.
4	Sounds forming **C**lusters	An evolving perception of *groups* of sounds, and the relationships that may exist between them.
5	Deeper structural **L**inks	A growing recognition of whole pieces, and of the *frameworks* of pitch and perceived time that lie behind them.
6	Mature artistic **E**xpression	A developing awareness of the culturally determined 'emotional syntax' of performance that articulates the 'narrative metaphor' of pieces.

Note: *From *The Principles of Psychology* (1890), by the early American psychologist, William James (available at http://psychcentral.com/classics/James/Principles/prin13.htm).

Level 1

In Level 1, there is no evidence of awareness of any sound, musical or otherwise (Figure 4.5).

Level 2

In Level 2, there is an emerging awareness of sound as a distinct perceptual entity, and a recognition of the variety of sounds that are possible (Figure 4.6).

Figure 4.5 *Sounds of Intent* Level 1: no awareness
of sound as a distinct perceptual entity

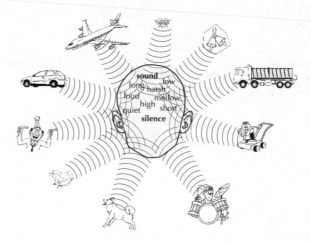

Figure 4.6 *Sounds of Intent* Level 2: an emerging awareness
of sound as a distinct perceptual entity and of the
variety that is possible within the domain of sound

Level 3

In Level 3, there is a growing awareness of the possibility and
significance of the *relationships* between single events or the basic
features of sounds. The notion of 'same' and 'different' evolves,
which, in due course (according to zygonic theory) underpins the

sense that, through imitation, one sound may be perceived as deriving from or generating another. As noted above, this is the point at which cognitive activity specifically pertaining to *music* can be identified – see Figure 4.7 (also see Chapter 3, pp.74–75) .

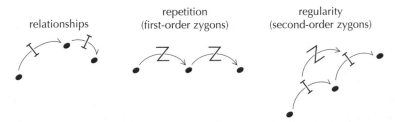

Figure 4.7 *Sounds of Intent* Level 3: a growing awareness of *relationships, repetition* and *regularity* in the domain of sound

A key question here is just when *repetition* – the notion of 'the same sound again' – becomes *imitation*: the idea that one sound is heard as copying another in the context of potential variety on account of human agency. Consider Scenario 8, in which Wendy giggles when she hears people repeating patterns of syllables such as 'ma ma ma ma' and 'ba ba ba ba'. To decide whether this represents auditory processing at Level 3, one would have to be persuaded that it was the relationships between a series of identical (or very similar) sounds rather than the quality of the sounds themselves that elicited Wendy's response. Hence, if a similar reaction were to be evoked by a *single* syllable or a stream of *different* vocal sounds, this would suggest that repetition was not an essential factor. Conversely, if the repetition of other sounds (but not changes in them) were to cause a comparable response, this would support the view that Wendy could recognise relationships of identity in the auditory domain.

But this does would not necessarily mean that Wendy could discern *imitation*, and therefore process sounds *musically*. This 'pre-musical' level of functioning would be indicated if the repetition of any sounds, irrespective of their source (such as the sequences of beeps on microwave ovens or even the ticking of clocks and timers) induced the same emotional reaction as vocalisations. The sense of human agency demanded by music is easiest to observe in *inter*action: see, for instance, Scenario 71, where Zeeshan laughs and rocks when he hears his teacher imitating Tom; Scenario 20, where Ellen laughs when people repeat her vocalisations (but not, we may assume, when they make different sounds); and, most compelling of all, Scenario 25, where Xavier tries to copy the high and low vocal sounds of another.

Level 4

In Level 4, children and young people have an evolving perception of sounds functioning as *groups*, and of the relationships that may exist between these. Groups of sounds are formed by their members having a quality or qualities in common that are not shared by non-members: invariably in relation to time, and often in relation to pitch, loudness or timbre too. According to zygonic theory, such similarity is deemed to occur through imitation. Relationships *between* groups can take one of two forms: where one is perceived to derive from another *as a whole*, and where one *aspect* of a group is perceived as deriving from one *aspect* of another (see Figure 4.8).

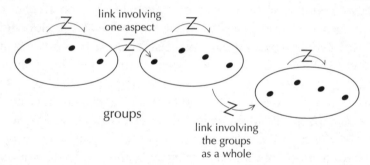

Figure 4.8 *Sounds of Intent* Level 4: an evolving perception of *groups* of sounds, and the relationship that may exist between them

An example of this theory in action is to be found in the description of Lottie's musical engagement set out in Scenario 17, which tells us that she likes to hum a distinct pattern of notes and repeat it (see Figure 4.2). Here, the primary grouping mechanism is temporal, in that the onsets of notes following the first are contiguous with the endpoints, in each case, of those that precede, and the boundary between groups is determined by the relatively long break between the end of one note and the beginning of the next. The sense that there are two distinct clusters of notes is reinforced through the repetition of the first group as a whole.

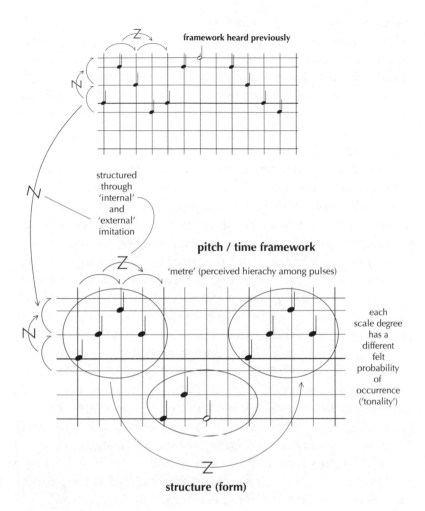

Figure 4.9 *Sounds of Intent* Level 5: a growing recognition
of whole pieces, and of the frameworks of pitch
and perceived time that lie behind them

Level 5

In Level 5, we have the cognition of abstract *frameworks* of pitch
(imaginary intervallic ladders upon which notes can be hung) and time
(equating to the apprehension of a regular beat that underpins rhythm)
(see Figure 3.16). In one form or another, such frameworks are common
to virtually all music. Internally, they are highly structured, repeatedly

using the same (or very similar) differences between pitches and the onsets of notes, although pitch frameworks have a slight asymmetry, which, as we saw in Chapter 3, means that notes can be used idiosyncratically with respect to the unique position that each occupies within a set. In zygonic terms, this implies derivation occurring *between* appearances of pitch-time frameworks and *within* them (see Figure 4.9).

Psychologists believe that such frameworks are internalised through repeated exposure, though it is not entirely clear, however, how the different elements evolve. For example, there are tentative signs that, in Ursula's case at least (Scenario 47), an awareness of pitch frameworks appears before a full appreciation of their idiosyncratic patterns of utilisation, as her improvised pentatonic tunes on the recorder have, over time, become increasingly likely to conclude with 'G'. More general evidence for the cognitive development of pitch and perceived temporal frameworks is to be found in children singing or playing increasingly in time and in tune over sustained periods (for the duration of whole songs): consider, for instance, Sabina's progress in her Suzuki cello group (Scenario 42) and Oscar's advances in singing (Scenario 62). Finally, note that a developing awareness of frameworks seems to go hand in hand with the recognition of pieces as holistic entities, and of the prominent structural features within them. Consider, for example, Scenario 22, in which Imogen gets excited in the middle of the 'Slowly/Quickly' song, to which she has recently learnt to tap to the beat, anticipating the sudden change of pace; and Scenario 75, in which Wallace, who is getting better at holding a steady tonal centre throughout songs, has recently started improvising short pieces that have a distinct 'beginning', 'middle' and 'end'.

Level 6

In Level 6, we are concerned with what I think of as 'mature musicianship' – when children and young people are aware of the conventions of performing and creating music within their culture, and intuitively understand the expressive and communicative intent of pieces to which they are exposed. In Western performance, functioning at Level 6 entails an awareness of how underlying musical content and structure may be enhanced perceptually through devices such as rubato, vibrato and dynamics (see Figure 3.17). Such perturbations to the stable, invariant, imaginary 'core' of a piece (which, as we have observed, experienced listeners are able to extract) are determined largely through convention (in terms of zygonic theory, through the imitation of previous performances) although some expressivity may be specific to a particular rendition, and may be passed between performers in ensembles (see Figure 4.10). In this way musicians articulate the 'narrative metaphor' of pieces (the abstract stories in sound that they tell).

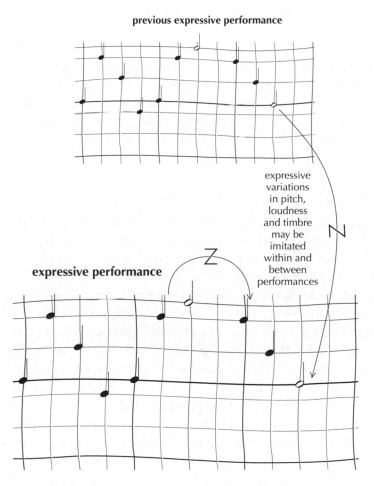

Figure 4.10 *Sounds of Intent* Level 6: a developing awareness of the culturally determined 'emotional syntax' of performance that articulates the 'narrative metaphor' of pieces

There are a number of examples of children and young people who appear to be functioning at Level 6 in the scenarios listed above, including, for example, Ciara (Scenario 52), who is developing her capacity to express a range of different emotions in her singing, and Mehul (Scenario 70), who plays the guitar expressively. However, it is widely noted (and, certainly, borne out by my own experience) that many children and young people with autism who would otherwise be regarded as competent players – even, technically, very able – do not play expressively, failing to use dynamics or rubato to colour their performances and so communicate the mood and fluctuating feelings that would typically be evoked in the course of a piece. It is as though this central role of music, as a conveyor of emotion, is of no interest to them. Rather, their whole attention seems to be taken up purely with the patterns of sounds that music makes. In my view, however, this by no means tells the whole story, and it is an area to which we will return in Chapter 7.

THE *SOUNDS OF INTENT* FRAMEWORK

Extending the six *Sounds of Intent* levels across the three domains of musical engagement (reactive, proactive and interactive) gave rise to the 'headlines' of musical engagement (see Figure 4.11). These are arranged as 18 segments in circular form, which were regarded as being the most appropriate metaphor for children's development, ranging from the centre, with its focus on self, outwards, to increasingly wider communities of others. For ease of reference, levels were ranked 1–6, each of which could be preceded with an 'R', a 'P' or an 'I', to indicate, respectively, reactive, proactive or interactive segments.

Each of these 18 descriptors can be broken down into four more detailed elements (see Figures 4.12a–c). Some relate purely to engagement with sound and music, others to sound and music in relation to other sensory input, and the remainder to technical matters pertaining to performance, which it was felt became important at Levels 5 and 6.

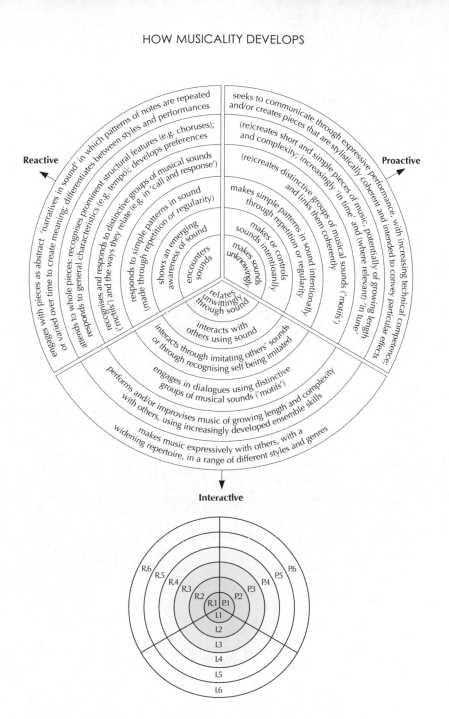

Figure 4.11 Visual representation of the *Sounds of Intent* framework

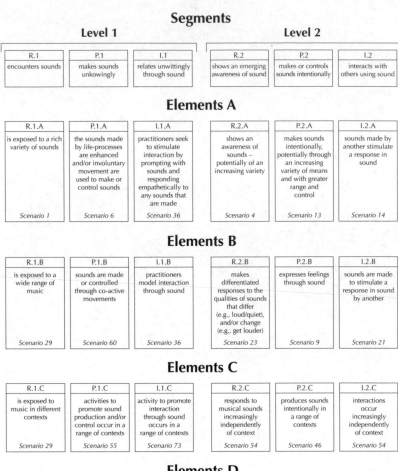

Segments

Level 1			Level 2		
R.1	**P.1**	**I.1**	**R.2**	**P.2**	**I.2**
encounters sounds	makes sounds unkowingly	relates unwittingly through sound	shows an emerging awareness of sound	makes or controls sounds intentionally	interacts with others using sound

Elements A

R.1.A	**P.1.A**	**I.1.A**	**R.2.A**	**P.2.A**	**I.2.A**
is exposed to a rich variety of sounds	the sounds made by life-processes are enhanced and/or involuntary movement are used to make or control sounds	practitioners seek to stimulate interaction by prompting with sounds and responding empathetically to any sounds that are made	shows an awareness of sounds – potentially of an increasing variety	makes sounds intentionally, potentially through an increasing variety of means and with greater range and control	sounds made by another stimulate a response in sound
Scenario 1	*Scenario 6*	*Scenario 36*	*Scenario 4*	*Scenario 13*	*Scenario 14*

Elements B

R.1.B	**P.1.B**	**I.1.B**	**R.2.B**	**P.2.B**	**I.2.B**
is exposed to a wide range of music	sounds are made or controlled through co-active movements	practitioners model interaction through sound	makes differentiated responses to the qualities of sounds that differ (e.g., loud/quiet), and/or change (e.g., get louder)	expresses feelings through sound	sounds are made to stimulate a response in sound by another
Scenario 29	*Scenario 60*	*Scenario 36*	*Scenario 23*	*Scenario 9*	*Scenario 21*

Elements C

R.1.C	**P.1.C**	**I.1.C**	**R.2.C**	**P.2.C**	**I.2.C**
is exposed to music in different contexts	activities to promote sound production and/or control occur in a range of contexts	activity to promote interaction through sound occurs in a range of contexts	responds to musical sounds increasingly independently of context	produces sounds intentionally in a range of contexts	interactions occur increasingly independently of context
Scenario 29	*Scenario 55*	*Scenario 73*	*Scenario 54*	*Scenario 46*	*Scenario 54*

Elements D

R.1.D	**P.1.D**	**I.1.D**	**R.2.D**	**P.2.D**	**I.2.D**
is exposed to music and musical sounds that are systematically linked to other sensory input	some activities to promote sound production and/or control are multi-sensory in nature	some activities to promote interaction through sound are multisensory in nature	responds to musical sounds linked to other sensory input	produces sounds as part of multisensory activity	interaction through sound involves activity that engages the other senses too
Scenario 78	*Scenario 3*	*Scenario 57*	*Scenario 15*	*Scenario 2*	*Scenario 32*

Figure 4.12a *Sounds of Intent* elements – Levels 1 and 2

Segments

	Level 3			**Level 4**	
R.3	P.3	I.3	R.4	P.4	I.4
responds to simple patterns in sound (made through repetition or regularity)	makes simple patterns in sound intentionally, through repetition or regularity	interacts through imitating others' sounds or through recognizing self being imitated	recognises and responds to distinctive groups of musical sounds ('motifs') and the relationships between them (e.g. in 'call and response')	(re)creates distinctive groups of musical sounds ('motifs') and links them coherently	engages in dialogues using distinctive groups of musical sounds ('motifs')

Elements A

R.3.A	P.3.A	I.3.A	R.4.A	P.4.A	I.4.A
recognises and responds to the repetition of sounds	intentionally makes simple patterns through repetition	shows awareness of own sounds being imitated	recognises and responds to distinctive groups of musical sounds – 'motifs'	(re)creates distinctive groups of musical sounds ('motifs')	produces musical motifs in the expectation that they will stimulate a coherent response
Scenario 8	*Scenario 16*	*Scenario 20*	*Scenario 64*	*Scenario 63*	*Scenario 19*

Elements B

R.3.B	P.3.B	I.3.B	R.4.B	P.4.B	I.4.B
recognises and responds to a regular beat	intentionally makes simple patterns through a regular beat	imitates the sounds made by another	recognises and responds to musical motifs being repeated or varied	links musical motifs by repeating or varying them	imitates distinctive groups of musical sounds – 'motifs' – made by others (as in 'call and response')
Scenario 10	*Scenario 48*	*Scenario 25*	*Scenario 44*	*Scenario 17*	*Scenario 19*

Elements C

R.3.C	P.3.C	I.3.C	R.4.C	P.4.C	I.4.C
recognises and responds to simple patterns formed through regular change	intentionally makes simple patterns through regular change	recognises own patterns in sound being imitated	recognises the coherent juxtaposition of different musical motifs	juxtaposes different musical motifs coherently	responds to others by using different musical motifs coherently (as in 'question and answer')
Scenario 41	*Scenario 56*	*Scenario 77*	*Scenario 31*	*Scenario 67*	*Scenario 72*

Elements D

R.3.D	P.3.D	I.3.D	R.4.D	P.4.D	I.4.D
responds to musical sounds used to symbolise other things	uses sound to symbolise other things	imitates simple patterns in sound made by another (through repetition, regularity and/or regular change)	responds to musical motifs being used to symbolise things	uses musical motifs to symbolise things (e.g. in 'sound stories')	interactions form coherent patterns of turn-taking, with the possibility of some simultaneity
Scenario 35	*Scenario 33*	*Scenario 12*	*Scenario 18*	*Scenario 50*	*Scenario 74*

Figure 4.12b *Sounds of Intent* elements – Levels 3 and 4

Segments

	Level 5			Level 6	
R.5	P.5	I.5	R.6	P.6	I.6
attends to whole pieces; recognises prominent structural features (e.g. choruses); responds to general characteristics (e.g. tempo); develops preferences	(re)creates short and simple pieces of music, potentially of growing length and complexity; increasingly 'in time' and (where relevant) 'in tune'	performs and/or improvises music of growing length and complexity with others, using increasingly developed ensemble skills	emgages with pieces as abstract 'narratives in sound' in which patterns of notes are repeated or varied over time to create meaning; differentiates between styles and performances	seeks to communicate through expressive performances, with increasing technical competence; creates pieces that are intended to convey particular effects	makes music expressively with others, with a widening repertoire, in a range of different styles and genres

Elements A

R.5.A	P.5.A	I.5.A	R.6.A	P.6.A	I.6.A
attends to whole pieces of music, becoming familiar with an increasing number and developing preferences	performs short and simple pieces of music, potentially of growing length and complexity; increasingly 'in time' and (where relevant) 'in tune'	performs simple pieces simultaneously with others, sharing a common part	develops a mature response to music, engaging with pieces as abstract 'narratives in sound'	plays or sings expressively using familiar conventions of performance, at the highest level producing original compositions	is aware of, and emulates the expressivity of others' playing or singing in ensemble performance
Scenario 59	Scenario 61	Scenario 43	Scenario 45	Scenario 52	Scenario 69

Elements B

R.5.B	P.5.B	I.5.B	R.6.B	P.6.B	I.6.B
recognises prominent structural features (such as the choruses of songs)	improvises on familiar pieces of music, varying the original material in simple ways	performs with others, using increasingly developed ensemble skills and maintaining an independent part	becomes familiar with an increasing number of styles and genres and develops preferences	improvises on familiar music to convey desired effects, potentially producing original versions of existing pieces (as in 'jazz standards')	contributes own expressivity in ensemble playing to infuence co-performers
Scenario 22	Scenario 68	Scenario 58	Scenario 70	Scenario 45	Scenario 28

Elements C

R.5.C	P.5.C	I.5.C	R.6.C	P.6.C	I.6.C
responds to general characteristics of pieces (such as mode, tempo and texture)	creates simple pieces, potentially of increasing length and complexity, whose general characteristics may convey particular moods or feelings, and which may be linked to external associations	improvises with others, repeating, varying and/or building on the material that is offered in simple ways	becomes familiar with different performances of pieces and styles of performance and develops preference	composes pieces in a familiar style or styles to convey desired effects, at the highest level producing original material judged to be of intrinsic musical value	improvises with others with stylistic coherence, sharing and developing material in increasingly sophisticated ways
Scenario 40	Scenario 75	Scenario 39	Scenario 45	Scenario 49	Scenario 34

Elements D

R.5.D	P.5.D	I.5.D	R.6.D	P.6.D	I.6.D
responds to pieces through connotations brought about by their association with objects, people ore events in the external world	has the physical capacity to produce short and simple pieces of music, potentially evolving to meet the needs of material of growing length and complexity	improvises with others, consciously offering material for them to use	becomes aware of how music as an abstract narrative in sound relates to other media (words, movement, etc.) to create multimodal meaning	technical proficiency develops to meet the demands of a widening repertoire	develops increasingly advanced ensemble skills, managing material of growing technical and musical complexity as part of a group
Scenario 5.53	Scenario 5.42	Scenario 5.66	Scenario 5.38	Scenario 5.65	Scenario 5.70

Figure 4.12c *Sounds of Intent* elements – Levels 5 and 6

Although Figures 4.12a–c are regular in appearance, the way that the level descriptors and elements relate to each other within and between the reactive, proactive and interactive domains is complex. Level descriptors form a hierarchy whereby, within each domain, achievement at higher levels is dependent on the accomplishment of all those that precede. So, for example, in the interactive domain, I.4, 'Engages in musical dialogues, creating and recognising coherent connections between groups of sounds', could occur only following I.3, 'Interacts by imitating others' sounds or recognising self being imitated' and (therefore) after accomplishing I.2 and I.1. *Between* domains, there is a broad flow of contingency that runs from reactive to proactive and then to interactive. For instance, in the proactive domain, intentionally making patterns in sound through repetition (P.3) depends on the capacity to recognise simple patterns in sound (R.3); while interacting with another or others using sound (I.2) relies on the ability to cause, create or control sounds intentionally (P.2), which in turn requires an awareness of sound (R.2).

The pattern of contingencies that links the 72 elements is more complex, however. Although in some cases there is a necessary connection between elements at different levels *within* domains (for example, a pupil could not engage in intentional repetition – P.3.A – before having the wherewithal to make a variety of sounds – P.2.B) and *between* them (for instance, imitating the sounds made by another – I.3.A – similarly requires functioning at the level of P.2.B), this is not always the case. It is perfectly conceivable that a child could intentionally make simple patterns through a regular beat (P.3.B), for example, before using sounds to symbolise particular people, places or activities (P.2.D).

However, the *Sounds of Intent* research team felt that intricacies of this type were an inevitable consequence of the complicated nature of musical development: multilayered and multi-stranded. At any given time, it was unlikely that the framework would indicate a pupil as being at a particular *point* on a developmental scale, but, rather, having a music-developmental *profile*, incorporating attainment at different levels in relation to a number of different elements.

Given these complexities, though, the challenge was to find a way of making the framework accessible to practitioners as a tool for assessment, enabling them to record pupils' levels of achievement and change, to draw comparisons between the attainment and progress of individuals and groups, and to gauge the potential impact of different music-educational and therapeutic interventions. This was achieved by creating a new, interactive website that encapsulates the information set out above, and a good deal more besides. To try it out, go to www.soundsofintent.org. There are many video clips of children on the autism spectrum engaging in musical activity at all levels, as well as downloadable materials for teachers, therapists, parents and carers to use.

AN EXAMPLE OF AN ASSESSMENT USING THE SOUNDS OF INTENT FRAMEWORK: SHIVAN

Shivan was 11 years old when the level of his musical development was assessed. He had been born after 24 weeks' gestation, weighing 660g, and was diagnosed as being on the autism spectrum, with cerebral palsy (which meant he used a wheelchair), and was registered blind.

Shivan understood some simple, everyday language that was relevant to him, but he spoke very little, sometimes talking quietly to himself using unrecognisable words and sounds. When conversing with others, although his articulation was louder and clearer, the single words that he used usually repeated what he has just heard ('echolalia' – see p.238), rather than *meaning* anything in the semantic sense. This corresponds to element [I.3.B] in the *Sounds of Intent* framework.

According to his mother, music had played an important role in Shivan's life from the time that he was less than a year old. She recalled how, when he was little, music would help him go to sleep, and that he would start crying if it was turned off. When asked to explain the significance of music to Shivan, his parents reported that it was vital to him as 'he does not seem to enjoy anything else'. His mother described how 'music is the only way for him…to relate to the world'. She did not see music as his talent, but as 'a way to be, the only way for him to be', since 'he can't move, he's trapped [and he] can't read'. He enjoyed listening to music for all his waking moments – twelve hours a day when he was at home. Music was used both for stimulation and comfort, and was particularly important at certain times: for example, Shivan would not eat at home unless music was being played [R.1.C].

During a home visit, at four o'clock in the afternoon, Shivan's mother revealed that he had already been listening to music since nine o'clock that morning. A number of CDs were available to him, including albums by Fats Domino, Bob Marley and Elvis Presley, as well as Indian chanting. Shivan's mother reported that he usually had about 15 CDs in use at any one time, getting through about eight to ten different disks a day, and making himself heard when he wanted one changed [R.1.B].

Shivan's mother said that she replaced CDs that were broken or worn out, or if Shivan indicated that he was bored with them [R.5.A]. As well as replacements, she also provided new CDs every now and then. It was difficult to predict which ones Shivan would take to and which he would not like – either way, he decided very quickly (within hearing a few seconds of the first track), and immediately rejected those that did not find favour [R.4.A]. Shivan's mother revealed that she had about 50 CDs that he refused to listen to. In contrast, he occasionally took to a new CD so ardently that he would listen to it exclusively for several days (this had been the case with *Sesame Street*). It was reported that Shivan's tastes had changed over the years – that he no longer enjoyed nursery rhymes, for example [R.5.A].

Shivan's mother described how, even among his favourite CDs, Shivan did not listen to whole albums, but quickly learnt how to locate the tracks that he wanted to hear. He was not even interested in hearing the whole of these, but just played snippets of music, usually only a few seconds long, over and over again [R.4.A, R.4.B]. To do this, he skipped tracks very quickly and then fast-forwarded within a track to find the fragment he was looking for – a skill that he had taught himself. Sometimes he would even find the pauses *between* phrases and listen to those repeatedly.

Shivan's parents said that they only occasionally turned the player off, as, for instance, when he was being changed, although then he would usually take his portable tape player with him. This would also accompany him on walks [R.1.C]. His parents revealed that they were trying to wean him off music when he was outside, 'so that he listens to the wind and birds instead [R.1.A] – otherwise he is just hunched up in his chair listening to music, although sometimes he will not come out without it and then we give it to him. The swimming pool is the only other place he goes without it.'

Shivan's mother said that he occasionally engaged in active music-making at home by playing his keyboard. During the assessment, he was observed putting his hand on some keys to produce sounds, and he evidently enjoyed speeding up and slowing down the tempo of 'demos' such as 'Für Elise', and changing the volume from quiet to loud and back again [R.3.C, P.3.C]. His parents explained that 'we don't have him play the keyboard much at home because he does it a lot in school.'

Although Shivan did not sing during the assessment, according to his parents, he would occasionally vocalise along to music and sing short phrases from songs [P.4.A]. He always appeared to be in tune. His mother said that 'when he sings in the mornings, I know that he is up and wants to go downstairs' [P.4.D]. In addition, it was said that Shivan sang when he heard a song that he had not encountered for a long time, when he was particularly interested in something, or when approached by people he knew, such as his father and his sister. His father would then whistle the tune, and Shivan would sing along for one or two lines. If his father tried to whistle a *different* tune, Shivan would still sing the song that *he* wanted, and would continue until his father came into line [I.2.C, I.4.A, I.4.C]! His mother described how he pronounced the words of songs clearly, such as the phrase 'I'm such an ugly bug' from 'The Ugly Bug Ball' by Burl Ives, without knowing what it meant. The only instances of a purposeful use of language his mother could recall were when Shivan said 'change' to change a tape or CD and 'not working' if the batteries had run out, although, apparently, 'he won't always say it – often he just cries or taps when he needs something' [P.3.D].

It was reported that provision that sought to capitalise on Shivan's musical interests and maximise his potential had been extensive both at school and at home, including specialist one-to-one input organised by his parents over many years. For example, Shivan's mother said that he had had the services of an outreach worker for two years, during which time she had taken him to see musicals such as *The Lion King* and *Mary Poppins* and to shows such as *Stomp* (which combines percussion, movement and visual comedy) [R.1.B, R.1.C]. His mother explained how, after seeing the musicals, Shivan 'often couldn't sleep at all for a couple of days. Then, for a whole week after that, he slept in the day and was lying awake at night [R.5.A]. And when the girl came again two weeks later, Shivan was really excited.' Shivan's mother said that she had also taken him to the opera from time to time – to see, for example, *Pinocchio* at the Royal Opera House and *The Nutcracker* at English National Opera [R.1.B, R.1.C]. However, she had been finding it difficult to continue with these outings, as Shivan was getting physically bigger and consequently more difficult to manage.

Shivan was said to be working with a professional musician on listening skills, with a view to nurturing his love of recorded music. The musician, who described her work as being 'existential' rather than 'therapeutic', led the sessions by selecting tracks for Shivan to hear, mainly from the Western classical repertoire, and with an emphasis on piano music (she considered that he was particularly responsive to Mozart and Beethoven piano sonatas) [R.5.C, Not R.6.B]. She sometimes supplemented the recordings with extracts from pieces that she played 'live' [R.1.C]. As he listened, she observed that Shivan often extended an arm, gesturing for his hand to be held, occasionally moved his feet to the music, and sometimes reacted emotionally to pieces that he heard [R.5.A].

Shivan was also said to be receiving music therapy and creative music sessions out of school. Here, it was reported that he had improvised duets on the piano (though it was not clear what these were like) and moved rhythmically to fast violin playing. His therapist had said that 'the non-verbal quality of music seems important to Shivan, and allows him to be, and to show himself as he is in his world of sound.'

At the time of the assessment, Shivan attended a specialist primary school for children with visual impairments and additional disabilities. Here, music was reported to be integral to the school day: forthcoming activities were signalled with particular songs or sound cues, and rooms were labelled with auditory 'objects of reference' [R.1.D] (see p.162). Most curricular areas used recorded music to enhance learning [R.1.D]. Indeed, various subjects were founded on music, such as 'TacPac' sessions [R.1.D].[2] Shivan's class teacher, who

---

2 'TacPac' is a series of activities that, through combining touch and music, seek to promote communication and social interaction, and sensory, neurological and emotional development – see www.tacpac.co.uk.

was also the school's music coordinator, played the guitar and sang at different times throughout the day [R.1.D]. All members of Shivan's class were exposed to a wide range of recorded music [R.1.B], and, when he had a choice of activities, Shivan liked to select tracks to listen to using headphones [R.5.A].

In addition, Shivan had a weekly one-to-one session with Sally Zimmermann, the Music Advisor at the Royal National Institute of Blind People. She reported that Shivan continued and sometimes completed lines from familiar songs that are stopped mid-phrase, using both the correct words and notes [P.4.A]. He would also fill in the silences at the ends of phrases by repeating the last word or words that had just been sung [I.3.A]. Occasionally, he would sing phrases at the same time as someone else [I.4.D]. However, he did not sing entire songs from beginning to end unprompted [Not P.5.A]. If he wanted a song to be repeated, he sang or hummed the starting note [I.3.B]. Often, he was happy to hear a song many times over [R.5.A]. Shivan's contributions were usually quiet and reserved; occasional periods of higher energy and excitement appeared to have more to do with a self-awareness of his participation in a musical dialogue than as a result of recognising or responding particular features of the music [P.2.B].

Here is a transcription of one minute of a session, video-recorded when Shivan was nine years old, and judged by Sally to be typical of the nature of his interaction at the time (see Figure 4.13) [I.2.C]. This is available to view and hear on the *Sounds of Intent* website.

Sally further reported that Shivan's approach to hand-held percussion instruments was highly idiosyncratic. He rarely used them to sustain a line of music (as in accompaniments to songs) [Not I.4.D]. Instead, when offered an instrument, he would either put it on his lap and play with it at length (fiddling persistently with the beads on a cabassa, for example), showing considerable fine motor control [P.2.A, P.2.D], or he would mouth the instrument before quickly but gently handing it back to the adult concerned or placing it on the floor by the side of his wheelchair. He was very good at remembering where he had left instruments, and he could find them again some time after putting them down.

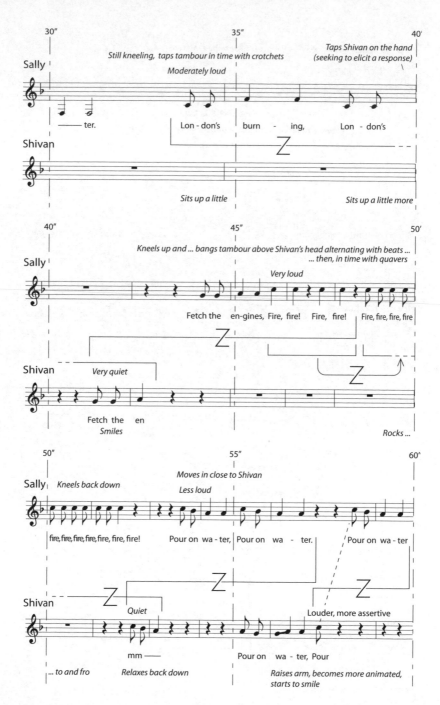

Figure 4.13 Shivan and Sally improvising vocally on 'London's Burning'

According to Sally, Shivan knew his way around a number of different keyboards, and was able to find the on/off buttons, tempo controls, 'fill' buttons and pitch-bend wheels. He could coordinate two button presses to change the beat or timbre [P.2.A]. However, his motivation for doing this appeared to be more to provoke a response from the person with him than for musical purposes [I.2.B]. This was shown by him repeating the button press if the adult responded (often becoming more animated if this process was repeated several times) and by the fact that he did not press the buttons at junctures that seemed to make sense musically [Not R.5.B].

Sally said that Shivan appeared to understand and would occasionally respond appropriately to some words used in a musical context, such as 'copy', 'play' and 'listen'. He knew that the interval of a falling fifth (G to C) was the cue for a recorded track in an otherwise live music session [R.4.D]. He sometimes waved his hands in anticipation of the song 'Music has Finished' following the appropriate verbal prompt. If he did not want to listen to a piece of music that had been offered, Shivan signalled this by becoming passive, or yawning and appearing to be tired [R.5.A].

What does this abundance of information tell us about Shivan's level of musical development? In seeking to gauge the nature of his engagement with music (and, at Level 1, the actions of those around him) in relation to *Sounds of Intent* elements, the crucial thing is the quality of the *evidence* that can be garnered to support the judgements that are made. Most powerful is the *direct* evidence in the form of the music that Shivan produced (a sample of which is transcribed in the 'London's Burning' interaction shown in Figure 4.13). *Indirect* evidence of Shivan's evolving musicality can be gleaned from his *non*-musical behaviours (for example, his reactions to a particular piece). Finally a *lack* of evidence (for instance, the fact that Shivan has never been observed to reproduce a whole song from beginning to end without prompting) can itself lead to certain reasonable assumptions being made. Inevitably, analysing data of this kind is to a greater or lesser extent subjective, though the validity and reliability of the findings can be enhanced by obtaining information from more than one source.

Here, then, is a detailed account of Shivan's engagement with music (see Table 4.2). Normally, one would expect such a profile to be built up by a teacher, therapist or team working with the pupil or client concerned over a substantial period of time, thus allowing any short-term variation in behaviour to be distinguished from longer-term, more significant patterns of change. Nonetheless, as the following analysis of Shivan's musicality shows, the *Sounds of Intent* framework can be used successfully to provide a 'snapshot' of a child or young person, given sufficiently contextualised, good quality evidence.

Table 4.2 A detailed analysis of Shivan's engagement with music using the *Sounds of Intent* criteria

Element	Evidence	Interpretation
R.1.A	Parents report trying to 'wean Shivan off music' to encourage him to listen to natural sounds when he is outside.	It is not clear what sense Shivan makes of many everyday sounds (see R.2.A).
R.1.B	Shivan listens to around eight to ten CDs a day. Shivan has seen a number of musicals, shows and operas. All members of Shivan's class are exposed to a wide range of recorded music at school.	A number of different people have been involved in determining which music Shivan experiences, albeit with some personal freedom for him to choose from a selection. (It may be that the impact of this exposure could be increased through coordination among the parties involved).
R.1.C	Music is played to Shivan in the context of different activities. Shivan's portable tape player accompanies him on walks. Shivan has been taken out to see live performances of musicals, shows and operas. Shivan works with a professional musician who plays him pieces of music both recorded and live.	Shivan is exposed to music in a range of different contexts, though the impact of these is unclear.
R.1.D	Music is integral to the school day, with songs and sound cues used to enhance learning across the curriculum.	It is not clear the extent to which sounds integrate with other perceptual input to assist Shivan in developing a fuller understanding of music and the wider world.

P.1.A	No evidence.	Other evidence (at level P.2) indicates that Shivan is beyond the need for support at this early developmental level.
P.1.B	No evidence.	Although other evidence (at level P.2) indicates that Shivan does not require co-active support to develop the notion of 'cause and effect', the fact that he is unable to see (and therefore lacks visual models to guide him) means that co-active assistance may still be needed, both in learning to make sounds with new instruments and in further developing his technique on familiar ones (such as the keyboard).
P.1.C P.1.D	No evidence.	Other evidence (at level P.2) indicates that Shivan is beyond the need for support at this early developmental level.
I.1.A I.1.B I.1.C I.1.D	No evidence.	Other evidence (at level I.3) indicates that Shivan is beyond the need for support at this early developmental level.
R.2.A	Implied by Shivan's responses to music.	It is interesting to reflect the extent to which Shivan processes all sound in a *musical* way, and the extent to which this may help or hinder his understanding of everyday life.
R.2.B	Implied by Shivan's differentiated responses to music.	It may be that Shivan's 'basic' responses to the qualities of sound are particularly important in his enjoyment of music (since, as we shall see, despite his obsessive interest in particular pieces and parts of them, Shivan does not appear to respond to works as 'narratives in sound'; cf. R.5.C).

Table continues

Table 4.2 A detailed analysis of Shivan's engagement with music using the *Sounds of Intent* criteria *cont.*

Element	Evidence	Interpretation
R.2.C	Implied by Shivan's reported desire to listen to music irrespective of the time of day, location or social context. Shivan has been taken out to see live performances of musicals, shows and operas.	It appears that Shivan's fascination for patterns of musical sounds is so powerful that it tends to overwhelm any appreciation of the context in which they are heard and their potential relationship with the wider world, although going out to hear live music may be an exception, and further work could seek to ascertain what it is about this context that has such a strong effect.
R.2.D	None.	Despite the integrated sensory programmes provided by Shivan's school, it is unclear (beyond his immediate capacity to make and control sounds by touching or manipulating instruments) whether he has a coherent sense of how musical sound can relate to other perceptual input.
P.2.A	Shivan 'plays with' instruments – for example, fiddling with the beads on the cabassa at length and with a high degree of fine motor control. He uses a range of controls on electronic keyboards – though not at junctures that seem to make sense musically.	These accounts suggest that, as far as instruments are concerned, Shivan is still at the stage of using them to enjoy making and controlling sound for its own sake rather than for musical ends – though other of his behaviours seem to indicate that he has the potential to develop this capacity (see observations at level P.4).
P.2.B	The character of Shivan's vocalising appears to depend on, and reflect, his feelings of the moment – often seeming to be introverted and reserved, but occasionally more extrovert, energetic and even joyful.	Shivan expresses his feelings in the way he vocalises – but this seems to have more to do with the sheer pleasure of producing sound or interacting with another person than factors relating to musical structure or content.
P.2.C	Implied in the accounts of Shivan vocalising, playing the keyboard and playing CDs both at home and school.	Context appears to be unimportant to Shivan in making sounds and music (cf. R.2.C).

P.2.D	Shivan fiddles persistently with the beads on the cabassa.	The relative importance of tactile and auditory input in experiences such as this is unclear; future work with Shivan could unpack the motivations underlying his participation in multisensory activities and suggest future programmes of learning based on perceptual integration.
I.2.A I.2.B	Shown in the interaction illustrated in Figure 4.13.	Shivan's 'music and communication' sessions incorporate interaction at this level and move beyond it to involve imitation too (see I.3).
I.2.C	Shivan responds vocally both to his father's singing or whistling and Sally's singing.	These observations suggest that Shivan's responses relate to qualities inherent in the music irrespective of (or as well as) the person interacting, although there may be subtle differences in the nature of the interactions.
I.2.D	Sally taps Shivan's hand in the course of their session to encourage him to respond musically. There is no immediate response, however (Figure 4.13).	It is not clear whether Shivan associates and can integrate other sensory input with musical interaction.
R.3.A	Shivan's recognition of repetition is implied through his musically coherent interaction using the material from 'London's Burning', whose every phrase embodies repetition as a structural element. Moreover, Shivan reacts to an unusual degree of repetition by rocking as Sally repeats 'Fire, fire' with increasing speed. Shivan then picks up on the final note of the repeated series of notes and sings the next phrase, evidently recognising Sally's extended repetition as a development of the repeated figure upon which it was based (Figure 4.11).	It is evident that Shivan has grasped the most fundamental form of musical structure – repetition – at least in one familiar context (which includes the novel development of material).

Table continues

Table 4.2 A detailed analysis of Shivan's engagement with music using the *Sounds of Intent* criteria *cont.*

Element	Evidence	Interpretation
R.3.B	Shivan's recognition of a regular beat is implied through his contributions to 'London's Burning', which conform to the even pulse that underlies it, even through silences, pauses and changes in tempo (see P.3.B).	Shivan can internalise regular beats – necessary for making sense of most music – at different tempi.
R.3.C	Shivan's recognition of regular change is implied by the fact that a number of his contributions to the 'London's Burning' interaction conform to the structure of the major scale, upon which the piece is based. Shivan's proclivity for changing the beat or pitch on keyboards may also be indicative of an appreciation of regular change in these dimensions of sound.	Shivan's use of the major scale indicates that he has internalised the intervallic framework, based on regular patterns of change, that characterises most Western music, and which is fundamental to understanding it. His interest in altering tempi (see also R.3.B) may indicate that he recognises regular change in the domain of perceived time too (cf. P.3.C).
R.3.D	Forthcoming activities are signalled with particular songs.	It is not clear the extent to which Shivan links these sound cues with other perceptual input to assist his understanding of music and the wider world (cf. R.1.D and P.3.D – though see evidence in R.4.D).
P.3.A	Shivan's contributions to 'London's Burning' involve repetition, either within the phrases that he produces (see Figure 4.13), or deriving from what Sally has just sung, or both (see I.3.A).	Shivan can reproduce the most fundamental form of musical structure: the imitation of a preceding note (cf. R.3.A).
P.3.B	Shivan conforms to the regular beat that is fundamental to 'London's Burning' – even through silences and changes of tempo (cf. R.3.B).	Shivan can reproduce a regular pulse at a variety of speeds, without the need for every beat to be realised in sound.

P.3.C	Shivan uses regular change in pitch to reproduce patterns in 'London's Burning' (cf. R.3.C). There is also evidence of Shivan starting his response on the 'incorrect' note of the scale (which he subsequently corrects). This implies that he has the capacity to take an abstract pitch contour and realise it at different degrees of the scale. Shivan enjoys bending pitches and changing the speed and of 'demos' on the keyboard (cf. R.3.C).	Shivan can (re)produce structures that are founded on regular change in the domain of pitch, and has the capacity to change the speed of a regular beat (cf. R.3.C).
P.3.D	Shivan occasionally says 'change' to change a tape or CD or 'not working' if the batteries run out – although he often just cries or taps if needs something.	Shivan appears to be on the cusp of using sounds symbolically. (The systematic use of musical sound-symbols in conjunction with language may promote further development in this area – see I.3.A).
R.4.A	Shivan usually plays only snippets of music from CDs, just a few seconds long. Although 'London's Burning' is made up of distinctive groups of sounds ('motifs'), Shivan rarely produces an entire motif alone (see P.4.A). Rather, his efforts tend to 'bridge' motifs, ending one and beginning another, emulating what Sally often does (presumably offering the *opening* of motifs in the intuitive expectation that these will be more likely to stimulate to Shivan to continue than would *complete* motifs, which provide a sense of closure).	The fact that Shivan is able to complete motifs once they are begun, and appears to have an expectation that Sally will complete those that *he* starts (cf. I.4.A), as well as occasionally producing entire motifs himself, suggests that he does appreciate, at some level, that the music he is familiar with comprises distinct 'chunks' of material. More information would be required about the 'snippets' he plays from CDs to ascertain whether these comprised what most listeners would regard as logical 'chunks' of music, implying that Shivan was attending to structural relationships beneath the perceptual 'surface', or whether he was just attracted to series of features of the sounds that were not of structural import.

Table continues

Table 4.2 A detailed analysis of Shivan's engagement with music using the *Sounds of Intent* criteria *cont.*

Element	Evidence	Interpretation
R.4.B	Shivan plays the same snippets of music over and over (cf. R.4.A). In 'London's Burning', he repeats a motif, and responds by rocking to the quickening repetition of 'Fire, fire!' (cf. R.3.A).	These behaviours are indicative of the fact that Shivan appreciates (at least in some contexts) that chunks of music can be repeated and varied – a feature of structure that is fundamental to all 'natural' musical grammars.
R.4.C	In his contributions to 'London's Burning', Shivan often anticipates the motif that follows (bridging between successive musical chunks) (cf. R.4.A).	Shivan's propensity to bridge motifs shows his intuitive understanding of how chunks of music can be linked coherently (cf. P.4.C).
R.4.D	Shivan knows that a falling fifth is the cue for a recorded track in an otherwise live music session.	This recognition suggests that at least one auditory pattern (a single interval) is understood symbolically, a comparable level of communication to his use of single words (cf. P.3.D).
P.4.A	Shivan sings short phrases from songs. In the course of 'London's Burning', Shivan largely bridges motifs, though he also produces complete ones (cf. R.4.C).	Shivan can produce entire motifs, but does not necessarily do this in the course of interactions, being content to let Sally start and complete them – arguably a stage in development that precedes producing entire motifs himself (cf. I.4.A).
P.4.B	Shivan links entire motifs through repetition in 'London's Burning', and with Sally's interpolations elsewhere. At one stage, he varies the preceding motif.	Repetition of motifs is (re)produced alone and with a partner; the variation he produces at one point is probably not intentional (see P.5.A).
P.4.C	Shivan juxtaposes different motifs coherently through 'bridging' Sally's contributions in 'London's Burning' (cf. R.4.C).	Coherent motivic connections are achieved with an interactive musical partner (cf. I.4).

P.4.D	Shivan sings in the mornings to indicate that he wants to go downstairs.	It is unclear whether Shivan always sings the same music, or whether he would use any song from his repertoire to achieve the same effect. The former would indicate that a given piece was being used symbolically; the latter would imply that music per se was being imbued with a contextually specific meaning.
I.4.A	Shivan sings when his father whistles or sings. In 'London's Burning', Shivan tends not to copy whole motifs exactly, though he evidently can, as in Segment 5 (cf. P.4.A).	It can be hypothesised that Shivan's tendency to 'bridge' motifs exemplified in 'London's Burning' indicates a stage of development that precedes a more 'antiphonal' style of interaction, in which whole chunks are passed between participants. It could be that Shivan's 'bridging' is a reflection of the scaffolding technique adopted by Sally, in which she provides the essential continuity and structural architecture of the song, upon which Shivan dips in and out with elements at the musical 'surface'.
I.4.B	Shivan's contribution in 'London's Burning' shows that he can respond coherently to another's input by linking complete (and different) motifs himself – although his habit of 'bridging' motifs (which may be different) tends to predominate.	See comment at I.4.A.
I.4.C	Shivan sings to encourage his father to whistle or sing. Shivan's interaction in 'London's Burning' shows him producing motifs, complete or in part, followed by periods of silence (in which Sally takes up the musical thread).	It is clear that Shivan wishes his father to imitate his singing through whistling. Shivan appears to use silence following a contribution as an indication to Sally that she should continue (cf. I.3.D).

Table continues

Table 4.2 A detailed analysis of Shivan's engagement with music using the *Sounds of Intent* criteria *cont.*

Element	Evidence	Interpretation
I.4.D	Shivan takes turns in 'London's Burning', though idiosyncratically, not respecting the structural boundaries of the song. In the excerpt that is transcribed, he twice sings *with* Sally in a fragmentary way. Shivan rarely uses percussion instruments to sustain a line of music, as in accompaniments to songs.	Shivan takes turns, though not within the conventional framework of the 'give and take' of improvised musical conversations. The more advanced skill of performing simultaneously with another – which implies hearing and concentrating on two parts at once, and adjusting one's contribution to fit another's in real time – appears to be at an early stage of development.
R.5.A	Shivan listens to many CDs and indicates his preferences; his tastes have changed over the years. Shivan's patterns of sleep were disturbed after hearing musicals (live). A professional musician who worked with Shivan reported that he sometimes reacted emotionally to the pieces he heard. Shivan enjoys listening to selected tracks at school using headphones. In 'music and communication' sessions, Shivan is often happy to hear a song many times over. Shivan signals if he does not want to listen to a piece of music that has been offered.	Shivan has heard many pieces of music in his life, though it is not clear how many he can remember. He has strong likes and dislikes, which he sometimes indicates clearly, and his preferences appear to have evolved over time. This may be through maturation or even boredom caused through self-induced excessive exposure to certain pieces. It is reported that music can have a powerful emotional effect on Shivan, though it is not clear what it is about pieces that move him (cf. R.5.B and R.5.C): there is no evidence that Shivan engages with pieces of music as a whole as they unfold over time as abstract narratives in sound (R.6.A). Based on what he produced in the 'London's Burning' interaction, it seems more likely that is the basic qualities of sound (R.2) and simple 'surface' structures based on immediate repetition or regular change (R.3 and R.4) that appeal. Hence it probably would not really matter to Shivan if, for example, elements of different pieces were strung together in the manner of the 'potpourri' songs typical of three-year-olds.

R.5.B	Shivan presses buttons on the keyboard to change the beat or the timbre, but such button presses do not occur at junctures that seem to make sense musically.	This suggests that Shivan is not aware of (or does not perceive the significance of) prominent structural features – a view that is reinforced by his willingness to ignore motivic boundaries when interacting – adding up to a view of Shivan's perception of music as near the 'surface'.
R.5.C	The professional musician who worked with Shivan considered that he was particularly responsive to Mozart and Beethoven piano sonatas. In 'London's Burning', Shivan maintains the same diatonic pitch framework (F major) throughout.	If this first observation is correct, it would indicate that Shivan has a sophisticated stylistic awareness (at R.6.B). This would not accord with the other evidence as to Shivan's probable level of musical development. However, it could be that Shivan is attracted not to the music of Mozart and Beethoven *per se*, but to piano music of the 'common practice' period, which would suggest that Shivan can recognise the general attributes of music (such as the mode, tempo and texture), rather than the niceties of style at the level of individual composers. This view is supported by his contributions to 'London's Burning'.
R.5.D	There is no evidence that Shivan responds to pieces through connotations derived from their association with events or people outside music.	Shivan does not yet appear to be processing music at this associative level.

Table continues

Table 4.2 A detailed analysis of Shivan's engagement with music using the *Sounds of Intent* criteria *cont.*

Element	Evidence	Interpretation
P.5.A	Shivan does not sing entire songs from beginning to end unprompted. This assertion is supported by the excerpt from 'London's Burning'. However, Shivan's contributions do indicate a secure underlying pitch framework.	It may be that Shivan has an unusually well-developed sense of pitch (perhaps evolving absolute pitch), which gives him an apparently skewed profile of musical ability, whereby he perceives pieces in terms of an overall pitch framework, but not yet as a structural whole. This is shown by him tending to use the notes to start motives with which Sally ended hers, rather than the correct ones that would make longer term structural sense. For example, he twice starts 'Pour on water' with A (the note that Sally has just sung) rather than C. On both occasions, he corrects himself. However, it is as though the individual percept of the note was temporarily more powerful than the relationships that contextualise it structurally. Typically, at this stage of development, one would expect the *contour* of the melody (its basic pattern of ups and downs) to be correct, rather than this being compromised through a focus on individual pitches. Yet that is what Shivan does. This is discussed further in Chapter 6.
P.5.B	There is no evidence of Shivan improvising on known material.	The variation that does exist seems to be unintentional (see P.5.A).
P.5.C	There is no evidence of Shivan creating his own musical material.	Many of the building blocks that would enable Shivan to create music appear to be in place – his interest in and knowledge of many pieces, his well-developed sense of pitch, his capacity for spontaneous musical interaction – but the capacity and/or motivation to create new material (generally typical of children at this stage of musical development) appears not yet to have evolved.

P.5.D	Shivan's contribution to 'London's Burning' shows that he appears to have the physical capacity to produce short and simple pieces of music.	Cognitively, this ability has not yet developed, though.
I.5.A I.5.B I.5.C I.5.D	No evidence.	Shivan does not yet appear to be functioning at this level.
R.6.A R.6.B R.6.C R.6.D	No reliable evidence (see comments at R.5.A).	Shivan does not yet appear to functioning at this level.
P.6.A P.6.B P.6.C P.6.D	No evidence.	Shivan does not yet appear to functioning at this level.
I.6.A I.6.B I.6.C I.6.D	No evidence.	Shivan does not yet appear to functioning at this level.

In summary, Shivan's *Sounds of Intent* profile can be represented as shown in Figure 4.14. This shows at a glance that Shivan is functioning in most respects at Level 4. However, his well-developed sense of pitch enables him to attain certain aspects of Level 5 in the reactive domain. That is, he has an uneven profile of musical development, which may or may not equalise over time. In relation to Shivan's general level of cognitive functioning, it is evident that music is, by a considerable margin, his greatest area of achievement.

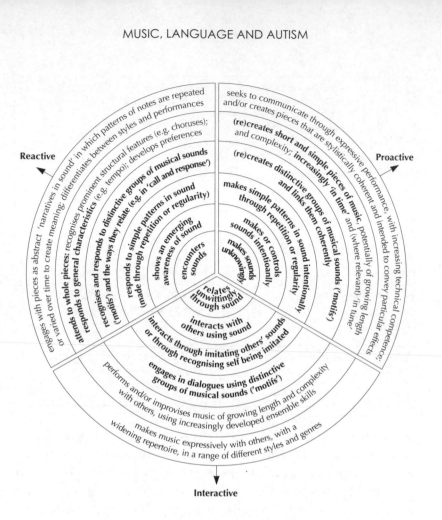

Figure 4.14 Visual representation of Shivan's level of musical development using the *Sounds of Intent* framework

CONCLUSION

In this chapter we presented evidence as to how a sense of derivation through imitation in sound – and, therefore, an awareness and appreciation of music – may develop in children with autism. Six stages in this process were identified, which were set out in relation to three domains of engagement with music: reactivity, proactivity and interactivity. The resulting *Sounds of Intent* developmental framework was shown in action with Shivan, a boy with severe learning difficulties and autism, in whose life music is a central element.

CHAPTER 5

Music, Language and Communication

INTRODUCTION

Previous chapters have examined definitions and the implications of autism, how language works, how music conveys meaning, and how musicality evolves in children. We now move on to consider communication more broadly, and how linguistic and musical development may advantageously be linked in the lives and learning of some children on the autism spectrum. (The potential role of music in promoting linguistic development in children with autism is recognised in an increasingly wide range of research: see e.g. Lim 2012; Simpson and Keen 2011; Yan and Schlaug 2010; Yan *et al.* 2010.)

THE DEVELOPMENT OF EARLY COMMUNICATION – AND AUGMENTATIVE STRATEGIES

Although the development of communication is continuous and irregular, it is possible, rather as the *Sounds of Intent* framework does in relation to music, to identify different stages in the evolution of children's capacity to receive information from others (the 'receptive' element in a dialogue) and convey information to them (the 'expressive' component): see Ockelford (2001). The five stages are shown in Figure 5.1.

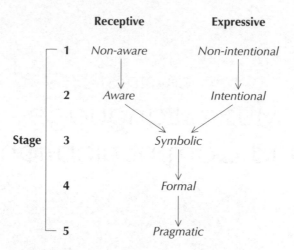

Figure 5.1 Five stages in the development of human communication

The earliest stage of communication is characterised, in expressive terms, by a child's unthinking reaction to basic needs – crying in response to physical discomfort, for example: an unwitting plea for help that may be detected by carers, who vest in the sounds a communicative intent, and act accordingly. This form of communication is termed '*non-intentional*'. Receptively, at this stage, children do not recognise the attempts by others to make their thoughts and feelings known. They are communicatively '*non-aware*'.

Gradually, youngsters may grow to realise that crying, other vocalising and particular expressions or gestures have an effect on others: this is termed the '*intentional*' stage in the development of communication. Here, children commonly draw people's attention to things by taking an adult's hand and putting it on something, or by handing over an object (or making it clear that they wish to take it back), or by pointing – perhaps relishing the shared external interest that this may arouse. Receptively, they come to appreciate that others can impart information through the sounds or gestures that they make; communicatively, they become '*aware*'.

Next comes a growing appreciation of '*symbolic*' communication, in which *one thing is understood to stand for another*. A child may flap her hand consistently to mean 'yes', for example, or she may use the made-up word 'bo-bo' in referring to her rocking horse. Similarly, an adult may show the child her coat to indicate that it is time to go out.

These symbolic personal gestures and vocalisations may eventually become standardised in conventional signing or speech, or lead to literacy. At this point, communication is said to be '*formal*'.

Finally, children become aware of how context contributes to meaning, including a knowledge about those involved and the inferred intent of the speaker. This social understanding of communication is termed '*pragmatics*'.

As we saw in Chapter 1, children on the autism spectrum often find communication challenging, with delays in developing receptive and expressive language and, in those who can and will speak, difficulties in initiating and sustaining conversation, and the use of stereotyped phraseology. In terms of social communication more broadly, there may well be a lack of eye contact, a failure to understand the significance of facial expressions, or to produce them appropriately, and an inability to grasp the significance of posture, gesture and personal space when interacting with others. Such children are likely to benefit from specialist intervention to help them develop the communication skills that usually evolve quite naturally, with little or no conscious effort on the part of parents, teachers, therapists or carers.

In Chapter 2, we saw how complex spoken language is, how ambiguous and even capricious (since words can mean different things according to the manner and context in which they are said), and how intangible: passing by fleetingly with a huge reliance on working memory to extract meaning. To ameliorate these difficulties, a common approach is to *augment* receptive language through enhancing or replacing the spoken word with symbolic information in other domains that is more distinct and accessible, both in sensory and cognitive terms. For example, accompanying speech with signing will mean that ideas are represented multidimensionally, yielding symbols that are perceptually richer and therefore more likely to be recognised and remembered, and allowing a greater margin for error in the transmission and reception of messages. Nonetheless, signs, like words, are ephemeral, and other systems of augmentative communication, such as PECS (see p.27), have sought to crystallise the symbolic meanings usually conveyed by words in the form of pictures, which have a certain permanence, and which can be viewed and rechecked over a period of time. Using PECS also tends to simplify what is expressed, since only the key features of language can be relayed. Both PECS and signing offer children with autism and learning difficulties forms of symbolic communication that they can readily perceive, are capable of understanding, and can physically manage.

However, a very special group of young people exists who, in addition to finding communication challenging on account of autism and learning difficulties, are also severely visually impaired, and in the late 1980s and 1990s, working with colleagues at Linden Lodge School in London, I pioneered using an approach to augmentative communication that had been developed with deafblind children by Jan van Dijk in the 1960s in the Netherlands (see e.g. Macfarland 1995). This involved the use of 'objects of reference' – largely everyday objects that were given symbolic meanings. For example, a spoon may be taken to mean 'food', a piece of towelling may mean 'swimming', and a bell may mean 'music'. Objects of reference may represent *activities, places* or *people*. In terms of symbolic logic, they may derive from a thing that is used in an activity (a cup meaning 'drink', for instance), or be part of something that is used (a stirrup meaning 'horse-riding' for example), or be linked through association (as in the case of a jangly bracelet that someone wears consistently). Objects of reference may be used be receptively, to inform a child what was going to happen next, for example, or expressively, to enable a pupil to choose, for instance, between two types of drink.

An issue raised by teachers at the time was at what point it was appropriate to introduce objects of reference in relation to a child's broader development. To this end, I developed a framework, showing how the five stages of communication identified in Figure 5.1 work in each of four domains: vocal, gestural/visual (person-based), gestural/visual (externally based) and tactile/haptic (see Table 5.1).

Table 5.1 Framework of the development of communication

Stages	Domain				
	Vocal	Gestural / visual (person-based)	Gestural / visual (externally based)	Tactile / haptic
1 Non-aware, Non-intentional	Receptive	Does not interpret human voices in the context of communication.	Does not interpret (for example) on-body signs or other physical cc-activity in the context of communication.	Does not engage in shared attention.	Does not recognise that being brought into contact with things could have significance or meaning.
	Expressive	Cries in response to need (without thinking).	May make reflex movements; for example, arching bcck in displeasure.	Appears to derive no meaning from any visual perception that may be present.	May bring himself/ herself into contact with things (accidentally).
2 Aware, Intentional	Receptive	Understands that the vocal sounds made by others may have meaning.	Recognises simple non-symbolic gestures in others; for example, adults extending their hands out to pick the child up.	Engages in shared attention, and understancs references made by others to things by pointing.	Understands others' manipulation of objects to communicate: for example, putting the child's hand on a beaker with juice in it, to indicate that a drink is available.
	Expressive	Deliberately vocalises to show needs and wants.	Makes simple non-symbolic gestures to communicate with others; for example, extending an arm to attract attention.	Engages in shared attention, for example, by pointing to things in the immediate environment.	Consciously manipulates others in relation to objects to communicate: for example, proffers a guitar in the hope the adult will strum the strings.

Table continues

Table 5.1 Framework of the development of communication cont.

Stages		Domain			
		Vocal	Gestural / visual (person-based)	Gestural / visual (externally based)	Tactile / haptic
3 Symbolic	Receptive	Understands personal utterances: for example, adult says 'timo' meaning a favourite soft toy.	Understands personal signs (which could be on-body): for example, a tap on the shoulder for 'stand up'.	Understands the significance of another pointing at pictures.	Understands 'objects of reference'.
	Expressive	Makes personal utterances: for example, says 'mmm' meaning 'hairdrier'.	Makes personal signs: for example, flaps hand for 'yes'.	Points at pictures or picks up picture-cards to communicate; draws.	Uses 'objects of reference'.
4 Formal	Receptive	Understands speech.	Understands conventional signs.	Reads (print).	Reads Braille or Moon (another tactile reading system).
	Expressive	Speaks.	Uses conventional signs.	Points at symbols or words writes.	Writes using Braille (it is difficult to write using Moon).
5 Pragmatic	Receptive	Appreciates the social contexts in which speech is used and the impact these have on meaning.	Appreciates the social contexts in which signs are used and the impact these have on meaning.	Understands that there are different kinds of writing for different occasions and audiences.	Understands that there are different kinds of writing for different occasions and audiences.
	Expressive	Speaks using language appropriate to a given social context.	Signs using language appropriate to a given social context.	Writes for different audiences and different occasions appropriately.	Writes for different audiences and different occasions appropriately.

Table 5.1 merely presents an outline of the ways in which communication may but need not occur. In reality, things are not as neat and tidy as this, of course: communication, like all spheres of human endeavour, is a 'fuzzy' enterprise. A communicative action may cross sensory domains, for example, involving sight, hearing and touch at the same time; and stages in a given domain are subsumed, one within another – for instance, formal communication is, by definition, both symbolic and intentional. Stages may also overlap, with intentional expression, for example, occurring alongside communication of a more symbolic or formal nature. It is quite common to encounter children on the autism spectrum who can read and write fluently, yet who are unwilling or unable to use spoken language, receptively or expressively, and much prefer to take adults by the hand to indicate what they want in everyday situations.

Development may well be inconsistent across domains: indeed, this is one of the principles upon which augmentative communication is founded – to ameliorate weaknesses in one domain with potential strengths in another. Children's levels of communication, particularly the use of expressive language, may well fluctuate, and some may be prepared to speak only on particular occasions or in certain contexts (with a given person in a familiar situation, for example). Some children make consistent progress in developing the confidence and skills to communicate, while others may plateau: augmentative communication methods seek to maximise the possibility of progress, as well as increasing the effectiveness of information transfer at any given level.

It is worth noting that, while objects of reference have proved a highly successful intervention with some blind children on the autism spectrum, they are rarely considered an option for those who are not visually impaired. I believe this is an area that should be explored further, since objects offer a degree of abstraction less than the representation of things as pictures, and may well constitute the appropriate means of symbolic communication for those who find two-dimensional depiction problematic. Indeed, objects of reference, which can be simplified and made more abstract over time, may assist in developing two-dimensional representational skills.

USING SOUND AND MUSIC TO AUGMENT COMMUNICATION

During the 1990s and early 2000s, I took the step of adding music and musical sounds in to this scheme – a form of augmentation that, as we shall see, can be used in two ways: as a system of communication in its own right, as well as supplementing and supporting communication in other domains.

This is how the *Sounds of Intent* framework fits within the broader development of communication (set out in Table 5.1) – see Table 5.2.

One immediate issue is that the framework outlining the development of communication has two domains (receptive and expressive), whereas *Sounds of Intent* has three: reactive, proactive and interactive. This reflects the special place of interaction in music, in which performers can play or sing simultaneously, whereas linguistic communication and its proxies tend to be turn-taking in nature. That is, while the 'interactive' domain in music is to an extent a combination of the 'reactive' and 'proactive' domains, it also exists as a distinct sphere of endeavour in its own right.

In the first two phases of communication and musical development, there is a clear overlap: neither language nor music has evolved as a distinct entity within a child's growing awareness of sound and of the conscious capacity to produce or control it. It is at Stage 3 (communication) and Levels 3 and 4 (music) where a distinction begins to materialise. Here, an appreciation of simple repetition and imitation – the beginnings of musical syntax – emerges, while in the realm of language, symbolic understanding evolves. Both these cognitive processes rely on relationships: in the case of the former, between sounds the same (see Figures 3.8 and 3.9), and in the case of the latter, between a sound and a phenomenon in world beyond (see Figure 5.2).

Table 5.2 Combined framework of communication and musical development

Stage of communication	Sounds of Intent level and description		Sounds of Intent Reactive	Sounds of Intent Proactive	Sounds of Intent Interactive
1 Non-aware, Non-intentional	C	1 Buzzing, blooming confusion	Encounters sounds.	Makes sounds unknowingly.	Relates unwittingly through sound.
			Is exposed to music and musical sounds that are systematically linked to other sensory input R.1.D.	Some activities to promote sound production and/or control are multisensory in nature P.1.D.	Some activities to promote interaction through sound are multisensory in nature I.1.D.
2 Aware, Intentional	I	2 Awareness and intentionality	Shows an emerging awareness of sound.	Makes or controls sounds intentionally.	Interacts with others using sound.
			Responds to musical sounds linked to other sensory input R.2.D.	Produces sounds as part of multisensory activity P.2.D.	Interaction through sound involves activity that engages the other senses too I.2.D.
3 Symbolic	R	3 Relationships, repetition, regularity	Responds to simple patterns in sound made through repetition or regularity.	Makes simple patterns in sound intentionally, through repetition or regularity.	Interacts through imitating others' sounds or through recognising self being imitated.
			Responds to musical sounds used to symbolise other things R.3.D.	Uses sound to symbolise other things P.3.D.	

Table continues

Table 5.2 Combined framework communication and musical development cont.

Stage of communication	Sounds of Intent level and description		Sounds of Intent Reactive	Sounds of Intent Proactive	Sounds of Intent Interactive
3 Symbolic	C	4 Sounds forming clusters	Recognises and responds to distinctive groups of musical sounds and the relationships between them.	(Re)creates distinctive groups of musical sounds ('motifs') and links them coherently.	Engages in dialogues using distinctive groups of musical sounds ('motifs').
			Responds to musical motifs used to symbolise other things R.4.D.	Uses musical motifs to symbolise other things P.4.D.	
4 Formal	L	5 Deeper structural links	Attends to whole pieces; recognises prominent structural features; responds to general characteristics; develops preferences.	(Re)creates short and simple pieces of music, potentially of growing length and complexity; increasingly 'in time' and (where relevant) 'in tune'.	Performs and/or improvises music of growing length and complexity with others, using increasingly developed ensemble skills.
			Responds to pieces through connotations brought about by their association with objects, people or events in the external world R.5.D.		
5 Pragmatic	E	6 Mature artistic expression	Engages with pieces as abstract 'narratives in sound' in which patterns of notes are repeated varied over time to create meaning; differentiates between styles and performances.	Seeks to communicate through expressive performances, with increasing technical competence; creates pieces that are intended to convey particular effects.	Makes music expressively with others, with a widening repertoire, in a range of different styles and genres.

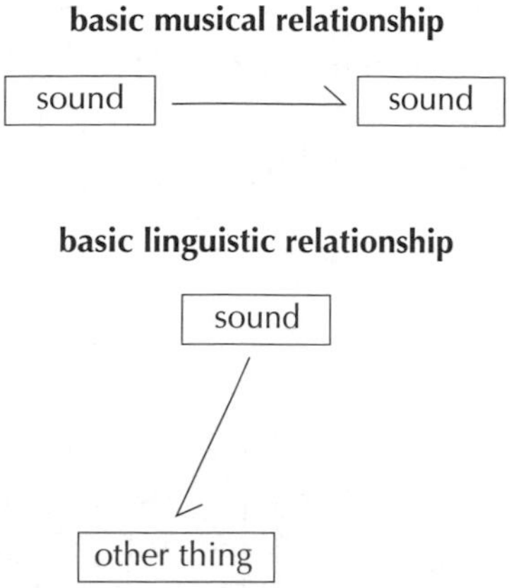

basic musical relationship

basic linguistic relationship

Figure 5.2 Both music and language work through relationships,
(a) between sounds and (b) between sounds and other phenomena

It is in these two types of relationship that the fundamental difference between language and music exists (see Figures 3.2 and 3.3). The musical relationship is simpler because it exists between phenomena in the same sensory modality (sound), because musical events (notes) tend to be simpler perceptually than linguistic events (words), and because there is none of the ambiguity associated with semantic relationships (for example, the 'other thing' represented could actually be a class of other things or any individual member of that class – hence, potentially many different things; see p.38).

Stage 4 (communication) and Level 5 (music) both show the impact of a child's prevailing culture: the words and syntax of a given language (or languages) start to become established, as do the tonal and temporal frameworks of the musical style or styles to which he or she is exposed. Stage 5 (communication) and Level 6 (music) are about understanding the effect of social contexts on language and music, and their potential impact on others.

The development of music and language together can be represented as shown in Figure 5.3 (see Miller and Ockelford 2005). This illustrates the notion that, initially (from three months before birth), the brain does not process the sound in terms of its discrete functions (musical and linguistic); rather, it seems that this distinction evolves during the first 12–18 months of life. This notion fits well with the thinking of cognitive neuroscientist Aniruddh Patel, who believes that some brain resources are shared between music and language, and some are discrete (see p.107).

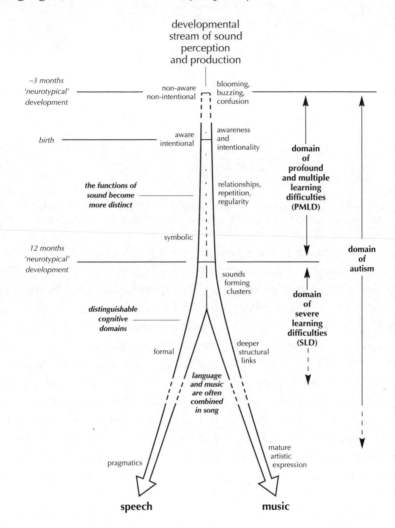

Figure 5.3 Representation of the development of language and music

It is possible that the phases of linguistic and musical development – fuzzy though they are – develop, at least as far as the receptive and reactive domains are concerned, more or less in kilter, in the way suggested in Figure 5.3. However, in Western cultures at least, music generally loses out proactively at Level 6 to language, Stage 5, since, as observed above, relatively few people go on to become advanced performers, capable of what would generally be recognised as mature artistic expression. However, most of us *do* develop an advanced sense of pragmatics in language, and, as adults, can convey a wide range of thoughts and feelings appropriately through everyday improvised speech.

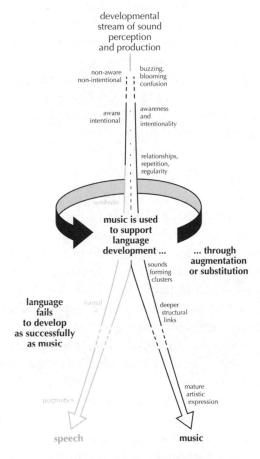

Figure 5.4 Musical development may outstrip linguistic development in some children on the autism spectrum

In engaging with any child, adults use music before language takes hold to convey feelings and promote social bonding (p.45), and subsequently to scaffold and augment language through songs, chants and musical games. As we noted above, many children on the autism spectrum or with learning difficulties have uneven profiles of development, which may well include linguistic development lagging behind the emergence of musicality (expressively or receptively or both). That is to say, the two prongs of communication in the auditory domain (music and language) may evolve unevenly. (In my experience, it is very unusual for uneven profiles of this type to occur the other way round, with language dominating music.) Indeed, in extreme cases it is possible for musical development to occur – even for a child to reach an advanced level of performance – in the absence of *any* expressive language. Here, music may be of particular value in promoting linguistic development, through augmenting the message of words or even substituting for them, by functioning symbolically in its own right (Figure 5.4). In the next section, we consider the practicalities of making this happen.

SOUND AND MUSIC AS SYMBOL

As we saw in Chapter 3, music and other organised sounds (in addition to speech) can fulfil a range of symbolic functions in everyday life. Consider, for example, the signature tunes that are used to introduce television and radio series: just a few notes are sufficient to remind regular viewers and listeners of their favourite programmes. Other familiar sound-symbols include church bells, door chimes, fire alarms and the referee's whistle in sport. These supply information about what is currently happening, what has recently taken place, or give warning of what is about to occur. They are used in preference to speech for a number of reasons: their immediate impact may be greater, for example, or they may be more aesthetically pleasing. However, it is through verbal explanation that people typically become familiar with the meaning of sound-symbols such as these. This need not be the case, however, and the principle of using sound symbolically can be extended to augment the receptive communication of children with autism and learning difficulties, and to assist them in their efforts to communicate expressively.

The *Sounds of Intent* framework indicates that the symbolic use of sound and music occurs at Levels 3 and 4 – the stage at which the use of words typically manifests itself (see Table 5.2). The framework distinguishes between musical *sounds* being used to represent other things (at Level 3) and musical *motifs* (at Level 4). We will deal first with the former.

There are various categories of day-to-day information that can be symbolised through sound, including *activities, places* and *people* (see Ockelford 1998). Sound-symbols can relate to these areas in two ways. There may be a direct link, where a sound is integral to a given activity, for instance, such as a small cluster of bells being used to represent a music session. Other sound-symbols work through being associated with the activity concerned, and so operate at a more abstract level. For example, a horn may be taken to mean 'ride the bike'. This type of connection can also be applied to places and people. For instance, the windchimes chosen to help characterise a room may also be used to represent it symbolically (see Figure 5.6), while the jangling bracelets or bangles worn to enhance the individuality of key figures in a child's life may acquire referential status too (see Figure 4.4).

The use of sound-symbols like these can be reinforced by placing them in the structured context of especially designed songs such as those from *All Join In!*, a set of 24 songs that I wrote in the 1990s for children with a range of learning difficulties, including those with sensory impairment and autism, which are now available in their original form on the *Sounds of Intent* website, from where they can be freely downloaded. All the songs are included in this chapter, some updated slightly, based on my two decades of experience in using them with a wide range of children, young people and adults with autism. The topics of the songs are 'self and other', 'time and place', 'things around' and 'music and sound'. They can be used to structure music sessions in their own right, with the fixed introductory songs (A and B) and concluding numbers (D and E), and a menu of possibilities in between (C_1 to C_5) – see Figure 5.5. Alternatively, the songs can be used independently in support of individual communication programmes.

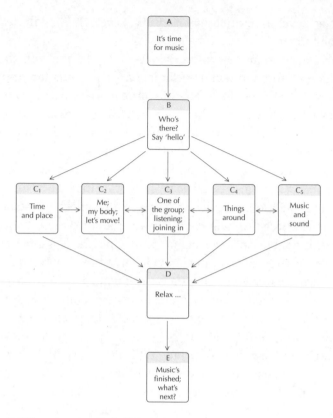

Figure 5.5 The structure of *All Join in!*

Throughout, the language used is simple and concrete, with the conscious avoidance of abstract concepts or metaphor, which, as we have seen, can be characteristic of children's songs. Key words and phrases are consistently allocated the same rhythm and, where possible, melodic shape (see Figure 5.6), opening up the possibility of musical fragments acquiring symbolic meaning in their own right. The tunes are constrained in pitch range and repetitive. Each of the 12 different available keys is used – making each piece as distinctive as possible, particularly for those children with autism with absolute pitch, for whom every note sounds quite different. In summary, the songs are intended to have a high degree of individuality, yet to be as easy to learn and engage with as possible.

Here is an example of a song that utilises sound-symbols of place (Figure 5.6).

Audio, MIDI and simplified versions of this song are available at **www.soundsofintent.org**

Figure 5.6 Sound-symbol (windchimes) used to represent a child's classroom, and incorporated into a song from *All Join In!*

Sound-symbols will often have tactile and visual qualities that may be exploited within multisensory communication programmes, just as some objects of reference, which are principally identified through touch and vision, have the capacity for making characteristic sounds. For example, a carved wooden rattle may be distinct and attractive visually, while a small bag of coins may make a unique jingling sound. In either case, the objects can be used in combination with other forms of communication, including speech and signing, as part of an integrated approach.

Practitioners and parents need to give careful attention to the circumstances in which sound-symbols are used, especially in the early stages. They are not something to be learnt about in isolation, but should be introduced in everyday situations, growing naturally from children's first-hand experiences, *whenever the need to communicate arises*. It is particularly important, in embarking on a communication programme, to consult widely and plan thoroughly, taking account of any strong interests or preferences a child may have.

Sound-symbols may be used first to augment *receptive* communication. They may be of particular benefit to children whose capacity for absorbing information in tactile form is limited, and who may find objects of reference physically difficult to manage. The aim is to move to a position where a sound that is typically associated with something or someone can be removed from this context, and, appearing as a stimulus in its own right, bring to mind the activity, place or person with which it was originally connected. In practical terms this may be achieved through presenting the sounding object to a child immediately before undertaking the activity of which it forms a part, or just prior to encountering the person or place with which it is associated. For example, a designated cluster of bells may be handed to a child shortly in advance of a music session, or a set of windchimes, identical to those in the doorway of the classroom, may be introduced on the way to class (see Figure 5.6).

Some children with autism and learning difficulties may make the link between a sound and its symbolic meaning straight away, while the same connection may continue to elude others. For many, interactions of the type described will have to be repeated time and again, over an extended period, before their significance is grasped, highlighting the importance of a well-planned and consistent approach to communication. Gradually, it may be possible to separate the sound-symbol further and further in time from that to which it refers, and eventually, two or more symbols may be presented in succession to indicate a forthcoming sequence of events. Some pupils may progress to using 'auditory timetables', which represent a series of events (Figure 5.7).

Figure 5.7 Using an 'auditory timetable'

Beyond this, time itself may be represented symbolically: for example, each day of the week may have a sound (or, eventually, a piece of music) associated with it. These can be introduced using songs such as 'What Day is it Today?' from *All Join In!* (see Figure 5.8). This has the advantage of running through all the days in sequence, and so reinforcing the place of any particular day in the context of the others.

Once children and young people have become familiar with receiving information through sound-symbols, to indicate what is going to happen next, for example, they may be encouraged to use them in an expressive way. Pupils may be able to choose the next activity for themselves, for instance, from among a selection that is offered. Sound-symbols may be employed retrospectively too, in reviewing events that have occurred.

They can also be used, receptively and expressively, in the context of make believe – giving an added auditory dimension to stories, for example, and enhancing the development of imaginative play, often a particular area of challenge for children on the autism spectrum (see Chapter 1). The effects chosen may be representative to a greater or lesser extent, ranging from the literal use of recorded animal sounds, for instance, to a roll on a suspended cymbal, which may be used in an entirely symbolic way to indicate the sun coming out. One approach is to assemble and maintain a collection of objects, with various sensory qualities, that are relevant to each story in a class's repertoire (Figure 5.9).

Spoken: **Today is ... [today's sound]**

Audio, MIDI and simplified versions of this song are available at **www.soundsofintent.org**

Figure 5.8 'What Day is it Today?' from *All Join in!*

Figure 5.9 Telling a story with sounding object

So much for musical *sounds* functioning symbolically. As we observed above, musical *motifs* can also fulfil this role (*Sounds of Intent*, Level 4). Such motifs may be presented initially by adults, or invented by children themselves, and used receptively or expressively.

Take, for example, Romy, who is on the autism spectrum and has no expressive language. However, she evinces exceptional musicality, including absolute pitch, and has a passion for playing the piano. She gleefully engages in improvised musical dialogues, largely using melodic fragments from the one hundred or so pieces she has learnt, interspersed with some material that she has created herself. Much of the interaction that occurs uses 'absolute' music, with no meaning beyond its inherent capacity to convey emotion (to which Romy is acutely sensitive). Motifs appear in succession and are connected or transformed using purely musical logic (imitation), an approach that enables Romy to control what goes on – something that she is unable to do through speech – and is thus a source of huge satisfaction for her. Musically, *she* initiates things, and expects her musical partner to continue what she begins (either alone, or simultaneously with her as she carries on playing, in the appropriate key and at the tempo she sets), or to provide an accompaniment, typically using material that she dictates.

This works well for Romy, provided that her musical collaborator is both able and willing to fulfil her wishes. However, over the years (Romy is now 11) I have seen it as part of my role as her teacher and musical 'friend' to challenge what she does and from time to time introduce new material – to provide some balance to the musical relationship, whereby *I* also influence what *she* does. However, Romy is a dyed-in-the-wool neophobe, who tends to resist novel experiences with an extraordinary fervour. Moreover, once something – anything – has acquired a negative emotional tag, it can be very difficult to override, and within a few seconds, psychological discomfort can become anger, upset and fear, which has the capacity to explode into full-blown panic. Hence I have always taken extreme care when presenting Romy with new musical materials, and tried to be sensitive to any signals of displeasure that she may seek to convey. But in the absence of language, how has she been able to make her feelings known?

Initially, she resorted to the simple expedient of seizing my hands and removing them from the keyboard, often accompanied by a warning vocalisation. If I attempted to continue, her physical intervention would become more powerful and insistent, pushing me bodily off the piano stool with a squeal of annoyance. Beyond this (which is not somewhere I willingly went, but which would sometimes occur through mutual misunderstanding) Romy would be likely to have a tantrum or run off (or both). However, after a few months of working together, she came to realise that she had a more subtle and ultimately more effective tool at her disposal: music itself. She developed a musical 'warning' sign, a rocking figure comprising oscillating pitches, three notes apart, which sounded rather like a two-tone police siren. Typically these would be played in a different key to the one I was using, so the overall effect was one of discord. The meaning was clear. 'Stop it'. And I quickly learnt to realise when my putative zygonic advances of the moment, 'Romy, would you like to copy what I'm doing?', were being spurned.

Romy's use of the 'stop it' motif can be heard in action around 45 minutes into an early session with her (available on the *Sounds of Intent* website – www.soundsofintent.org). At this stage in proceedings, there was as yet no sign of any diminution in her customary frenetic energy. I began to play what I knew to be one of her favourite pieces, Beethoven's 'Für Elise', whose opening segment was programmed into the first keyboard that she owned. Romy watched and listened to me intently. I continued playing into the second section of the piece to see how she would react, since her father had made me aware that her new keyboard included this additional material, and that Romy found it disconcerting, quickly turning the machine off whenever this point was reached. What would she do in the context of a human performer? Would she seek to influence the course of events, and, if so, how?

The answer became clear only a few seconds into my rendition of the second section of 'Für Elise'. Romy introduced her rocking motif. At the time, I suspected that her intention, as usual, was to force me to lose the thread of the musical conversation in which I was temporarily taking the lead, and to stop playing. On this occasion, however (somewhat to my amusement), Romy misjudged things, in that the constituents of her alternating figure, the notes A and C, could be heard as deriving from elements of 'Für Elise' (that is, resulting from 'unintentional' zygonic relationships) and the effect was not as deleterious in musical terms as she would have liked. In other words, her sound-symbol 'stop it', fitted rather well with what was going on, and did not sound like 'stop it' in musical terms at all. Rather, it had the effect rather of saying 'carry on while I join in'.

To give some idea of what happened in musical terms, try this verbal equivalent with a partner (see Figure 5.10).

Voice 1 (quite loud): The racing car
                       Is coming in
                       For a
                       Pit stop, pit stop, pit stop, pit stop, ...
Voice 2 (quieter):   Stop it, stop it, stop it, stop ...

together

Figure 5.10 Verbal equivalent of Romy's 'stop it' music symbol acquiring a different meaning through the context in which it is heard

On its own, Voice 2's message is clear, but in the context of Voice 1, the ear hears the two words in a different way, and 'stop it' is transformed to 'pit stop', even though the sounds remain the same.

Romy endeavours to remedy this accidental congruence and exert her authority by playing more loudly, but this has no effect, and a critical point is reached when 'Für Elise' changes key (moving back from F major to A minor). Here, Romy's two notes become fully compatible with those used by Beethoven, and her strategy of calculated discord is subverted by harmonic happenstance.

Her efforts at disruption in the domain of pitch having been foiled, Romy abruptly changes tack and modifies the tempo twice in rapid succession as she strives to avoid conformance with, and so unsettle, the regular beat of the Beethoven. This tactic too is ignored. Romy is not to be deterred, however, and she proceeds to take more direct action, pushing my hands off the keyboard with her right elbow, while, through a considerable contortion, simultaneously playing a series of chords (new sound-symbols for 'stop it') with her right hand that clash stridently with the harmonies of 'Für Elise' at this point.

At this point, all logical connections with preceding material are lost: there is no sense of the music I was playing exerting any influence on Romy, and the interaction is momentarily halted. Having succeeded in her aim of terminating the middle section of 'Für Elise', Romy squeals with delight, before setting off once more with her familiar rocking motif, this time on C and E. Here the message has changed somewhat: 'This is me again, and I am in charge.'

© Adam Ockelford, 1996/2013

Audio, MIDI and simplified versions of this song are available at **www.soundsofintent.org**

Figure 5.11 'Music has Finished' from *All Join In!*

Given Romy's evident capacity for imbuing musical motifs with symbolic meaning, I subsequently taught her short pieces with specially designed symbolic meanings from *All Join In!* It struck me that one of the most useful symbolic messages for Romy to be able to express was 'finished', so that she could indicate when she had had enough of something (similar to, though potentially with a broader range of applicability than, her 'stop it' motif). Hence the song 'Music has Finished' was among the first that she learnt (Figure 5.11).

I consistently used the song at the end of sessions, and Romy quickly picked up on its import, often trying to close the piano lid before my fingers had left the final notes. Before long, she started using the melody expressively as well, to bring a lesson to an end that she felt had gone on for long enough. Sometimes she would indulge in the musical equivalent of 'synecdoche' – a figure of speech in which a part stands for the whole – by just playing the opening three or four notes: rather like saying 'see you' instead of 'I'll see you later'. On occasion even the first note would suffice – at least, as far as she was concerned: it was often difficult to pick up this most aphoristic of messages amidst the many musical fragments that were usually swirling around!

Shortening motifs in this way also enabled Romy to indulge in another of her favourite pastimes: teasing me by seeming to indicate that she had chosen a particular tune (by playing just the opening note or notes) but then (whatever I played) choosing a different continuation – accompanied with a beaming smile. Clearly, this diversion (at once an entertainment and a musical re-routing) depended on the fact that different melodies begin in the same way, and in the case of 'Music has Finished', opening with an upbeat on the fifth degree of the scale. There were plenty of options for Romy to choose from, and typically she would plump for the spiritual 'Oh Freedom', the Irish song 'Cockles and Mussels' or the Christmas carol 'Away in a Manger'. Playing with the ambiguity of a symbol for humorous ends is not, of course, uniquely musical – consider, for example, the 'double entendre' in language – though its combination with a form of musical alliteration (whereby motifs rather than words begin with the same sound) was, I believe, entirely Romy's invention. To make things even more complicated for her co-performer, already struggling to keep up with her quick-fire musical repartee, Romy would sometimes introduce 'Music has Finished' as a joke, not really intending things to be over at all.

Humour of this type – the musical double entendre and the deception – requires 'theory of mind' of some refinement, since it means that Romy was able to step outside the immediate musical dialogue in which she was participating, and appreciate the impact of her actions on my thoughts: namely, making me believe the opposite of what she was thinking, and also the reverse of what was actually going to happen. Hence music provided Romy with a medium with which to explore the dynamics of social interaction in the absence of language, and, by the same token enabled her father (who was present at the sessions) and me to recognise her capacity for a deft and witty engagement with others without a word being spoken.

Romy extended the meaning of the 'Music has Finished' motif too, using it not only to signal her wish to end a session, but also to terminate a train of thought in one of our musical conversations. For example, in a recent session, after around half an hour of improvising with her on some of the themes from the first movement of Beethoven's Violin Concerto, I decided to 'ask' if we could change tack, by playing the first few notes of Pachelbel's *Canon*. Romy swiftly retorted with the first two notes of 'Music has Finished', and returned to the Beethoven. Later in the session, she noticed that her father was texting on his mobile phone (which she dislikes because of the unpredictable appearance of message notification sounds), looked at him and played the opening of 'Music has Finished' again!

Interestingly, unlike tunes with no symbolic meaning, which Romy habitually transposes to a wide range of keys, 'Music has Finished' is always played at the original pitch when it is intended to convey a concrete meaning. It seems that, for Romy, a crucial part of the identity of this 'finished' music symbol is vested in the actual pitches, not just in the relationships between them, something that is not surprising given her sense of absolute pitch, which means that she experiences the tune in quite a different way from most listeners. However, when she treats 'Music has Finished' as pure music, linking it, as we noted above, to tunes that begin on the same scale-step and with a similar rhythm, then she is likely to transpose it, so that a different set of pitches are involved.

Hence, Romy derives multiple functions and meanings from this one simple musical idea – variously reliant on an acquired symbolic meaning, on the zygonic links between the qualities of the sounds themselves, and on the context on which they are heard (the equivalent of 'pragmatics' in speech); see Figure 5.12. For her, music can truly be considered a proxy language.

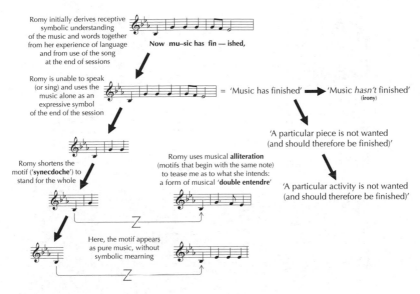

Figure 5.12 Romy derives a range of functions
and meanings from a single musical motif

© Adam Ockelford, 1996/2013

Audio, MIDI and simplified versions of this song are available at **www.soundsofintent.org**

Figure 5.13 'Can You Find...?' from *All Join In!* uses music
to add interest to a simple exchange of words

Audio, MIDI and simplified versions of this song are available at **www.soundsofintent.org**

Figure 5.14 'Finding/Giving' from *All Join In!* enhances an everyday verbal exchange with music

MUSIC AND SPEECH

As we have seen, music and speech are closely linked products of the human psyche, which share the same early developmental journey, and continue to enjoy a special relationship throughout life in songs and chants. This affinity can be particularly useful in promoting communication and fostering its development among children who have autism and learning difficulties. In the early stages, for example (*Sounds of Intent*, Level 2), exposure to music may elicit vocalisation. At more advanced levels of functioning, music can play a significant role in *motivating* children to use language, through the many songs that have been especially written or have evolved over the years for their edification and pleasure. Whether counting songs, playground chants or action songs, game songs or songs that tell a story...music adds another dimension to the verbal messages presented, enlivening everyday expressions and imbuing them with extra colour and interest. As we have seen, though, such songs typically make use of language and concepts that are likely to be difficult for children on the autism spectrum – particularly those with learning difficulties – to grasp, and *All Join In!* seeks to address this issue by contributing pieces to the children's repertoire that are inclusive by design. Among those that have proved their worth in motivating children to use language both receptively and expressively are 'Can You Find…?' (Figure 5.13), 'Finding/Giving' (Figure 5.14) and 'Wiggle' (Figure 5.15).

Audio, MIDI and simplified versions of this song are available at **www.soundsofintent.org**

Figure 5.15 'Wiggle' from *All Join In!* sustains the interest of a repeated three-word phrase

Music can also help to *structure* language. This may be particularly important for children who are on the autism spectrum, who, as we saw in Chapter 2, may often have to contend with a baffling array of different words and phrases from adults who, in the face of little or no immediate reaction from those they are addressing, are culturally programmed *not to repeat themselves*. As we observed on p.33, everyday language abhors immediate repetition, and if at first you don't succeed in being understood, there is a strong inclination to try again, using *alternative* means of expression. Experience suggests that scenarios such as the following, in which an adult is addressing a child with autism and learning difficulties, are not untypical:

'It's time for lunch.'

[Pause. No response]

'Come and get something to eat.'

[Longer pause. Still no response]

'Aren't you hungry? – I expect there'll be something nice for us today.'

[Further pause, then, encouragingly…]

'Come on. Food! My tummy's rumbling, isn't yours?'

[Final check for any response, then…]

'Ready, then? Off we go…'

Yet what the child seeking order and regularity may need most is *simplicity* and *consistency*. Here, music can help. By setting selected phrases to characteristic snatches of melody, reinforced where appropriate with signing and objects of reference, the consistent delivery of key messages is assured; one form of complex auditory input (speech) is supplemented with a simpler overlay (melody). The message is given a stronger identity, which is consequently more memorable, and which children may find easier to recognise. Examples pertaining to 'swimming', 'music' and 'home time' are to be found in Figure 4.3. The fact that it was time for lunch can be communicated as shown in Figure 5.16. That is not to say that carefully structured fragments such as this should be all that is communicated, but that they should form salient features in a rich and diverse landscape of multisensory interaction.

Figure 5.16 Setting a key verbal message to music ensures the consistency of its delivery

Songs can be devised to *add interest* to language while *structuring it tightly*. The clarity of design may be enhanced through direct repetition, which is common in words set to music, but (to reiterate) rare in speech alone. Consider, for example, 'Wiggle' (Figure 5.15) and 'What is it?' from *All Join In!* (Figure 5.17).

© Adam Ockelford, 1996

Audio, MIDI and simplified versions of this song are available at **www.soundsofintent.org**

Figure 5.17 'What it is?' from *All Join In!* uses the immediate repetition of words to enhance the clarity of the message

The melody of the 'Goodbye' song from *All Join In!* relies on repetition to an even greater extent (Figure 5.18).

Audio, MIDI and simplified versions of this song are available at **www.soundsofintent.org**

Figure 5.18 'Goodbye' from *All Join In!* uses motifs consistently and repetitively to enhance the symbolic meaning of the key word ('goodbye')

As we saw in relation to Romy, it is possible for short snatches of melody like the three-note 'goodbye' motifs to function symbolically in their own right, expressively and receptively. As well as substituting for speech, as in Romy's case, music symbols such as this, and those shown in Figures 4.3 and 5.16, may assist children who find it difficult to produce speech sounds accurately to make themselves understood more readily – the rhythm and shape of the tunes holding things together, and even if individual vowels and consonants are not quite as standard, other people can understand what is meant.

© Adam Ockelford, 1996

Audio, MIDI and simplified versions of this song are available at **www.soundsofintent.org**

Figure 5.19 'Music Time' from *All Join In!* can played in the environment to indicate that a music session is about to begin

Having observed children on the autism spectrum over many years, it is evident that language directed at them is often a source of anxiety – even, perhaps, perceived as a threat. Little wonder when, in the absence of the customary pleasantries of social chat, they are typically receiving instructions to do something, or to stop doing something, or to choose what they would like to do next, using a form of communication that can be like 'dynamite going off in the ears' (Barrett 2006). Times of change – transitions – can be particularly challenging (see e.g. Sterling-Turner and Jordan 2007), and language is typically used to signal that things are about to happen, albeit in combination with picture symbols or objects of reference. Very often it is the conveyor of the message that has to bear the brunt of any negative reaction. However, if we remove the words and the messenger from the situation, things can be very different. Musical cues can be incorporated into the environment at the appropriate junctures to signal that change is about to occur – for example, by playing a particular piece five minutes before it is time to go to school or get ready for bed. Once the connection between music and symbolic meaning is established, it does not need to be augmented: there is no need to say anything. However, direct communication can occur to reinforce what is happening once the message is received and understood, and a safe interpersonal space exists. The first song in *All Join In!* is designed to set the scene for music sessions. It takes the 'music' motif (see Figure 4.3) and extends it into a piece that can be repeated as often as required (Figure 5.19).

Finally, it is worth bearing in mind that, since music and speech are in part processed differently in neurological terms (see p.170), some children who are normally unable to speak, or who find verbalising difficult, may nevertheless be able to communicate by singing words and phrases, or at least intoning them within a rhythmic structure. For example, the psychologists Anne Anastasi and Raymond Levee (1960), in their report on a musical savant whom they referred to as 'S', observed that

> before he could talk, S was able to hum tunes he heard on the radio or phonograph. To capitalize on this propensity, a speech therapist was engaged and S was eventually taught to talk through the medium of lyrics. To this date, a sing-song quality is discernible in his speech. (Anastasi and Levee 1960, p.696)

It is interesting to compare this approach with the one adopted by Romy, who is generally unwilling to hum or sing tunes, but will *play* them – an exceptional ability that relies on her sense of absolute pitch.

MUSIC AND UNDERSTANDING

Music can assist children to grasp the *meaning* of words in three ways:

(a) since the sounds that make up pieces have perceptual qualities, and these can be experienced at the same time as the verbal labels associated with them are enunciated (such as 'sound and silence', Figure 5.20, and 'quiet and loud', Figure 5.21 – *Sounds of Intent*, Levels 1 and 2)

(b) through body movements that are synchronised with the beat alone (such as 'slowly and quickly', Figure 5.22), or with the beat in combination with the repetition of motifs (such as 'to and fro', Figures 5.23 and 5.24, 'left and right', Figure 5.25, and 'round and round', Figure 5.26), or even with a *lack* of movement (see Figure 5.27) – *Sounds of Intent*, Levels 3 and 4)

(c) through direct mapping between perceptual domains, whereby a rise in pitch of a piece is felt to correlate with physical height (as in 'up and down', Figure 5.28), a connection that can be made explicit using devices such as the Soundbeam®, which converts movement into sound through a MIDI interface, see Figure 5.29; or where movement away from the body (or a rise in tension) is felt to correspond to an increasing number of scale-steps up from the 'home' note of a piece (see p.87), as in 'stretch and bend', Figure 5.30; cross-modal relationships that pertain to musical understanding at Levels 3, 4 and 5 of the *Sounds of Intent* framework.

Audio, MIDI and simplified versions of this song are available at **www.soundsofintent.org**

Figure 5.20 'Sound and Silence' from *All Join In!* can assist in learning the meaning of the word 'sound'

Audio, MIDI and simplified versions of this song are available at **www.soundsofintent.org**

Figure 5.21 'Quiet and Loud' from *All Join In!* can support children in learning to understand the concepts and the words

© Adam Ockelford, 1996

Audio, MIDI and simplified versions of this song are available at **www.soundsofintent.org**

Figure 5.22 'Slowly and Quickly' from *All Join In!*
provides an example of the adverbs in action

Audio, MIDI and simplified versions of this song are available at **www.soundsofintent.org**

Figure 5.23 'To and Fro' from *All Join In!* offers a repetitive auditory framework with which to synchronise repetitive movements

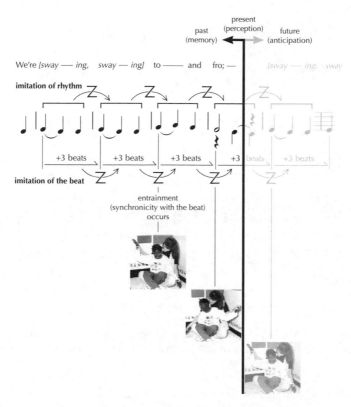

Figure 5.24 The rhythmic regularity of music can be used to reinforce the meaning of words describing regular movement

Audio, MIDI and simplified versions of this song are available at **www.soundsofintent.org**

Figure 5.25 'Left, Right' from *All Join In!* also offers a repetitive auditory framework with which to synchronise repetitive movements

© Adam Ockelford, 1996/2013

Audio, MIDI and simplified versions of this song are available at **www.soundsofintent.org**

Figure 5.26 'Round and Round' from *All Join In!* offers a further repetitive auditory framework with which to synchronise repetitive movements

© Adam Ockelford, 1996/2013

Audio, MIDI and simplified versions of this song are available at **www.soundsofintent.org**

Figure 5.27 'Now it's Time to Rest' from *All Join In!* has a slow place, suggestive of relaxation

Audio, MIDI and simplified versions of this song are available at **www.soundsofintent.org**

Figure 5.28 'Up and Down' from *All Join In!* uses differences in pitch height to refer directly to changes in body position

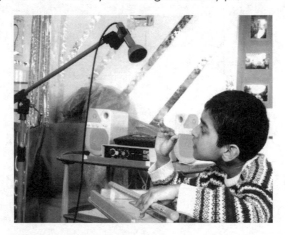

Figure 5.29 The Soundbeam® converts movement into sound through a MIDI interface

Figure 5.30 'Stretch and Bend' from *All Join In!* uses differences in scale-step to refer directly to changes in body position

In relation to (c), it is interesting to note that 'synaesthesia', whereby a stimulus in one sensory modality (such as hearing) triggers an automatic, consistent response in another modality (such as sight), which is usually very rare (around one in a hundred), may be more common among children on the autism spectrum (see Cytowic 1997). This may have to do with the relative prevalence of absolute pitch among this group (see p.20), since this is often linked with sound-colour synaesthesia. For example, Joshua, who was part of a study by Christina Matawa and me on the musicality of premature babies, reports hearing the note B as green, whereas B flat elicits the image of a light blue room with large windows in the distance (Ockelford and Matawa 2009). This is despite Joshua being almost totally blind! However, among children with severe visual impairment, both absolute pitch and synaesthesia appear to be relatively common. The important point to take from this in the current context is that when some children with autism hear music, they are likely to be experiencing visual sensations too. These should not cut across the perceptual mapping between changes in pitch and movement that some *All Join In!* songs use, though it would be as well for practitioners to be aware that music teaching schemes and children's instruments that link colour and pitch may be very disconcerting for some (synaesthetic) pupils on the autism spectrum.

There is a further way in which music can help illustrate the meaning of words directly, and that is through the emotional reactions that pieces can evoke, which, as we have seen, are likely to be a mixture of hard-wired and learnt responses. The songs from *All Join In!* were not designed to deal with this issue: they are largely upbeat, though some could be used to illustrate happiness (for example, 'Hello!') or sadness ('Goodbye'). The issue of whether and to what extent children on the autism spectrum 'feel' music in the same way as their 'neurotypical' peers, and how it can be used to assist in learning about one's emotions and reflecting on them, is discussed in Chapter 7.

MUSIC AND SOCIAL INTERACTION

According to my music psychology colleagues David Hargreaves and Adrian North (1997), music may have many different functions in life, but nearly all of them are essentially social – that is, involving other people. In terms of children on the autism spectrum, although listening to music, exploring the multisensory properties of sound-makers, singing, playing instruments and inventing new pieces are activities that can be satisfactorily undertaken alone, music sessions offer a unique and secure framework through which many of the skills and disciplines of social interaction can be experienced and developed. This is particularly true for young people who have difficulty in processing or managing visual information, whose awareness of other people may be more than usually reliant on the sounds they make.

Teachers, therapists and carers may provide structured opportunities for children in the early stages of musical development (*Sounds of Intent*, Levels 1, 2 and 3) to listen to the sounds that others are making, in a variety of contexts, and to respond appropriately to them. It may well be appropriate for at least some of these activities to be undertaken on a one-to-one basis, with teacher and pupil (or comparable combination) working in close proximity, sound featuring as one element in a broader pattern of multisensory contact. Here, there is likely to be an intimate connection between the shared activity and the relationship between the adult and the child; the one enabling the other to occur, and permitting it to evolve (see Figure 5.31).

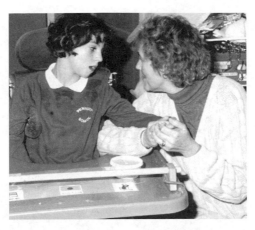

Figure 5.31 Intense one-to-one interaction involving sound and music at Level 2 of the *Sounds of Intent* framework

In these circumstances, young people functioning at Level 2 of the *Sounds of Intent* framework or above may initiate sound-making themselves, and by offering an appropriate response, teachers and others can reinforce children's awareness that what they do can have an effect – contributing, perhaps, to their developing cognisance of a sentient 'other' out there. Alternating patterns of sounds and responses may be built up: 'proto-conversations', in which the teacher, carer or therapist reacts sensitively to the child's efforts, promoting interactive play. At first, in responding to what they hear, children may produce sounds that bear no immediate resemblance to the ones with which they are presented. Teachers may nevertheless copy what their pupils do, encouraging them to do the same (*Sounds of Intent*, Level 3), both vocally and using sound-makers, through providing a model of imitation. Initially, two adults may interact in this way themselves, with children listening. Subsequently, teachers and others may act on behalf of pupils, gradually fading support as the children themselves become active participants. Songs such as 'Can You Copy Me?' can be used to set the scene for activities of this type (see Figure 5.32).

Audio, MIDI and simplified versions of this song are available at **www.soundsofintent.org**

Figure 5.32 A musical framework for imitation provided by the song 'Can You Copy Me?' from *All Join In!*

Audio, MIDI and simplified versions of this song are available at **www.soundsofintent.org**

Figure 5.33 The song 'All Join In!' is designed to be customised to suit individual experiences, interests and abilities

Some children may be able to participate in more formal sequences of interaction, whose scripts are taken from a standard repertoire. For example, there are many nursery songs and games which set up the expectation that a particular event (such as being tickled) will occur at a given juncture, and others in which the child is required to supply certain features from a familiar selection (for instance, 'actions' in 'If You're Happy and You Know It'; and 'animal sounds' in 'Old MacDonald Had a Farm'). Often, the challenge for teachers is in providing material for older children that is appropriate to their age, culture, social background and interests, and which plug into their experiences, both conceptual and linguistic. The songs in *All Join In!* seek to address topics and to use language which have broad-based, everyday relevance. They are designed to be customised to suit individual needs. For example, the content of 'All Join In!' (the title song from the *All Join In!* set) is largely determined by those who use it (see Figure 5.33).

Whatever its context and content, music is particularly effective in supporting the development of early social interaction. Because pieces are generally made up of sequences of identical or similar events, which divide time into manageable chunks and constitute predictable patterns, music provides a secure framework for the risky business of reaching out into the far from predictable world of other people, setting parameters and establishing the boundaries within which socialisation can occur; building confidence through a medium which the great majority of young children find enjoyable and motivating.

Although, in the early stages of development, listening to sounds can induce attendant vocalisation, producing coherent streams of sound simultaneously is a more advanced stage, which involves listening and producing a coordinated response at the same time – or at least, switching attention rapidly between the two (*Sounds of Intent*, Level 4). However, the context of group performance can be valuable in enabling children whose music-making powers are limited to find a satisfactory means of musical expression. For example, producing simple, repetitive patterns on percussion may have little aesthetic appeal in the long run unless they are part of a larger experience, and their combined effect can indeed be musically pleasing and motivating.

Particular forms of social interaction can be structured through especially designed or adapted songs. These set occasions include 'good morning' routines, using material such as the 'Hello!' song from *All Join In!* (see Figure 5.34).

© Adam Ockelford, 1996

Audio, MIDI and simplified versions of this song are available at **www.soundsofintent.org**

Figure 5.34 'Hello!' from *All Join In!* can assist in structuring and simplifying, formal social situations, making them more predictable and so easier to manage

On occasions such as this, it is suggested that the group sits in a circle, singing to each member in turn. Some participants may be able to choose whom they wish to sing to next. Positions in the circle may vary from one occasion to another, or a more consistent approach may be adopted if this is felt to be particularly important. If people are away, their absence may be noted. Support workers can, of course, be included in the greeting too. In undertaking activities of this type, it is important to remember that receptive language develops before the capacity to express thoughts and feelings, and that just *listening* is as valid a form of participation as any other – an essential developmental stage. In songs such as 'Hello!' where support workers may be singing on behalf of individuals, it will make more sense of names and pronouns, and therefore assist understanding, if only one person performs, effectively functioning as the voice of the youngster concerned. At other times, everyone can join in.

Each person can use a personal sound-maker (see pp.115–116) to enhance his or her presence in sensory terms, helping to establish the identity of participants who have no expressive language. Examples of sound-makers include: a little bell, a squeaker, a wooden rattle, a tiny tambourine, a miniature drum, a shaker, a whistle, a small net of pebbles, porcelain windchimes and a scraper (see Figure 5.35). It may be advisable not to use conventional instruments in order to avoid potential confusion in other music sessions.

© Adam Ockelford, 1996

Audio, MIDI and simplified versions of this song are available at **www.soundsofintent.org**

Figure 5.35 'Who's Sitting Next to Me?' from *All Join In!* offers opportunities for the use of personal sound-symbols in a structured social context

'Listen!' from *All Join In!* encourages different roles in social interaction – proactive and reactive (*Sounds of Intent*, Levels 2 and 3) – see Figure 5.36.

Audio, MIDI and simplified versions of this song are available at **www.soundsofintent.org**

Figure 5.36 'Listen!' from *All Join In!* structures reactive and proactive contributions in an interactive context

'Together and Alone' from *All Join In!* provides a musical structure for children to contribute to a social situation on their own, and then in combination with others (*Sounds of Intent*, Levels 4 and 5) – see Figure 5.37.

Once 'set-piece' songs are familiar, it will be possible to use them in a wide range of social situations, with or without accompaniment: music can inform and enrich living and learning throughout the day.

Finally, it is worth remembering that musical activities give children who are on the autism spectrum the opportunity for experiencing a wide range of social situations. Music-making takes place indoors and outdoors, in concert halls and sitting rooms, with small groups of friends and among thousands of strangers. Each occasion has its own atmosphere and code of conduct to which participants are expected to adhere. Hence the kinds of extrovert behaviour that are the norm at a rock concert staged in a large arena, for example, are not likely to find favour among devotees of classical chamber music, listening in the relative intimacy of a small concert hall. The extent to which pupils and students can gain awareness of these issues will vary from one individual to another: the key thing is for teachers and carers to find ways of offering them fulfilling musical experiences – experiences which typically occur in the company of other people.

© Adam Ockelford, 1996

Audio, MIDI and simplified versions of this song are available at **www.soundsofintent.org**

Figure 5.37 'Together and Alone' from *All Join In!* enables children to contribute to a social situation alone and with others

CONCLUSION

This chapter explored how music and language typically develop together in the early years, and how they may evolve separately in some children on the autism spectrum – specifically, with musical skills outstripping the growth of linguistic abilities. The consequences of this are discussed in some depth, and a number of strategies are presented through which music can be used by practitioners and parents to support the development of language in children and young people with autism, or even, in some cases, substitute for it, serving as an alternative form of communication.

CHAPTER 6

Exceptional Early Cognitive Environments (EECEs)

INTRODUCTION

In Chapter 5, it was suggested that the developmental trajectories of music and language, which usually proceed in parallel, may diverge in some children on the autism spectrum, with a delay in linguistic understanding and use. It was proposed that music may be used to ameliorate this state of affairs, supporting the development of language, or even acting as its proxy. Romy's story (pp.179–185) hinted at something further: that the music-developmental strand not only may be *intact* alongside profound linguistic impairment, but also may, by any standards, be *advanced*. This is borne out by examples in the academic literature (see e.g. Miller 1989), in the popular media, and from my own experience of teaching many children and young people with autism since the early 1980s, which suggest that special – even extraordinary – musical abilities are not uncommon among those on the spectrum. In this chapter, we consider why this is the case, and what the critical factors underpinning exceptional musical development are.

EVERYDAY SOUNDS

First, let us return to the model of the development of sound perception and production set out in Figures 5.3 and 5.4. Here, two strands were identified, pertaining to language and music. However, there is a third area in which auditory perception functions, with which we will now be concerned: 'everyday sounds' (see Figure 6.1).

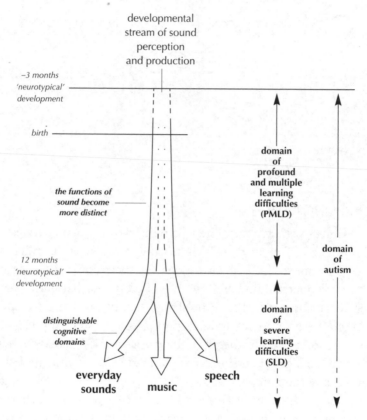

Figure 6.1 Three-strand model of the functional processing of sound in early development

Evidence that some children may attach particular importance to everyday sounds and that, in some cases (presumably as a result), auditory perceptual skills may become heightened in this domain, comes from my studies of young people who are born blind or who lose their sight in the first few months of life. Parents report that almost all this group have a special interest in everyday sounds (around two or three times as many as those who are fully sighted). It seems that, in the absence of vision, sound has a distinctive appeal and offers a ready source of stimulation. For example, one mother commented that her blind three-year-old daughter was interested in sounds of 'anything and everything since this is a huge part of her learning experience'. Other visually impaired children appear to be attracted to sounds for the sheer pleasure they bring. For instance, the mother of a five-year-old boy noted that 'he loves repetitive sounds – [he] will press toys which make noises over and over to hear the sounds'. Other favourite sources of sound that parents mentioned included windchimes and birdsong, and one five-year-old boy was said to love listening to the rain and the sea: 'he loves the sound of breaking waves'.

Sound-making may also have an exploratory element. For example, one 18-month-old boy constantly 'takes objects and toys and attempts to make sounds out of them by banging them together, shaking, throwing'. And the functionality of sound was evidently important to a two-year-old girl who 'has excellent hearing and immediately recognizes the sound of cars pulling up and parking outside of our house'; she 'often motions that someone is at the front door before her mother has heard them'.

Sometimes, such auditory pleasure seems to have developed atypically and become a fixation. For instance, one mother wrote of her six-and-a-half-year-old son with retinopathy of prematurity being

> obsessed with the noise of the microwave, so much so that he becomes upset if he can't make it into the kitchen before it is finished. More recently he has become interested in the tumble drier. He lies on the floor and listens to it and gets upset when it stops. He also loves the noises of the vacuum cleaner, washing machine and dish washer.

Similarly, a three-year-old boy was reported to be passionate about 'any type of fan (table fan, exhaust fan, pedestal, box fan, computer fan etc.)'. It is of interest to note (in view of the discussion that follows) that all these sounds are inherently 'musical', comprising distinct pitches and tone colours that are rich in harmonics.

The importance of sound to children and young people may become evident not only through particularly attentive or sustained listening but also through mimicry. For instance, the 18-month-old who was reported to enjoy exploring toys through the sounds they make 'also mimics a lot of sounds – not just words – like clearing your throat', while another boy of the same age was said to copy unusual animal sounds. Similarly, one mother of a three-year-old boy described his liking of the sounds that 'different surfaces make when tapped or banged' and his enjoyment when 'imitating vocal sounds we make'.

As we noted in the Introduction, some children with autism display a similar fascination for everyday sounds, and I suspect that a number of parents of autistic children reading the descriptions above will find the types of behaviours that are described very familiar: recall from the Introduction Jack, who is obsessed with the sound of the microwave (and, increasingly, the tumble drier), and we shouldn't forget Freddie's flowerpots. When I first met Freddie (aged nine years), he indulged in a range of pursuits that bemused his parents, including habitually flicking any glasses, bowls, pots or pans that were within reach, and, one day, removing a dozen or so flowerpots (and their contents) from the garden and bringing them into the kitchen. Freddie arranged these on all available surfaces, like some earthenware gamelan, and he ran around gleefully, playing his newly constructed instrument with characteristic flicks of the fingers. Woe betide his mother if she tried to tidy the pots up, shifting any of these by even the smallest degree, while Freddie was at school! Any slight rearrangement would instantly be noticed and rectified on his return.

So what is happening here? One might reasonably expect that blind children, in the absence of the visual input that would otherwise be their main source of information about the world around them, would be particularly attracted to salient features in the *auditory* landscape. One might also predict that, without the visual data to contextualise what is heard – to know *what* is making a particular sound and *why* – that at least some auditory information would remain at the perceptual level, rather than acquiring a functional gloss. Hence the whirr of the tumble drier and the hum of the vacuum cleaner would remain as ends in themselves, as perceptual experiences to be relished, rather than portending dry laundry or a clean carpet. (And, as one would expect, a key element in supporting young blind children's development is to help them link what they hear with tactile input and, where appropriate, verbal explanation.)

But why do some children on the autism spectrum treat sound in the same way? Are there the same cognitive mechanisms at work here, or different ones that have similar consequences? For sure, a proportion of autistic children have problems in processing visual information, which may partly account for the tendency to behave in certain respects as though they were visually impaired. And many autistic children have difficulties with 'sensory integration': linking incoming data from different sensory modalities. That is, the processes through which incoming streams of perceptual information in the domains of sight, sound, touch, smell and taste (as well as balance and proprioception) are typically bound together to produce single, coherent experiences and concepts, appear not to be fully functional. One can speculate that this cognitive anomaly is linked to 'weak central coherence', in which, as we saw in Chapter 2, there is a tendency to focus attention on parts of things rather than wholes. So, in summary, a child on the autism spectrum may be facing the double challenge of finding it difficult to link information received in *different* sensory channels, as well as successively in *one* domain.

MUSIC AND EVERYDAY SOUNDS

This I describe as an Exceptional Early Cognitive Environment (or EECE), one outcome of which seems to be that certain sounds, especially those that are particularly salient or intrinsically pleasing (given that what is pleasurable to one ear may be irritating to another!), do not acquire wider meaning or functional significance. Rather, they tend to be processed purely in terms of their sonic qualities: that is, *in musical terms* (see Figure 6.2). Similarly, other everyday sounds that involve repetition (like the beeping of the microwave or the ticking of clocks or timers – see p.75) may, I believe, be processed *in music-structural terms* (since, as we have seen, the way that music is organised is through patterns of sameness and similarity).[1]

---

1 The extent to which such repetitive patterns are heard as 'narratives in sound' (*Sounds of Intent*, Level 6) is a moot point; but then, as we have seen (p.132), it may be that some children with autism hear music as pure pattern rather than as emotional journeys that ultimately depend on the sense of one musical event *deriving* from another that is the same or similar, rather than merely occurring after it.

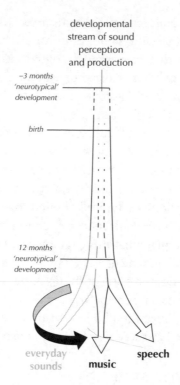

Figure 6.2 Everyday sounds may be processed in musical terms by some children on the autism spectrum

This tendency is likely to be reinforced by the prevalence of music in the environment, estimated to be present around 80 per cent of the time in the lives of babies: as well as computers, the television and radio, young people are often surrounded by electronic games and gadgets, toys, mobile phones, MP3 players, iPads and so on, all of which make use of music to a greater or lesser extent. In the wider environment too – shops, restaurants, cafés, cinemas and waiting rooms, in cars and aeroplanes, and at many religious gatherings and ceremonies – music is ubiquitous. Hence, given that children are bombarded by *non*-functional (that is, musical) sounds (designed, in one way or another, to influence emotional, behavioural or even what people take to be spiritual states), it is perhaps of little surprise that the *functional* sounds with which they are often jumbled together should become processed in the same way.

This confusion was brought home to me vividly many years ago when working with Derek Paravicini (then aged ten or so) – a blind, autistic musical savant,[2] with severe learning difficulties, of whom we shall hear more later. He was playing through a Chopin waltz on the piano, in his usual, jaunty, fluent style, only to stop, briefly and unexpectedly, mid-phrase, and tap the fingers of both hands vigorously on the music rack above the keyboard, before continuing with the performance as though nothing had happened. Derek's language was not, at the time, sufficiently well developed for me to be able to ask him why he had stopped playing in mid-flow, so I just assumed it was 'one of those things' – perhaps he had suddenly thought about something else, and had become distracted. However, a couple of days later, I heard him play the waltz again, and exactly the same thing occurred. Baffled, I decided to check it out with the pianist who taught Derek classical pieces at the time – Susan Wynn. She couldn't immediately think of a reason for his extramusical antics, and so we looked over the score to see if that would help solve the mystery. Sure enough, the reason quickly became clear: the point where Derek interrupted his playing occurred at a page turn, and it seemed that he had absorbed not only the music as he listened to Sue, but also the extraneous sound of her flicking the page over (which, of course, would have meant nothing to him). In that moment, it struck me powerfully that, sophisticated young musician though Derek may be in many respects (he had recently performed at the Barbican Centre in London with the Royal Philharmonic Pops Orchestra), in functional terms, his understanding of sound was still in some ways naive. For him, the everyday sound of a page being turned was as much a part of the music as the notes that Chopin had prescribed: in his mind, he evidently did not distinguish between the two.

Romy (whom we met in Chapter 5) is also in the habit of introducing everyday sounds into her playing, though in a rather different manner from that adopted by Derek at the same age. As soon as Romy hears certain sounds, including her father's mobile phone ringtone and aeroplanes as they come in to land (one of the rooms we

---

2   A savant is someone with an exceptional ability or abilities in the context of learning difficulties – see, for example, Miller (1989), Ockelford (2007) and Treffert (1989). Savants' areas of special interest include music, art and maths.

use for sessions is only a few miles from Heathrow), she reproduces them on the piano, incorporating them into her improvised dialogues with me. The extraneous sounds *become* part of the music. But unlike Beethoven's cuckoo in his 'Pastoral' Symphony (see p.106), Romy's extramusical interjections are not (I believe) intended to have a residual symbolic meaning, borrowed from their original contexts.[3] Her aim is not to create a piece, for example, about a plane coming in to land (in fact, as far as I'm aware, she has no concept of an aeroplane landing): the whine of the jet engines is pure sound as far as she is concerned – grist to the mill of her musical creativity.

ABSOLUTE PITCH (AP)

It seems that the modus operandi in the auditory domain, through which attention is paid to each sound as a phenomenon in its own right, means that young children may develop an unusually strong focus on 'absolute' perceptual qualities, in some cases, as we shall see, potentially at the expense of the more typical 'relative' way of processing certain stimuli. This is particularly noticeable in relation to pitch, where children on the autism spectrum are around 500 times more likely to have highly developed 'absolute' perceptual skills than those in the general Western population (1 in 20 – the same as advanced musicians – as opposed to around one in ten thousand).

To appreciate what a difference this makes, consider that most of us are able to assign pitches heard in isolation only to around one in seven categories (say, 'extremely high, very high, fairly high, mid-range, fairly low, very low, and extremely low), whereas a child with 'perfect' or 'absolute' pitch (the two labels mean the same thing – here we will use the abbreviation favoured by psychologists, AP) may be able to distinguish a hundred or more levels. To put this in perspective, there are 88 notes on a standard piano keyboard, which make up the range of pitches used in the great majority of Western music of all styles. In other words, to a child with AP, each musical note sounds recognisably different.

But for many children with autism, there is more to AP than this. While for some musicians, particularly those who develop the

---

3   For more on how the meaning of musical quotations can be transferred to their new contexts, see Ockelford (2005a).

ability relatively late in childhood (from four to ten years old), AP is often limited to one instrument (usually the piano), constrained in range, adversely affected by factors such as fatigue, and may well operate only reactively rather than proactively, for children on the autism spectrum, such restrictions do not, in my experience, appear to prevail. Such children have 'universal' AP, which applies to all categories of sound, irrespective of context. However, the children themselves (and those educating and caring for them) may not be aware of their unusual skill. Once, after giving a public lecture on the impact of autism on the development of auditory perception, I was approached by a man in his fifties who, through the examples I had provided of people with universal absolute pitch finding certain types of everyday sound distinctive and memorable, came to realise, for the first time, that he himself had AP. He could recall, for example, the pitch of a buzzing fluorescent light at home. However, no one had ever taught him the names of the notes in music, and so, up to that point lacking the vocabulary to talk about what he heard, he had been unaware that the way he perceived sound was at all unusual.

This man's story shows, contrary to what some academics believe, that pitch-labelling is *not* an essential element in AP (see e.g. Miyazaki 2004). This is in any case obvious to anyone who works with very young autistic children, since AP almost invariably develops before any language associated with music theory. Indeed, I suspect there are many young people on the autism spectrum, who, having little or no language, and, therefore, no immediate way of demonstrating their special skill, have undetected AP. Time after time, when I visit schools and units specialising in autism spectrum conditions, I find pupils and students who, for example, are obsessively interested in certain music-like sounds in the environment (to which they may be acutely sensitive), or who are habitually singing, humming or even whistling snatches of melody in a particularly tuneful way, or who, like Freddie, have rearranged everyday objects according to the different sounds that they make. Whenever I see children behaving like this, I immediately wonder whether they have AP – whether there is a latent musicality waiting to be released through the development of the necessary technical wherewithal, enabling the youngsters to express themselves through playing or singing, and, above all, to be guided into the wider world of musical interaction with others.

Of the many autistic (and blind) children I have known with AP, this ability had invariably manifested itself by the age of two years. This is according to the accounts of teachers and parents and, on a number of occasions, through direct observation on my part. The effects can be very striking. For instance, I remember encountering a 12-month-old baby boy who was totally blind with a condition known as *Leber Congenital Amaurosis* (LCA). It later emerged that he was autistic and had severe learning difficulties as well. His mother brought him to meet me at the school for blind children where I was then head of music. When she arrived, an older boy (who, by chance, also had LCA, learning difficulties and autism) was playing the organ. On hearing the sound, the little boy stilled in his mother's arms, apparently transfixed. He listened, intently, for around a quarter of an hour, while the organ music continued. I remember thinking then (and mentioning to his mother) that here was a child who evidently showed signs of exceptional musical *interest*, which may or may not translate into exceptional musical *ability* as he grew up. At any event, it seemed important to ensure that he was exposed to a wide range of different musics in the coming months and years, had access to instruments and other sound-makers to explore freely and to play with, and had plenty of close, enjoyable musical interactions with his adult carers through voice, movement and touch.

I next met the little boy, six months later, when he was eighteen months old. This time, his mother lifted him up onto the piano stool, and he proceeded to pick out a series of nursery rhymes (all in C major, I noticed – using only the white keys). This suggested to me that he had encoded the melodies using 'relative' rather than absolute pitch: that is, through patterns of intervals (the differences between notes) rather than the notes themselves, since there would be no particular reason why the tunes he had learnt to play should all have appeared in one key.

A further six months passed, and we met again. As the boy sat on his mother's knee at the piano, I hummed 'Twinkle, Twinkle' in A major (which uses a combination of white and black notes on the keyboard). What would the boy do, reproduce the notes themselves (suggesting that he may have AP) or, as before, replicate only the differences between them (indicating that 'relative' pitch was still his predominant processing strategy)? The answer came straight away. Not only did he reproduce the tune in the correct key – starting on A – but also it appeared with a rudimentary accompaniment (comprising individual notes) in the left hand. Further simple copying games, involving single pitches, as well as chords comprising two or three notes, confirmed that the boy did, indeed, have absolute pitch.

The latter capacity, to disaggregate two musical sounds or more that are heard at the same time, is often associated with AP. Without it, the task appears to be very difficult. Indeed, most people struggle even to hear *how many* notes there are in a chord or cluster, let alone identify which they are.

Have a friend play clusters of three, four or five notes simultaneously on the piano. For example, see Figure 6.3.

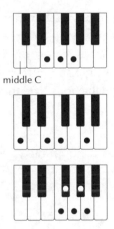

Figure 6.3 Clusters of three, four and five notes

Just by listening (without looking), can you tell how many keys have been pressed down?

There are a number of implications of the ability to hear several notes at once as individual entities. To put these in perspective, we will consider first the position that 'neurotypical' listeners find themselves in as they attend to music.

Play a music track that involves a number of musicians performing at once (such as a band, orchestra or choir). What do you hear? Probably your attention will immediately be drawn to a tune (which you may be able to sing along to). This will usually be at the 'top' of the musical texture, using the highest pitches of those present.

Keep listening. What else do you hear? In the case of the choir, it may just be a general sense of 'harmony' – the notion that there are other voices present, which are somehow merged into a pleasing auditory meld. With the band or orchestra, which are less homogeneous in auditory terms, it may be easier to have some sense of what else is going on apart from the lead vocals or main theme; unpitched percussion instruments (drums, cymbals, and so on), for example, are usually relatively easy to pick out, since they cut through the texture.

However, given that a symphony orchestra may comprise upwards of 50 musicians, between them playing a dozen different lines of music, it is reasonable to ask what is going on with regard to auditory perception: how is it that we get an impression of a single, composite musical fabric and yet be unable to isolate the detail of more than one or two strands within it?

To get a sense of what is happening musically, consider the following visual analogy. Glance quickly at Figure 6.4, and then look away.

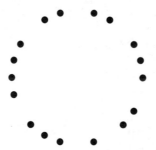

Figure 6.4 The impact of 'Gestalt' perception in the domain of vision

What did you see? Probably, your initial impression was of a circle, made up of a number of dots. But without checking, would you be able to say how many dots there are, where they are positioned, and how many are missing?

This capacity of the brain to see pattern in a group of isolated objects is known as 'Gestalt' perception ('Gestalt' being the German for 'shape' or 'form'). Through this process, separate stimuli fuse together in the brain to form an impression of one thing. Gestalt perception works in both the visual and the auditory domains. Visually, it is relatively easy to take the time to review an illustration such as that shown in Figure 6.4 and isolate its constituents – 17 dots. Indeed, as we saw in Chapter 1, it is a feature of the way that some people with autism process information, that they may be more likely to see the detail than the overall effect or function of something.

For 'neurotypical' brains, however, as you probably discovered through the listening experiment set out above, groups of simultaneous notes are much harder to disentangle than patterns of dots on a page. There are a number of reasons for this, not least the fact that musical sounds, each being made up of many pitches (see Figure 3.4), tend to interfere with each other: there is a good deal of overlap. With extensive experience or conscious practice or both, musicians without AP can learn to disembed the different components of a chord, particularly if they are used to playing with other musicians, and so get to know how each part sounds from hearing it performed by a colleague, distinct from others. In contrast, many children with AP – whether on the autism spectrum or not – just seem to be able to disaggregate chords without thinking about it. Those who are verbal, and have learnt the names of the notes, will able to say which pitches are present when they listen to chords. Others, who can't or won't talk about what they hear, may play music with two parts or more by ear on a keyboard or piano. Indeed, some people with autism are very good at this task. Derek Paravicini famously demonstrated his capacity for chordal disaggregation on CBS's 60 Minutes programme in the USA. The host, Lesley Stahl, played large, complex combinations of notes on the piano, and Derek was able to imitate them all immediately without error. Subsequent tests showed that even with nine or ten note chords, he can achieve over 90 per cent accuracy. Beyond this, with only ten fingers at his disposal, testing gets more difficult, although on another television programme (Extraordinary People), Derek did reproduce the sounds of a whole symphony orchestra by scurrying up and down the keys!

Another important feature of the way that Derek and other musical savants – and the most skilful 'neurotypical' musicians with absolute pitch – appear to process chords, is from the 'bottom up'. That is, their attention seems to be drawn most strongly to the lowest pitches in harmonies (those to the leftmost end of the keyboard) with relatively less importance being attached to higher notes. We know this because of the findings of a series of experiments undertaken by one of my PhD students, Annamaria Mazzeschi, who had six musical savants and around 20 advanced music students (all with AP) attempt to play a series of 120 chords of four, five, six, seven, eight and nine notes on the piano, just by copying what they heard. All the savants and some of the music students achieved high scores, and a common characteristic of these most successful participants was 'bottom-up' listening. The music students who did less well tended, on the whole, to get the top notes correct, but were not as good at hearing 'further down' into each of the clusters. As we observed, this strategy is the one that 'neurotypical' listeners appear to adopt, with most attention devoted to melodies that are usually topmost in a musical texture.

So, Mazzeschi's data suggest that two different listening strategies were in play, and that one ('bottom up') was more effective than the other ('top down'). To understand the significance of this in musical terms, it is important to appreciate that the lowest note in a chord has a special significance in determining the type of harmony that is heard, and defining in its function in relation to neighbouring sonorities. That is, the lowest note carries greatest structural weight, and so 'bottom-up' hearing implies a deep harmonic understanding. Interestingly, this runs contrary to the tendency, observed in other contexts, of the autistic mind to be attracted primarily to surface detail. And it could be, unlike many other domains of human engagement and activity, that music perception is not adversely affected by 'weak central coherence' (see p.25).

This proclivity for structural hearing can be seen in other characteristics of the savants' chordal processing style too: even Derek, who consistently managed to replicate nine out of ten notes in the most complex combinations, was better at dealing with some groups of sounds than others. In particular, 'conventional' chords, that formed recognisable auditory 'shapes', were more likely to be reproduced entirely correctly than clusters of pitch that were irregular or unusual or both. And this was true to an even greater extent with the other participants, including all the savants. In other words, the savant musicians, just like their 'neurotypical' counterparts with AP, were perceiving the 'Gestalts' of the chords to which they were exposed *as well as* their individual components. Again, this appears to imply a form of music-perceptual processing in these exceptional autistic people that diverges from the general principle of weak central coherence.[4]

Savants are very rare, and so (inevitably) they are in some respects atypical of the autistic population as a whole. However, there is anecdotal evidence that the 'bottom-up' auditory processing strategy that seems to be favoured by musical savants may be used by other children on the autism spectrum (or with broadly comparable neurodevelopmental conditions). Here is a description written by another student of mine – Anna Powell (2011) – of an excerpt from a lesson with Avni, a seven-year-old girl with Williams syndrome.[5]

> The following week, when Adam suggested that they play *Over the Rainbow*, Avni began to pick out a bass line in the lower register of the piano. She was playing in C major and it was not very clear what she intended to do. Adam started to play the melody in E♭ major (as he had done in the previous week) to remind her of the tune but Avni stopped him and instructed him to start on C, while she continued to pick her way through a bass line in C major. It seemed that she had assimilated the overall harmonic structure of the piece rather than just the melody, and she was eager to reproduce this harmonic bass line. Avni's mother informed us that, in fact, she had played several different arrangements of *Over the Rainbow* to Avni during the previous week, which explained why she had learned the piece in a different key. Her eagerness to play the bass line, rather than

---

4 For further evidence of this phenomenon, in relation to melodies, see Mottron, Peretz and Ménard (2000), and for related findings pertaining to the visual domain, see Mottron *et al.* (2003).

5 Williams syndrome was first identified in 1961 in the context of cardiology by Dr J.C.P. Williams and colleagues. It is now known to be caused by a deletion of genetic material from region q11.23 of chromosome 7. Physically, people with Williams syndrome have supravalvular aortic stenosis and 'elfin' facial features. Functionally, it is a neurodevelopmental genetic disorder that is characterised by uneven mental functioning, with cognitive impairment in areas such as reasoning, arithmetic ability, and spatial cognition, and relatively preserved skills in social domains, face processing, language and music.

the melody, in the first instance, demonstrates Avni's keen sense of harmony, and the facility that she has in reproducing that harmony. (Powell 2011, p.48)

So what does all this mean for children with autism? It seems as though, for some of them at least, their experience of music is likely to be very different from that of the majority: more vivid, more intense, more exciting, more exhausting. For those with AP, each pitch may be like a familiar friend in an otherwise confusing world; each with the capacity to evoke a strong emotional response. Little wonder, then, that children such as Freddie and Romy will play notes or clusters or short melodic patterns over and over again to get the emotional 'kick' that they elicit. When he was younger, Derek would strike particular notes forcefully and repeatedly until, after weeks of such treatment, the hammer or the string would often give way, and (according to the nature of the damage) his musical friend lost her voice or at least displayed a new-found huskiness. Whereas neurotypically we habituate to such stimuli (whereby their impact upon us diminishes with repeated exposure) children with autism seem to hear them afresh on each occasion – as though listening for the first time. And when, as supporting adults, boredom with a child's latest auditory obsession is a distant memory, his or her level of emotional engagement and arousal appears, if anything, to have increased.

The same may well be true of what (to the neurotypical brain) are *everyday* sounds (but which, as we have seen, autistic children may process musically). To a child on the autism spectrum, the soundscape of the shopping centre, the airport or the classroom may be overwhelming. Each stream of sound – the humming of the air-conditioning, the ticking of the clock, the musical tones that precede each announcement on the PA system, the babble of people chatting – has its own, distinct characteristics, and the child may not be able to 'turn them off' mentally. Most of us (through Gestalt perception) instinctively draw some stimuli into the foreground of our attention, while pushing others into the background, where they can be ignored. However, as Romy's reaction to aeroplanes and mobile phones shows, this may be difficult (or even impossible) for some children with autism.

> Some idea of how effective our continuous auditory filtering mechanism is can be gleaned by sitting for a time alone with one's eyes closed in a busy public space (such as a shopping centre or school) and letting one's auditory attention wander freely. Over a period of five minutes or so, how many different sounds did you hear?
>
> As composers such as John Cage observed, as far as humans are concerned, there is no such thing as silence!
>
> Now imagine lacking the capacity to ignore any of those sounds – even those that are more or less constant (such as the hum of electrical appliances). What strategies would you adopt to make things tolerable? Put your hands over your ears? Move around to try to escape the constant sonic mélange? Vocalise to block the sounds out?

We can surmise that, for a proportion of children on the autism spectrum, being assailed with unfiltered auditory clutter is the norm. For them, 'multitracking' is unexceptional and, indeed, they may even seek out auditory complexity: for example, both Freddie and Romy enjoy having other music sounding (even from two or three sources, such as the radio, an iPad and a noisy toy) as they play the piano (unlike their music teacher, who cannot cope with the resultant cacophony!).

We all have the capacity to 'hear sounds in our heads', without the presence of any physical correlate, as a combined function of memory and imagination. Indeed, most people are thought to have 'earworms' from time to time – fragments of tunes that go round and round unstoppably in our minds. The possession of AP implies that the mental imagery of sounds may be more vivid than for those who are reliant on relative pitch alone, since in the former scenario the 'inner sounds' one hears are memories of percepts themselves, rather than having to be reconstructed via remembered relationships (see p.69). From observing many children on the autism spectrum over the years, I am of the view that earworms are relatively commonplace, particularly among those with AP, for whom, I suspect, they form potent elements in the youngsters' streams of consciousness. Evidence for this includes the frequency with which children repeatedly hum, whistle or sing snippets of tunes, presumably as an expression of what they can hear in their heads, often with fingers placed firmly in the ears, to block out possible external distractions. Sometimes, I have had pupils continuing to hum or sing under their breath while they play a *different* piece on the piano – further testimony to the auditory 'multitracking' of which they appear to be capable. Occasionally the two worlds are coordinated: for example, both Freddie and Romy will *pretend* to play, by touching the appropriate keys, but without them actually sounding. Clearly, for them, and others like them, there is a sense in which physically causing a pitch to occur when an intense mental image of it has already been heard is tautological – irritating, even, if the piano is slightly out of tune. Always making notes on instruments sound when performing is just another thing that 'neurotypical' people do that children with autism have to get used to!

There is a line of thinking that holds that AP, and the characteristics of auditory perception described above that sometimes coexist with it, is something that we all have very early in life, but quickly lose, as relative pitch processing comes to dominate. This is thought to be because important information, such as the vocal inflections that modulate speech, and (as we have seen), musical structures, are essentially about pitch differences rather than absolute values. According to this view, we can surmise that a feature of auditory perception prominent in some people on the autism spectrum is shared by *all of us* in the first few months of life. It is just that the Exceptional Early Cognitive Environments of those with autism (and those who are blind) mean that they have a far higher probability than most of us have of retaining AP.

However, the account of the blind baby, given above, who played nursery rhymes in C major at 18 months (suggestive of relative pitch) but subsequently, at two years, in the key in which he had heard them (indicative of AP) runs counter to this. That is, a sense of absolute pitch was something that he apparently acquired in his second year of life, not an ability that he had once had and then failed to lose. Two other observations are relevant to the 'acquisition' argument. First, we have already noted that the later AP is (re)acquired, the 'weaker' it is: more context-bound by instrument and pitch range, less consistent, and more susceptible to fatigue. Second, there is anecdotal evidence that a strong sense of AP can improve: the absolute pitch discrimination abilities of a number of the children I have worked with appear to have become more refined as they progress through childhood – through a developing awareness of microtones, for example (meaning they are able to recognise very small discrepancies between pitches heard at different times). These developments of or improvements in AP do not appear to be consistent with a skill that was once present but was somehow lost.

THE CONSEQUENCES OF AP FOR MUSICAL DEVELOPMENT

Another contention is that the development of AP is contingent on music education – in particular, instrumental tuition. Now, it may be the case that, for some children, learning to play a pitched instrument early in childhood has an impact on the development of their absolute pitch perception abilities. However, given that young children are thought to be exposed to music around 80 per cent of time (see p.216) *whether or not* they have music lessons, and since it is not necessary to play an instrument to develop AP, one has to question the extent to which specialist music input actually plays a part. Indeed, one could argue the converse, that those young children who are attracted to play instruments (or whose parents consider that they should) are those that in any case have noteworthy auditory skills.

Whatever the general picture, there is no doubt that, for the great majority of children on the autism spectrum with AP, the ear leads the hand, as it were. That is to say, it is absolute perception that drives them towards playing any instruments that they may find in their living or learning environments at home, in the nursery or at school – typically the keyboard or piano – something that very often occurs with no adult intervention. As Francesca Happé (2011) said at a Royal Society Lecture, it is the autistic child's eye for detail (in this case, *ear* for detail) that kick-starts special talents. I would go further and say AP is the fire that fuels savant abilities in the domain of music, an issue that is discussed at length in Chapter 7. Here, we consider how the kick-starting and the subsequent fuelling of proactive musical engagement work.

Let us return for a moment to Lottie's song, which sounds rather like a playground chant, and which she repeats from one day to the next, though not always starting on the same note (see Figure 4.2). That is to say, she has encoded and memorised the melodic motifs not as individual pitches in their own right, but as a series of differences between them. (We can surmise, though, that absolute representations of pitch are not entirely absent for Lottie, since the notes she uses on separate occasions are broadly similar.) However, for children such as Faisal (p.118) and Romy, who both have AP, the position is rather different, since, as we have seen in relation to the 'chord experiments' described above, they have the capacity to encode the pitch data from music directly, rather than as series of intervals. So in seeking to remember and repeat groups of notes over significant periods of time, they have a processing advantage over Lottie, since she has to extract and store information at a higher level of abstraction.

It is this that explains why children on the autism spectrum with AP are able to develop instrumental skills at an early age with no formal tuition, since for them, reproducing groups of notes that they have heard is merely a question of remembering a series of one-to-one mappings between given pitches as they sound and (typically) the keys on a keyboard that produce them. These relationships are invariant: once learnt, they service a lifetime of music making, through which they are constantly reinforced. Were Lottie to try to play by ear, though, she would have to master the far more complicated process of calculating how the intervals that she hears in her head map onto the distances between keys, which, due to the asymmetries of the keyboard, are likely to differ according to her starting point. For example, producing the interval between the first two notes of Lottie's song, which musicians call a 'minor third', can be achieved through 12 distinct key combinations, comprising one of four underlying patterns. Even more confusing, though, virtually the same physical leap between keys may sound different (a 'major third') according to its position on the keyboard (see Figure 6.5).

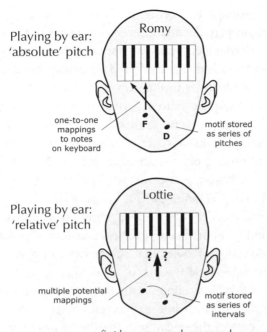

Playing by ear: 'absolute' pitch

Romy

one-to-one mappings to notes on keyboard

motif stored as series of pitches

Playing by ear: 'relative' pitch

Lottie

multiple potential mappings

motif stored as series of intervals

first key press produces sound
mental calculation of interval from this sound
(initial) trial and error to find second key (to match the interval)
there are 12 possibilities: four different patterns
confounding factor: the same pattern and similar ones produce different *intervals*

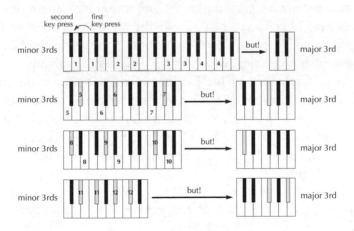

Figure 6.5 Different mechanisms involved in playing by ear using 'absolute' and 'relative' pitch abilities

For sure, many children with AP who learn to play by ear rapidly develop the skills to play melodies beginning on different notes too, and some, including a proportion of those with severe learning difficulties, are able to play fluently in every key (a capacity that, as a teacher, I strongly encourage). This may appear contradictory, in the light of the processing advantage conferred by being able to encode pitches as perceptual identities in their own right, each of which, as we have seen, maps uniquely onto a particular piano or organ key. But the reality of almost all pieces is that motifs variously appear at different pitches, and so to make sense of music, young children with AP need to learn to process pitch relatively as well as absolutely. This begs the question of how the two forms of processing evolve and interact in a child's musical development.

Let us take the case of Romy once more, who today has a repertoire of around a hundred song excerpts and fragments of other pieces from a wide range of styles that she enjoys using as material for improvised interactions on the piano. In re-creating these motifs, she largely plays the melody alone with the right hand, although she sometimes supplies a bass-line in the left, occasionally adding chords and, in the case of the opening of the theme from the second movement of Beethoven's 'Pathétique' Sonata, a moving inner part. Apart from being an utterly joyous musician with whom to work, Romy is fascinating from a music-psychological point of view because she does not always get things right, and it is in her pattern of errors that one can obtain a rare glimpse into the workings of an exceptional musical mind: in particular the relationship between absolute and relative pitch processing, which, in her case, is still evolving.

For example, one of her passions of the moment is the theme from *Vltava* by Smetana. I first played Romy the tune in E minor (the key in which it initially appears in the symphonic poem), and she quickly picked it up using her AP ability, invariably reproducing the outline of the melody correctly, sometimes adding new details of her own (see Figure 6.6).

Figure 6.6 A typical rendition of the *Vltava* theme in E minor by Romy

This seems straightforward enough. But Romy is what can only be described as an obsessive transposer. She will very often play the same motif over and over again, frequently starting on a different note each time, and sometimes even changing key *within* a particular appearance of the musical fragment concerned. As she likes me to provide an accompaniment, the latter tendency is particularly challenging! It may be, though, that it is this very challenge that offers one possible explanation for Romy's maverick modulations, since they keep her firmly in control of the shared musical narrative. This is a subtle development of the influence that she previously had exerted through playing material in different keys to *prevent* me from joining in (see p180). She is now content for me to participate in her creative flow provided that she feels in charge of what is happening.

Another reason, I believe, for Romy's constant key changes is the buzz she gets from hearing things that are at once well known and novel: 'so familiar and yet so strange'.[6] Only someone with her powerful sense of AP could experience shifts of key in this way: she will often leap up and shriek with excitement as she hears the impact of a motif that she knows well appearing as a fresh set of pitches – seeing old friends in a new light. And yet, she sometimes makes mistakes that remain uncorrected at the time, and which are repeated on future occasions. For example, in her version of the introduction of the *Vltava* melody in F minor, she plays a B instead of a C (see Figure 6.7). This is a blatant error; observers in Romy's lessons notice it straight away.

It seems inconceivable that, at a certain level, Romy, does not recognise that something is wrong, given her advanced music-processing abilities. Yet at the same time, we can assume that she *wants* to play things correctly (she very rarely makes mistakes, and is somewhat intolerant of any changes that I may try to introduce within the accompaniments with which she is familiar). So what is going on?

---

6 See Kayzer's (1995) book, which features an interview with Derek Paravicini.

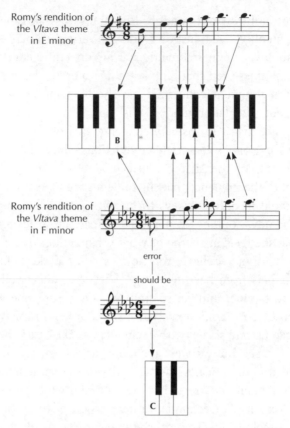

Figure 6.7 Romy's uncharacteristic error as
she transposes the *Vltava* theme

To find out, let us take a step back and consider again Lottie and her
musical motif. Since Lottie reproduces her tune at different absolute
pitches, we previously made the assumption that this information
is encoded largely as differences in pitch. Now, imagine Lottie is at
the stage of beginning to sing the first note. Without thinking, she
chooses a pitch (which will approximate to the ones she has used
in earlier renditions of the same motif). We can surmise that this
will be stored in working memory and become a reference point
for those that follow, functioning as a temporary 'absolute' in the
domain of pitch (you followed a similar process in singing 'Frère
Jacques' in Chapter 3). In much the same way, the second note will
be retained, as a potential benchmark for others. Hence the third note
will have two possible points of reference, the fourth three, and so on:

the unfolding network of relationships creating an embryonic pitch 'framework' (see Figure 3.12) through which the notes are mentally locked together (Figure 6.8). There are no conflicts, and the structure is self-sustaining. (Although, as amateur choirs know to their cost, temporary 'absolute pitch' markers can drift over time without the singers being aware of it.)

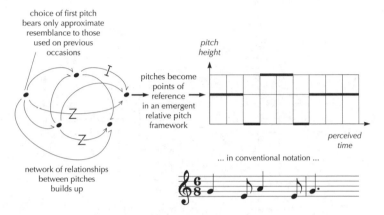

Figure 6.8 A 'relative pitch framework' emerges from Lottie's production of her motif, beginning at an unspecified pitch level

How does this differ from Romy's position? We know that she initially encoded the *Vltava* theme as a series of pitches pertaining to E minor (and therefore starting on a B). When retrieving the melody at this pitch level, the task appears (for her) to be straightforward, and she re-creates it without error (Figure 6.6): we can assume that she plugs into her absolute pitch memories (which are, of course, not unique to this melody) and reifies them on the piano.

It is not clear whether she *also* encoded the melody in relative terms, distinct from the 'absolute' memories, although, as we shall see, the error she makes throws this into doubt. Let us assume for the moment that the pitches were stored only as absolute values. Given a series of data in this form, there are two strategies that Romy could adopt when she tries to transpose. The first would be to draw into working memory her long-term recall of absolute pitches, and calculate a transposed version of each. Inevitably, this would produce interference, since the values being calculated anew would conflict with those being remembered, yielding the potential for confusion and – therefore – error (see Figure 6.9). Similar incompatibilities would arise if an attempt were made to extract information concerning intervals from the series of absolute pitches as they were recalled.

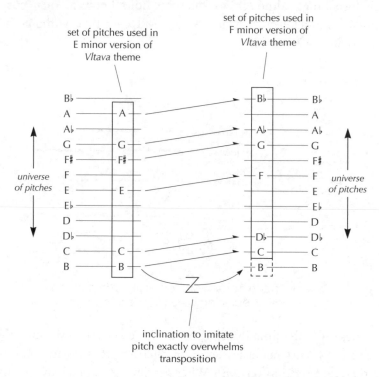

Figure 6.9 The conflict between absolute memories recalled and transposed is thought to result in confusion and induce error

However, if relative data, in either of these two forms, were *dissociable* from the absolute, conflicts would not arise, and, we can surmise, errors would be less likely. Hence, one explanation for Romy's mistakes in transposition may be a lack, or partial lack, of discrete relative encoding of pitch in her long-term memory.

Most children with AP sooner or later find ways of resolving the potential conflicts like this, between the 'absolute' and 'relative' encoding of pitch. Freddie, for example, learnt to play major and minor scales in every key on the piano by ear – but he required only C major and minor as models. These provided him with all the information he required. When asked to play the scales on other notes, I could hear him singing the next note that was required, and then finding the relevant key on the piano, which he did very rapidly since, as we have seen, his AP means that he knows precisely what each note sounds like. Any mistakes he made (largely due to difficulties with fingering, which he continues to learn much more painstakingly through physical demonstration and support) were immediately corrected. Hence we can assume that Freddie encoded the initial scale patterns on C absolutely, abstracted the necessary information about pitch differences from those traces, and subsequently drew on this when transposing, plugging the nodes of the intervals back into his absolute pitch framework (at a different level from the original) – see Figure 6.10.

In summary, then, despite the conflicts that may arise from retrieving pitches encoded relatively and absolutely, there seems to be little doubt that the possession of AP offers a huge advantage to the musical development of children with autism and learning difficulties, for whom many of the more conventional ways of learning (through emulating peers working in social groups or through being taught using notation, for example) may not be available. In short, AP may well enable children to function at *Sounds of Intent* Level 4 and above who would otherwise be unable to do so (see Chapter 4) and, beyond this, it is AP that catalyses the exceptional achievement found in musical savants (see Chapter 7).

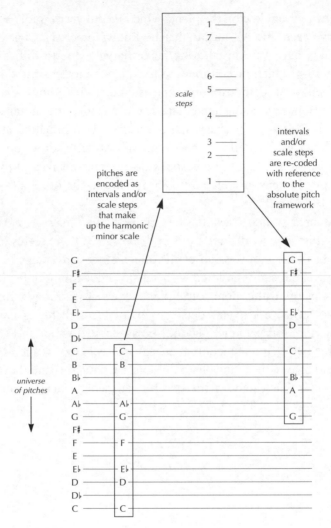

Figure 6.10 Example of Freddie's hypothesised mental processing in transposing a scale

MUSIC AND LANGUAGE

There can be a further consequence of the Exceptional Early Cognitive Environment that autism causes, which pertains to language: echolalia. This feature of speech is widely reported among autistic children, and was originally defined as the (apparently) meaningless repetition of words or groups of words. Echolalia can occur immediately after the language in question has been heard, or its reoccurrence may be delayed. Barry Prizant was among the first to observe that echolalia actually can fulfil a range of functions in verbal interaction, such as turn-taking and affirmation, and often finds a place in non-interactive contexts too, where it can serve as a self-reflective commentary or rehearsal strategy (see e.g. Prizant and Duchan 1981).

Why does echolalia occur? It is a feature of normal language acquisition in young children (one to two years old) – when the urge to imitate what they hear outstrips semantic understanding.

To get a sense of why echolalia may occur, imagine someone says to you:

'Hvað segirðu?'

You don't know what he or she means. For the purposes of this scenario, you're not allowed to say, 'Do you speak English?' or 'Sorry, I don't understand'! Nonetheless, you have a strong sense that a reply is required.

What do you do?

The only logical thing is somehow to make use of the material to hand, but without semantic understanding (and, therefore, without syntax), you have little alternative but to punt the phrase, or at least part of it, back. For example:

'Segirðu?'

And what do we have? Echolalia.

As we saw in Chapter 3, imitation lies at the heart of musical structure – so one could argue that echolalia is the organisation of language (in the absence of semantics and linguistic syntax) through musical structure. It is as though the words (bearing little or no meaning) become musical objects, to be manipulated purely through their sounding qualities (see Figure 6.11).

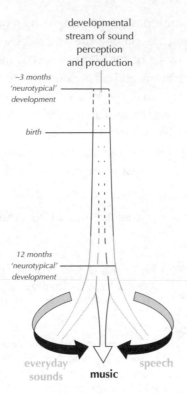

Figure 6.11 Everyday sounds and speech may be processed
in musical terms by some children on the autism spectrum

It is worth noting that even music can become 'super-structured' with
additional repetition, as the account, for example, of Shivan in Chapter
4 shows: it is common for children on the autism spectrum to play
snippets of music (or videos with music) over and over…and over…
again. It is as though music's 80 per cent proportion of repetition is
insufficient for the mind ravenous for structure, and so it creates even
more! Speaking to autistic adults who are able to verbalise why (as
children) they would repeat musical excerpts in this way, it appears
that the main reason (apart from the sheer enjoyment of hearing
a particularly fascinating series of sounds again and again) is that
they could hear more and more in the sequence concerned. Bearing
in mind that most music is, as we have seen, highly complex, with
many events occurring simultaneously (and given that even single
notes generally comprise many pitches in the form of harmonics),
to the child with finely tuned auditory perception, there are in fact

many different things to attend to in even a few seconds of music, and many relationships between sounds to fathom. That is, while listening to a passage a hundred times may be extremely tedious to the 'neurotypical' ear, which can detect only half a dozen composite events, each fused in perception; to the mind of the autistic child, which can break down the sequence into a dozen different melodic lines, the stimulus may be rich and riveting.

CONCLUSION

In this chapter I set out a new theory of autism and music, which can be summarised as follows. Autism creates what I term an 'Exceptional Early Cognitive Environment'. This can pose challenges in terms of language (both receptively and so, inevitably, expressively) and in grasping the functional importance of everyday sounds, which are more likely to be processed for their perceptual qualities. Add into this mix the ubiquity of music in early childhood, and music's self-referencing structure (requiring no symbolic understanding), and there is a tendency for *all* sounds to be processed as though they were inherently musical, and in terms of musical structure (repetition). This has a number of consequences. Critically, as we have seen, it is estimated that around 5 per cent of children on the autism spectrum develop AP (experience suggests that this percentage is unduly low, but assessment can be difficult). The fact that AP tends to appear around 24 months – the same time as language would generally emerge – has been noted by researchers such as Leon Miller (1989), who investigated the abilities of a number of musical savants whose verbal communication skills were limited; his suggestion was that music comes to function in some respects as a proxy for verbal communication in the auditory domain. I have worked with a number of children for whom this is the case, including some instances where music substitutes entirely for language (as it does, for example, for Romy). Notwithstanding Miller's (1989) observation, AP is not a necessary factor in this unusual developmental journey, however.

The area where AP does usually appear to play an important role, though, is in the tendency of some children to teach themselves to play an instrument (typically the keyboard) by ear at any early age. As we saw in the example of the young, blind, autistic boy cited above, some initial learning may occur in the absence of AP, but more advanced skills do seem to depend on it. This thinking is captured in Figure 6.12. The critical thing for parents and practitioners is that such abilities have the opportunity to develop, through access to musical instruments that are manageable with small hands, and (preferably) encouragement to explore them, and have fun experimenting with the sounds that they can make. It is crucial that appropriate adult support be provided to guide the development of technique and a love of playing in social contexts is available as soon as possible.

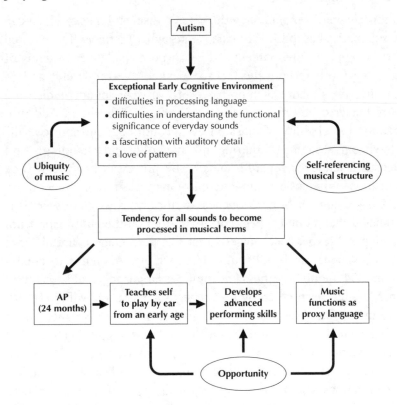

Figure 6.12 The supposed impact of 'Exceptional Early Cognitive Environments' caused by autism on musical and wider auditory development

CHAPTER 7

Teaching the '1 in 20'

INTRODUCTION

In Chapter 6 we saw how exceptional cognitive environments can result in exceptional musical potential. For those with high levels of general intelligence, unusually advanced auditory processing and a well-developed capacity to engage with music may merely be features in a rich and balanced landscape of talents. Certainly, such children will require specialist input, but, in most cases, the approaches that music teachers would use with any pupil of outstanding ability are likely to be appropriate – albeit in conjunction with an autism specialist who can advise on managing the relationship with the pupil concerned, and how to deal with anxieties, obsessive behaviours and so on. The important point is that the child's learning strategies pertaining to music are likely to be similar to those of others with prodigious abilities.

However, where exceptional musicality occurs as part of a markedly uneven profile of cognitive development, which characterises many children on the autism spectrum, then the challenge for teachers and their pupils will be much greater. In this chapter, we consider some of the practical consequences of working with children with unusual musical potential (which, as we have seen, is likely to be at least 5% of the autism population), which occurs in the context of pervasive developmental delay.

The first thing to bear in mind is that having an exceptionally good 'musical ear' – including AP – does not necessarily equate to wanting, or indeed having the capacity, to become an advanced performer. Actively engaging in music-making requires an array of abilities, in addition to those in the auditory domain: a range of motor skills, coordinated with what is heard; and concentration, memory, and executive planning – all of which can be challenging for children on the autism spectrum. However, for those who show signs of wishing to acquire the skills necessary to play an instrument, or at least have the potential to do so, then they should be given the opportunity to learn, not only for the musical benefits this may bring, but also since the extra-musical rewards for them as individuals can be so huge, in terms of improved self-esteem, communication, emotional awareness and social skills.

How does one recognise exceptional musical interest and potential? Not all children with outstanding musicality start teaching themselves to play an instrument. The signs may not be immediately obvious. We have already encountered Freddie and his flowerpots. Other indications, as we have seen, may be a marked interest in, or even an obsession with, certain everyday sounds. A child may exhibit a tendency to whistle, hum or perhaps sing tiny fragments of melody that sound beautifully in tune. He or she may tap rhythms repeatedly on and with anything that comes to hand (see p.120).

Those who do start to play by themselves typically choose the keyboard (or piano), partly, one suspects, because that is most likely to be the instrument that is immediately to hand, partly because keyboards have an immediacy and consistency that not all instruments do (press a given key and the same pitch will always sound), and partly because the keyboard itself has a pleasing symmetry – captivating, even, with its line-up of black and white keys, whose pattern repeats every 12 notes. However, autodidactic children can present particular challenges for a would-be teacher: their learning styles, having been self-directed, may well be unorthodox; similarly, they may have eccentric – and ingrained – ways of playing (or singing) that have arisen in the absence of formal tuition; they will probably have little or no awareness of music and music-related ideas as *concepts*, despite an advanced level of *implicit* understanding; they may have limited and idiosyncratic patterns of receptive and expressive language with which to communicate *about* music; and they may have an unwillingness (or inability) to accept assistance or advice, often with little or no idea of what a conventional 'teacher–pupil' relationship may entail. Nonetheless, the rewards of working with such children – for both parties – can be immense.

TEACHING STRATEGIES

If there is one golden rule in working with children with autism, it is that there are no golden rules! I remain suspicious of *any* system or approach that claims to offer the best for all, or even the majority, of children, since the spectrum of their abilities, needs, propensities, motivations, likes and dislikes is so vast. That is not to say, of course, that one should not in time develop longer-term aims (taking into account the views of parents and other significant figures in a child's life), and have to hand a battery of potential strategies (at least some of which will perhaps be tried and tested in other contexts) to support the child in moving forward. But to approach music education with a severely autistic youngster with a more or less fixed plan is likely to be a frustrating experience for all concerned. Indeed, it may do more harm than good.

So, as a teacher, what approach should you take? Above all, listen, listen, listen again, and look. Open your ears (and your eyes) to whatever children do, whether exploring or playing the instrument that they have chosen (or have been presented with), or vocalising, or moving. They may even seem to do nothing at all or they may engage in apparently random behaviours, but I am convinced that everything a child does (or fails to do) occurs (or fails to occur) for a reason. The challenge, of course, is trying to fathom what that reason may be.

Having said there are no golden rules, I am about to make an exception: *don't talk too much* (if at all)! Language is so often a barrier or, worse, a threat or, at best, auditory clutter. (Be prepared, though, to listen carefully to anything the child may choose to say to you.) Save verbal interaction for the parents, *after* the lesson – which, unless there are exceptional circumstances, I believe they should attend. The relationship you may develop with their child through mutual, enjoyable musical engagement is far too precious to keep to yourself (certain music therapists take note). It must be seen as a stepping-stone to a wider and, let's hope, deeper, purposeful connection with others.

And if the child does nothing? Discreetly introduce fragments of music. 'Talk' to children through pure sound. Improvise. Entice them to engage with you musically, excite them, tease them with single notes and exotic chords, a metronomic beat and quirky rhythms. Above all, be musically interesting; make your playing or singing *irresistible*.

Irrespective of what you do, children may vocalise or play. It can be beneficial for you and your pupil each to have a similar instrument available, since this assures an affinity in sound and the possibility of imitation without compromising a child's personal space. *Sharing* may be an unfamiliar notion, as shown in this account of my first attempt to teach the young Derek Paravicini (aged five), having met him once before (Ockelford 2007).

> As I had done at Linden Lodge, I reached forward and this time as gently as I could, started to improvise a bass-line below what he was doing. The notes were barely audible to me, but Derek was on to them immediately. His left hand shot down to where my fingers had trespassed, shooed the intruders away with a flick, and instantly picked up from where I had left off.

> Round 1 to Derek.

> Leaving my chair, I walked round to the other side of the piano and starting improvising an ornamented version of the tune high up – as far away as I could from his right hand. In a flash he was there again, pushing my hand out of the way. Then once more he began imitating what I had just played before extending it to fit in with the changes in harmony.

> End of Round 2, and Derek was clearly ahead on points.

> Still, by following me to the extremes of the keyboard, he had left the middle range of notes temporarily exposed and, surreptitiously leaning over Derek's shoulders, with a feeling of mischievous triumph, I started to add in some chords. My victory was short-lived, however. Without for one moment stopping what he was doing, he tried to push me away with the back of his head. This time, though, I was minded to resist.

> 'Do you mind if I join in, Derek?'

My words fell on deaf ears. Ignoring me, he pushed with increasing force, all the time continuing to play. His message was unequivocal, so I decided to let him have his own way. For now. As soon as the coast was clear, his hands darted back to the middle of the piano, to fill in the chords that were now missing, before scampering outwards again to catch up with the abandoned tune and bass-line.

'You need an extra hand, Derek,' I joked, as in my mind I conceded Round 3 to him. By a knockout. (Ockelford 2007, pp.81–82)

As you start to respond musically to your new pupil, pay scrupulous attention to how he or she in turn reacts to you. Doubling the melody as the child plays may be tolerated, for example, but not deviating substantially from it. An open-minded, flexible approach is most likely to succeed: be prepared to modify your input to accommodate your pupils' potentially roving musical focus. By providing an arresting model of musical responsiveness, the aim is to encourage them to evolve a sensitivity to the direction that others are taking, and a willingness to follow their lead. By stimulating the aural imagination of pupils the hope is that they will be fired with enthusiasm to explore new and exciting musical territories.

Matters of technique are likely to present a particular challenge, especially for those working with children who have previously taught themselves. For example, when he was very young, Derek, with very small hands but a huge determination to play the complex musical textures he could resolve aurally, used his wrists and even his elbows on occasions to play notes that would otherwise have been beyond his reach.[1] The main melodic line was typically placed in the middle of the texture and picked out with the thumbs, giving it a characteristic percussive prominence.

While technical idiosyncrasies such as these are ultimately neither 'right' nor 'wrong', certain methods of playing undoubtedly enable performers to fulfil their musical aims more effectively than others – indeed, some passages on the piano may even be rendered impossible unless a particular fingering is adopted. However, the prospect of changing aspects of a child's technique, which may have evolved wholly intuitively, can be daunting too. Those with severe learning

---

1 Eddie, the young savant with whom Leon Miller worked, apparently adopted the same approach (see Miller 1989, p.30)!

difficulties may have little capacity to reflect consciously on what they do, and lack the receptive vocabulary to make description or analysis of their efforts meaningful. Moreover, the challenges they face may be compounded with physical disabilities. In circumstances such as these, you may opt for compromise: seeking to modify a pupil's technique only where it is judged to be essential; adopting, where appropriate, an evolutionary rather than a radical approach to change; and, in a positive way, acknowledging and accepting the effects on performance – technically, stylistically and in terms of repertoire – that a child's disabilities may have. You may have to rely to a great extent on demonstration (rather than explanation). This may be based on the pupil seeing, feeling or listening to what is going on, or a combination of the three. Remember that 'hand under hand' demonstrations are most effective from behind. This is usually preferable to attempting coactive movements face-to-face, when sets of muscles work in opposition rather than together. Listening, and seeking to emulate the quality of sound made by you or other performers, may be a crucial factor in technical development too, since the pupil's desire to reproduce what is heard may encourage the necessary motor activity without needing conscious attention.

Whatever approach is adopted, the development of technique is likely to require many hours of painstaking work on the part of both you and your pupil. For example, as a little boy, Derek tended to play passages of consecutive notes by jumping from one to the next using the same finger – or sometimes even a series of karate chops with the side of his hand! Despite the extraordinary dexterity this entailed, it was clear that his playing would benefit enormously from incorporating the standard finger patterns associated with scales and arpeggios.

I decided to start with some five-finger exercises, the foundation of all keyboard technique: just up and down the keys, one note for each finger and the thumb. Would Derek find that sufficiently engaging? How would he react? But these questions were supplanted in my mind by a more immediate problem: how was I going to be able to get at the piano for long enough to play the notes that he was supposed to be copying?

Sitting next to him on the piano stool, I tried holding both his wrists with my left hand to give my right free rein on the keyboard. I reckoned that I only needed about ten seconds. But that was nine too many for Derek. He wriggled out of my grip in no time and struck the C that I had managed to play before being overwhelmed. I was afraid of hurting him if I held his wrists any tighter, so I had to try something else.

'Right, Derek,' I declared, 'we're going to play a game. You're going to sit over the other side of the room while I play something on the piano, then you can come over and see if you can copy it.'

I didn't really expect to him understand what I'd said, but in any case, without waiting to see his reaction, I picked him up and plopped down on the floor at the far end of the nursery. I strode back to the piano and quickly played the five-finger exercise. I'd only just finished when Derek, who'd been amazingly quick out of the starting blocks and had fairly scuttled across the room, was pushing me out of the way. That done, he reached across the stool, and played what I had – well, a version of it. He used both hands to play a series of chords, up and down. I had to laugh at his antics.

Then he stopped, waiting. This was a game whose rules he had somehow immediately grasped.

So I picked him up again, sat him as far away as I could from the piano, raced back and played the exercise once more – this time starting on the next note up, C sharp. Again, my thumb was barely off the last key when Derek was back with his response.

And so we continued up the chromatic scale, until we'd tackled all twelve different keys. That brought us back to C, and it felt right to stop there. Derek seemed to sense that feeling of completion too, and he was content to return to his familiar routine of taking requests for pieces to play. He still wouldn't let me join in, I noticed, but I didn't mind: I was convinced that the five-finger-exercise game had provided the breakthrough that I had been looking for. Now I had something to build on.

It was then a short step in the lesson that followed to leave Derek where he was on the piano stool, and to engage in the 'play-copy' dialogue with no physical intervention on my part at all. In due course, I started to imitate what *he* was doing too, enabling us to have a genuine musical 'conversation'. And it wasn't just a matter of a musical ball bouncing between us like echoes in an alleyway.

Whatever you lobbed at Derek would invariably come hurtling back with interest, and it was challenging to keep up with his musical repartee, which combined wit and ingenuity with an incredible speed of thought.

With no words to get in the way, a whole world of sophisticated social intercourse was now opened up to him. It was the second 'eureka' moment of his life: having first discovered that he was able to play what he could hear, now he came to realise that he could communicate *through* music. Indeed, for Derek, music came to function as a proxy-language, and it was through music that his wider development was increasingly channelled. (Ockelford 2007, pp.103–106)

However, Derek's fingering remained as eccentric as ever, and as he had no conceptual understanding of his thumbs and fingers as distinct entities, and was consequently unable to manipulate them appropriately in response to verbal direction, the problem of how to help him develop his technique remained. Although he could copy the notes that I played just by listening, he could not, of course, see how I held my hands at the piano, which fingers I used, and the fact that my elbows didn't figure at all in what I did!

To plug this gap in his experience, I tried putting his hands over mine, one at a time, so that he could feel the shape of my hand and, to an extent, what my fingers were doing. We tried it for a few weeks, but it didn't seem to make any difference: whenever it was his turn, Derek just carried on as before.

So I tried a different approach. I held his right hand on mine.

'Look, Derek, here's my thumb,' I said, giving it a wiggle as his fingers curled around it.

'Now, where's yours?' I guided him to feel his right hand with his left.

'That's it! Now, let's put your thumb on C, middle C.' He allowed me to help him find the correct note and to push it down with his thumb.

'There you are.' And I sang, 'thumb'.

Next I uncurled his index finger and placed its tip on D. He pressed the note.

'Second finger,' I sang.

And so we continued with his third, fourth and little fingers, before coming back down to the thumb. He sang along enthusiastically, and couldn't resist adding in an accompaniment below. When we swapped over to his left hand, he treated the five-finger exercise like a bass-line, and added tunes in the right. No matter, I thought. The main thing was that, for the first time in his life, he'd manage to play using something approaching a conventional technique. On that simplest of foundations we would subsequently be able to build.

Little did I appreciate at the time just how long Derek's technique would take to reconstruct. For a total of eight years we worked together, weekly and then daily, spending hundreds of hours physically going over all the basic fingering patterns that make up a professional pianist's stock-in-trade. From five-finger exercises we moved on to full scales: major, minor and chromatic, as well as some of the more exotic varieties – the so-called 'modals', the whole-tones and the octatonics. Scales had the additional complexity of requiring Derek to tuck his thumb under his fingers while his hand was travelling in one direction, and to extend his fingers over his thumb while it was coming back in the other. I had to use both my hands to help him get this action right. We also tackled arpeggios: major, minor, and dominant and diminished sevenths, followed by some of the more unusual forms – French sevenths, augmented triads and chords of the added sixth. Long after my threshold of boredom was a distant memory, Derek would be keen for more. There was something about the orderliness, not only of the scales and arpeggios themselves, but also the regular way in which they related to one another, that he clearly found deeply satisfying.

However, in spite of the tens – perhaps hundreds – of thousands of willing repetitions, Derek never did learn to tell which finger was which! And even today, if you ask him to hold his thumb up (rather than his fingers), he still can't do it reliably, and the capacity to distinguish one hand from the other continues to elude him. While this seems odd – incredible, even – given his dazzling virtuosity, with hindsight I've come to realise that being able to put a name to concepts such as 'left' and 'right' wasn't the most important thing.

What really mattered was achieving that very first aim I identified when I initially watched Derek play: that his technique should develop sufficiently so as not to trammel his vivid aural imagination. And that, over the years, is exactly what *did* happen. During all those hundreds of hours of practice he absorbed many of the standard fingering patterns, quite without being aware of it, and these slowly became assimilated into his own playing. Today his technique, as a mature adult performer, although still far from conventional, enables him to do whatever his musical imagination demands. (Ockelford 2007, pp.107–110)

Even those children who are (initially) self-taught may well need a high level of support between lessons for them to get the most from programmes of learning. Effective communication between you (the specialist music teacher) and those who you are supporting is essential. To this end, as we noted above, it will almost certainly be advantageous for parents and others to attend lessons, at least in part. As well as using those that are commercially available, teachers can make their own video and audio recordings for pupils, comprising simplified or modified versions of pieces. The right hand and left hand parts of keyboard music can be recorded separately, for example, played slowly, and broken down into sections to make learning easier. Pupils (and their helpers) will probably need to be taught how to derive the greatest benefit from resources such as these. Managing items of music technology, assembling and disassembling instruments where necessary, and ensuring that all equipment is properly maintained and is available when required, are likely to be among the key functions of supporting staff and carers. Deciding how much practice is appropriate each day may be an issue with some children whose interest in music is felt to be obsessive. Clearly, it is a question of balance: if a child's playing takes up so much time that many other forms of purposeful activity are excluded, this may reasonably be deemed excessive; conversely, to deny a child his or her principal source of pleasure and achievement would appear to be nothing less than abusive.

Children on the autism spectrum can perform with others more or less successfully, according to their levels of musical, cognitive and social development. They may show varying degrees of sensitivity to the fluctuating dynamics of a performing group. Some may be able to conceptualise and assume distinct roles; at different times consciously accompanying, for example, or taking the lead. The individuality of some young people may mean that they will always be more suited to solo performance. The greatest challenge in ensembles may be working together and making decisions using little or no language. Even relatively straightforward instructions such as 'play the final chorus twice' may have to be conveyed in purely musical terms. For example, an additional 'dominant seventh harmony' may indicate that more is to come, whereas a slight slowing may show that the end is approaching.

> Working with a large group of children who couldn't see, many of whom had complex needs, presented a number of challenges for teacher and pupils alike. Clearly, conducting was out of the question, so starting and stopping, slowing down and speeding up, and making expressive changes or effects such as getting louder or softer had to be co-ordinated non-visually: through sound, using speech or musical cues. As I soon discovered, calling out what was required was disruptive, and in any case spoken instructions meant little to several of the children, including Derek, on account of their learning difficulties. So, during a performance, the direction of the group had to come solely through inflections in the piano part, to which the children learnt to listen very attentively. For example, if a verse were to be sung sadly, then the accompaniment might reflect this through a reduction in tempo and dynamics and, perhaps, by moving to the 'minor' key. Conversely, the return to a happy state could be conveyed through an increase in movement, loudness and the use of 'major' chords. It was even possible to communicate a sense of irony, which could be appreciated by some of the older and more able pupils, by juxtaposing different pieces with contrasting connotations together – for example, by playing fragments of *Day oh!* while the children were singing *Morning has broken*.

> The accompaniment could relay simpler messages too. For instance, if a chorus were to be repeated at the end, this could be signalled through particular chords that suggested there was more to come. From time to time I would link songs together by improvising a 'bridge' between them. Musically, this would borrow material from the first piece and incrementally transform it into the introduction to the second, so it gradually became apparent what this was to be.

Sometimes the children would compete to see who could name the upcoming tune first. If things were becoming too straightforward, I would tease them by appearing to set off in a certain direction only to change course at the last moment. Increasingly, I was able to hold their attention by linking a whole sequence of pieces in this way. Indeed, I came to the conclusion that the most effective lessons were those in which there was little or no talking, and that the more one could teach music *through* music the better. (Ockelford 2007, pp.134–136)

Children on the autism spectrum (with or without learning difficulties) may play in public – just like any other musicians – enjoying a rapport with their audience and relishing the acclaim their performances bring. There should be no ethical difficulty here, provided the child concerned is aware of what is happening, consents to it, and is not being exploited. Indeed, I am constantly amazed at how some severely autistic children revel in the excitement of performing to a large group of people, and it would be wrong to deny them that opportunity. However, where individuals have only limited awareness of a situation, an informed decision may have to be made by those closest to them. A number of factors will have to be weighed up. For example, while there may appear to be little short-term advantage, it could be that playing in concerts, experiencing the special atmosphere they generate, and conforming to the patterns of behaviour they require, benefit a child's social development over a longer period. Repertoire and context are important considerations too. While it may be desirable, in the course of lessons, for pupils to attempt pieces in a wide range of styles, it may be inappropriate for them to perform a similar variety in public. For instance, a child whose speciality is jazz may be demeaned by unexpectedly improvising on a Beethoven sonata in the course of a formal concert of classical music. In other circumstances, however, such an exploit may be admired for its telling musicality and pungent wit.

For those supporting autistic children, playing in concerts is likely to raise a number of practical questions, such as attendance at rehearsals, setting up instruments and behaving appropriately on stage. It is essential that these areas of potential concern are acknowledged in good time and adequately addressed. Other issues, such as facing the audience, learning not to move excessively while playing, and receiving applause appropriately may need special consideration – and rehearsal – too. A child with severe learning difficulties may find it far more difficult to raise or lower the piano stool than to play the instrument once seated! Here is an account of Derek's first public performance, aged eight.

He was rocking slowly on the piano stool, his fingers fidgeting in readiness for their forthcoming workout. He smiled when he heard his name, and sat still for a moment to give his full attention to what Miss Lingard was saying.

'…and now he's going to play the *Streets of London.*'

Derek's smile widened into a broad beam that stretched right across his face. This was the moment that he'd been waiting for.

I decided to assert my authority straight away – and to keep Derek on his toes – by beginning in E flat major, a key in which he had not, as far as I could remember, ever played the song. I couldn't think of another child (except, perhaps, Philip) for whom such an act wouldn't have had disastrous consequences. But for Derek, the unusual was commonplace, and I had complete faith in his ability to follow me. My confidence was well-founded, and before the opening chord had faded away he was there alongside me, as though it were the most natural thing in the world to play a piece in an unfamiliar key before his first ever public audience. The hundreds of hours that we had spent practising all conceivable scales and arpeggios had refined his raw capacity to realise his entire repertoire starting on any note, and he was now equally at home playing pieces in any key – rather like being able to speak twelve languages with native fluency.

I led Derek resolutely through the first verse and chorus of the *Streets of London* and he obediently followed. I was longing to let him go in order to see just where his musical imagination, fired up by the excitement of the occasion, would take us, and as soon as I judged it was prudent to do so – towards the end of verse two – I gradually retreated into the background with a series of *sotto voce* chords. The instant that he sensed my musical grip was released, Derek was off, scampering up the octave with a series of broken chords. Up and up he took the music, ascending into higher and higher realms of musical invention. Just when it seemed as though he was going to run out of notes at the end of the keyboard, he came scurrying down in a series of tumbling scales and rejoined me in the middle register. Seizing my opportunity, I took the lead again and introduced a new syncopated rhythm in the bass. Without a moment's hesitation, his left hand too started skipping along to the new beat before he broke free once more, dancing out of my reach.

And so our pas de deux continued for a few minutes, until it felt appropriate to draw matters to a close, before Derek ran out of steam and his perambulations became repetitive. An almost imperceptible reduction in the pace of my accompaniment signalled that it was time to wind things up, and he fell back into step with a series of expansive chords that served as an effective climax to the piece. He held on to the last *fortissimo* cluster of notes waiting for me to lift my hands up first, and then he couldn't resist his trademark final plonk low down in the left hand.

The audience burst into rapturous applause – this was quite unlike anything they'd ever seen or heard before. There were shouts of 'Well done, Derek!' He was quivering with excitement, his face radiant, his hands alternately clapping and flapping energetically at his sides. I looked across at Nanny. She too was applauding vigorously, her eyes shining with pride. I felt relieved, delighted and (I had to admit) vindicated. From somewhere, Derek seemed to have acquired the instincts of a natural performer: a sense of occasion and the capacity to rise to it, the ability to communicate with an audience and a feeling of exhilaration when his playing was acknowledged. These were things that could not be taught, but with them, Derek's playing had the potential to reach heights that were as yet unexplored. (Ockelford 2007, pp.140–142)

Finally, we consider a question that I am often asked in relation to music-making by children on the autism spectrum: do they *feel* the music in the same way as their 'neurotypical' peers? This is a complex issue. Consider, for instance, Scenario 28 in Chapter 4 (p.118), in which Milán – lead singer in his pop group at school – slows down before the return of each chorus of 'Thank You for the Music' for expressive effect. Milán is autistic and severely developmentally delayed and, as he normally displays little or no emotion in everyday life, his teacher questions whether he actually understands the music on an emotional level and, if so, whether it is this affective engagement that drives the change of tempo; or (his teacher wonders) is it merely a device that Milán has copied unthinkingly from Agnetha Fältskog's performance with ABBA that he has accessed on YouTube. Evidence for the latter view comes from the fact that, although Milán uses similar conventions of Western musical expression in other songs, they always appear to match recordings that he has heard rather closely. And, as far as his teacher is able to ascertain, Milán does not transfer the interpretative gestures he reproduces in one context to novel scenarios.

Other performers, such as Derek Paravicini, in whom it is similarly possible to discern only a limited range of emotions in day-to-day life, seem to have taken the next step. Derek has learnt the 'emotional syntax' of expressive performance in a range of styles with which he is familiar: that is, he has acquired a repertoire of expressive devices that he can apply to new music in a rule-based way at appropriate points to communicate different feelings. For example in the documentary about him, *The Musical Genius* (originally screened in 2005 on Channel 5 in the UK and Discovery Health in the USA), I created a short sequence of chords on the computer that, in terms of performance, were devoid of any expressivity at all. However, in conversation with the music psychologist John Sloboda, Derek showed that he was able to convey different emotions (joy, sorrow and – least convincingly – anger) through improvising on the series of chords in different ways, which included the introduction of expressive devices (such as changes in dynamics and tempo) as well as structural alterations (including the introduction of the minor key).

On viewing the programme, a number of people have asked the same question that Milán's teacher was keen to answer, to the effect of: 'Derek may be able to convey emotion in his playing (he has evidently learnt the 'code' of expressive performance), but does he *feel* it himself?' Ultimately, since Derek has very limited powers of metacognition (his capacity to reflect on his own thinking), this issue may remain unresolved. However, there are two points that I think are worth making in this regard.

The first is, does it matter? Derek loves playing *for other people* (he rarely, if ever, plays at his own instigation for his own amusement) and since his performances bring him and his audience pleasure, is it critical to have a precisely shared message? Or is the fact that positive communication takes place (even if the message as transmitted and received is somewhat different) the important thing? This highlights an issue that is problematic for all performers: since, as we saw in Chapter 3 (p.102), music exists only in the ear of the beholder so, by definition, does musical *meaning*, and it is inevitable that in any live musical engagement, performers and members of the audience will experience subtly (even, on some occasions, radically) different things.

The second point is that Derek, and others like him, may come to learn about their own feelings *through music*, which they may then recognise in everyday life (rather than via the more common route of experiencing reactions to people and events, which are subsequently felt to be conveyed by music). Such responses may occur directly, as when Derek *feels* emotion as he listens to music (just as 'neurotypical' listeners do), or indirectly: for example, when he performs with others, and detects a communicative intent in the way they play or sing – intentions that may be confirmed verbally. (For more on emotional responses to music by people with autism, see Emanuele *et al.* 2009; Molnar-Szakacs and Heaton 2012; Quintin *et al.* 2011.)

CONCLUSION

In this chapter we have considered the musical abilities and needs of an exceptional group of children and young people on the autism spectrum, who have advanced skills in the context of pervasive developmental delay. While those with levels of talent that would be regarded as outstanding in any circumstances (that is, disregarding their disabilities) are extremely rare, uneven profiles of development – where musical attainment outstrips progress in other areas – are encountered rather more frequently. Indeed, it is quite likely that, within a class of autistic pupils, teachers will come across musical abilities that merit particular attention.

While there is no one approach to music education that is suitable for all musically talented autistic children, it is possible to identify approaches and strategies that have met with a broad range of success in relation to this group as a whole. The key point to bear in mind is that *all* such children, no matter how talented or disabled, or how extreme the disparity between the two, will benefit from systematic and sustained educational input. But teachers should not be surprised if work that lies even a little way outside a child's intuitively acquired domain of expertise or just beyond their preferred style of learning will need to be tackled primarily in the context of their cognitive impairment. Equally, it may be a considerable challenge to have the encapsulated skills associated with music-making accrue to wider learning and development.

Overall, the most important thing for those responsible for the education of children and young people on the autism spectrum who are (or may be) functioning at Levels 5 or 6 of the *Sounds of Intent* framework, is to ensure that specialist provision is put in place as early as possible, with the aim, always, of minimising the impact of disability through maximising musical potential.

Conclusion

This book has advanced a range of thinking, variously based on well-established research, the observations of fellow practitioners and parents, personal experience and the accounts of people on the autism spectrum themselves. If a number of the ideas that are presented are frankly speculative, that is because the relationship between music, language and autism is, on the whole, poorly understood. With one or two notable exceptions, music and auditory perception have been a poor relation in the academic discourse pertaining to autism, and if the assertions that are put forward stimulate further thinking, encourage new research and prompt practitioners to view their practice in a new light, then the book will have served a useful purpose.

At the very least, I hope that it will have provided (provisional) answers to the questions with which we began: why Jack is obsessed with the sound of the microwave, why four-year-old Anna repeats what her father says, why Ben persistently listens to the jingles from the internet, why Callum puts his hands over his ears and hums to himself whenever his mother's mobile goes off, why Freddie flicks any glasses, bowls, pots and pans that are within reach, why Romy sometimes only pretends to play the notes on her keyboard, why Bharat repeatedly bangs away at particular notes on his piano, and why Rachel cries whenever she hears 'Twinkle, Twinkle, Little Star'.

If music provides important intellectual and emotional nourishment for us all, one could argue that it is essential brain-food for children on the autism spectrum. Policy-makers and practitioners take note!

References

American Psychiatric Association (2013) *Diagnostic and Statistical Manual of Mental Disorders*, Arlington, VA: APA.

Anastasi, A., and Levee, R. (1960) 'Intellectual deficit and musical talent: a case report', *American Journal of Mental Deficiency*, 64(January), 695–703.

Balkwill, L.-L. and Thompson, W. (1999) 'A cross-cultural investigation of the perception of emotion in music: psychophysical and cultural cues', *Music Perception* 17(1), 43–64.

Ballard, K. (2007) *The Frameworks of English: Introducing Language Structures* (2nd ed.), Basingstoke, Hampshire: Palgrave.

Baron-Cohen, S. (1995) *Mindblindness: An Essay on Autism and Theory of Mind*, Cambridge, MA: The MIT Press.

Baron-Cohen, S. (2000) 'Theory of mind and autism: a fifteen year review', in *Understanding Other Minds: Perspectives from Developmental Cognitive Neuroscience* (2nd ed.), S. Baron-Cohen, H. Tager-Flusberg and J. Donald (eds), New York, NY: Oxford University Press, pp. 3–20.

Baron-Cohen, S. (2009) 'Autism: the empathizing–systematizing (E–S) theory', *Annals of the New York Academy of Sciences*, The Year in Cognitive Neuroscience 2009, 1,156, 68–80.

Baron-Cohen, S., Leslie, A. and Frith, U. (1985) 'Does the autistic child have a "theory of mind"?', *Cognition*, 21(1), 37–46.

Barrett, M. (2006) '"Like dynamite going off in my ears": using autobiographical accounts of autism with teaching professionals', *Educational Psychology in Practice*, 22(2), 95–110.

Bondy, A. and Frost, L. (2011) *A Picture's Worth: PECS and Other Visual Communication Strategies in Autism* (2nd ed.), Bethseda, MD: Woodbine House, Inc.

Boucher, J. (2009) *The Autistic Spectrum: Characteristics, Causes and Practical Issues*, London: Sage Publications Ltd.

Boucher, J. (2011) 'Redefining the concept of autism as a unitary disorder: multiple causal deficits of a single kind', in *The Neuropsychology of Autism*, D. Fein (ed.), New York, NY: Oxford University Press, pp. 469–482.

Charlop-Christy, M., Carpenter, M., Le, L., LeBlanc, L. and Kellet, K. (2002) 'Using the picture exchange communication system (PECS) with children autism: assessment of PECS acquisition, speech, social-communicative behaviour, and problem behavior', *Journal of Applied Behavior Analysis*, 35(3), 213–231.

Clarke, E. (1999) 'Rhythm and timing in music', in *The Psychology of Music*, D. Deutsch (ed.), New York, NY: Academic Press, pp. 473–500.

Cohen, J. (1962) 'Information theory and music', *Behavioral Science*, 7(2), 137–163.

Corpus of Contemporary American English (2012). Available at http://corpus.byu.edu/coca/, accessed 3 February 2013.

Crowder, R. (1985) 'Perception of the major/minor distinction: III. Hedonic, musical, and affective discriminations', *Bulletin of the Psychonomic Society*, 23(4), 314–316.

Cytowic, R. (1997) 'Synaesthesia: phenomenology and neuropsychology – a review of current knowledge', in *Synaesthesia: Classic and Contemporary Readings*, S. Baron-Cohen and J. Harrison (eds), Oxford: Blackwell Publishing, pp. 17–42.

Dale, N. and Salt, A. (2008) 'Social identity, autism and visual impairment (VI) in the early years', *British Journal of Visual Impairment*, 26(2), 135–146.

Davies, J. (1978) *The Psychology of Music*, Stanford, CA: Stanford University Press.

Emanuele, E., Boso, M., Cassola, F., Broglia, D., Bonoldi, I., Mancini, L., Marini, M. and Politi, P. (2009) 'Increased dopamine DRD4 receptor and mRNA expression in lymphocytes of musicians and autistic individuals: bridging the music-autism connection', *Activitas Nervosa Superior Rediviva*, 51(3–4), 142–145.

Fauconnier, G. (1994) *Mental Spaces: Aspects of Meaning Construction in Natural Language*, Cambridge: Cambridge University Press.

Fauconnier, G. and Turner, M. (2002) *The Way We Think: Conceptual Blending and the Mind's Hidden Complexities*, New York, NY: Basic Books.

Fox, R. (2008) 'Applied behavior analysis treatment of autism: the state of the art', *Child and Psychiatric Clinics of North America*, 17(4), 821–834.

Frith, U. (2001) 'Mind blindness and the brain in autism', *Neuron*, 32(6), 969–979.

Frith, U. (2003) *Autism: Explaining the Enigma* (2nd ed.), Oxford: Blackwell Publishing.

Frith, U. and Happé, F. (1994) 'Autism: beyond "theory of mind"', *Cognition*, 50(1–3), 115–132.

Fraigberg, S. (1979) *Insights from the Blind*. London: Souvenir Press.

Gall, C. (2009) BBC News Magazine. Available at http://news.bbc.co.uk/1/hi/magazine/8013859.stm, accessed 2 February 2013.

Global Language Monitor (2012) 'No. of words.' Available at www.languagemonitor.com/no-of-words, accessed on 21 March 2013.

Gundlach, R. (1935) 'Factors determining the characterization of musical phrases', *American Journal of Psychology*, 47(4), 624–644.

Happé, F. (1995) *Autism: An Introduction to Psychological Theory*, London: UCL Press Ltd.

Happé, F. (1996) 'Studying weak central coherence at low levels: children with autism do not succumb to visual illusions', *Journal of Child Psychology and Psychiatry*, 37(7), 873–877.

Happé, F. (1997) 'Central coherence and theory of mind in autism: reading homographs in context', *British Journal of Developmental Psychology*, 15(1), 1–12.

Happé, F. and Booth, R. (2008) 'The power of the positive: revisiting weak coherence in autism spectrum disorders', *The Quarterly Journal of Experimental Psychology*, Special Issue: A Festschrift for Uta Frith, 61(1), 50–63.

Hargreaves, D. (1986) *The Developmental Psychology of Music*, Cambridge: Cambridge University Press.

Hargreaves, D. and North, A. (1997) *The Social Psychology of Music*, Oxford: Oxford University Press.

Hatfield, E., Cacioppo, J. and Rapson, R. (1994) *Emotional Contagion*, Cambridge: Cambridge University Press.

Hevner, K. (1936) 'Experimental studies of the elements of expression in music', *American Journal of Psychology*, 48(2), 246–268.

Hill, E. (2004) 'Executive dysfunction in autism', *Trends in Cognitive Sciences*, 8(1), 26–32.

Hobson, P. (1993) *Autism and the Development of Mind*, Hove, East Sussex: Lawrence Erlbaum Associates.

Hobson, P. and Lee, A. (2010) 'Reversible autism among congenitally blind children? A controlled follow-up study', *Journal of Child Psychology and Psychiatry*, 51(11), 1, 235–1, 241.

Jairazbhoy, N. (1971/1995) *The Rāgs of North Indian Music: Their Structure and Evolution*, Bombay: Popular Prakashan Pvt. Ltd.

Juslin, P. (1997) 'Perceived emotional expression in synthesized performances of a short melody: capturing the listener's judgement policy', *Musicæ Scientiæ*, 1(1), 225–256.

Juslin, P., Friberg, A. and Bresin, R. (2001/2002) 'Toward a computational model of expression in music performance: the GERM model', *Musicæ Scientiæ*, Special Issue: Current Trends in the Study of Music and Emotion, 63–122.

Kayzer, W. (1995) *Vertrouwd en a zo Vreemd: Over Geheugen en Bewustzijn*, Amsterdam: Uitgeverij Contact.

Kearney, A. (2007) *Understanding Applied Behavior Analysis: An Introduction to ABA for Parents, Teachers and Other Professionals*, London: Jessica Kingsley.

Koelsch, S. and Friederici, A. (2003) 'Toward the neural basis of processing structure in music', *Annals of the New York Academy of Sciences*, The Neurosciences and Music, 999, 15–28.

Lakoff, G. (1990) *Women, Fire and Dangerous Things: What Categories Reveal about the Human Mind*, Chicago, IL: University of Chicago Press.

Lea, R., Rapp, D., Elfenbein, A., Mitchel, A., and Romine, R. (2008) 'Sweet silent thought: alliteration and resonance in poetry comprehension', *Psychological Science*, 19(7), 709–716.

Lim, H. (2012) *Developmental Speech-Language Training through Music for Children with Autism Spectrum Disorders*, London: Jessica Kingsley.

Macfarland, S. (1995) 'Teaching strategies of the van Dijk curricular approach', *Journal of Visual Impairment and Blindness*, 89(3), 222–228.

Malloch, S. (1999/2000) 'Mothers and infants and communicative musicality', *Musicæ Scientiæ*, Special Issue: Rhythm, Musical Narrative and Origins of Human Communication, 29–57.

Mesibov, G., Shea, V. and Schopler. E. (2004) *The TEACCH Approach to Autism Spectrum Disorders*, New York, NY: Springer Science+Business Media, Inc.

Meyer, L. (2001) 'Music and emotion: distinctions and uncertainties', in P. Juslin and J. Sloboda (eds), *Music and Emotion: Theory and Research*, Oxford: Oxford University Press, pp. 341–360.

Miller, L. (1989) *Musical Savants: Exceptional Skill in the Mentally Retarded*, Hillsdale, NJ: Lawrence Erlbaum.

Miller, O. and Ockelford, A. (2005) *Visual Needs*, London and New York: Continuum.

Miyazaki, K. (2004) 'How well do we understand absolute pitch', *Acoustical Science and Technology*, 25(6), 426–432.

Molnar-Szakacs, I. and Heaton, P. (2012) 'Music: a unique window into the world of autism', *Annals of the New York Academy of Sciences*, The Neurosciences and Music IV, Learning and Memory, 1,252, 318–324.

Morrongiello, B. and Roes, C. (1990) 'Children's memory for new songs: integration or independent storage of words and tunes?', *Journal of Experimental Child Psychology*, 50(1), 25–38.

Mottron, L., Burack, J., Iarocci, G., Belleville, S. and Enns, J. (2003) 'Locally oriented perception with intact global processing among adolescents with high-functioning autism: evidence from multiple paradigms', *Journal of Child Psychology and Psychiatry*, 44(6), 904–913.

Mottron, L., Peretz, I. and Ménard, E. (2000) 'Local and global processing of music in high-functioning persons with autism: beyond central coherence?', *Journal of Child Psychology and Psychiatry*, 41(8), 1,057–1,065.

Narmour, E. (2000) 'Music expectations by cognitive rule-mapping', *Music Perception*, 17(3), 329–398.

National Center for Voice and Speech (2005) 'Voice Qualities.' Available at www.ncus.org/ncus/tutorials/voiceprod/tutorial/quality.html, accessed on 21 March 2013.

Nielzén, S. and Cesarec, Z. (1982) 'Emotional experience of music as a function of musical structure', *Psychology of Music*, 10(2), 7–17.

Ockelford, A. (1996) *All join in! A Framework for Making Music with Children and Young People who are Visually Impaired and have Learning Disabilities*, (CD, 24 songs and teaching materials), London: Royal National Institute of the Blind.

Ockelford, A. (1998) *Music Moves: Music in the Education of Children and Young People who are Visually Impaired and have Learning Disabilities*, London: Royal National Institute of the Blind.

Ockelford, A. (2001) *Objects of Reference: Promoting Early Symbolic Communication* (Third Edition), London: Royal National Institute of the Blind.

Ockelford, A. (2005a) 'Relating musical structure and content to aesthetic response: a model and analysis of Beethoven's Piano Sonata Op. 110', *Journal of the Royal Musical Association*, 130(1), 74–118.

Ockelford, A. (2005b) *Repetition in Music: Theoretical and Metatheoretical Perspectives*, London: Ashgate.

Ockelford, A. (2007) *In the Key of Genius: the Extraordinary Life of Derek Paravicini*, London: Hutchinson.

Ockelford, A. (2012) *Applied Musicology: Using Zygonic Theory to Inform Music Psychology, Education, and Therapy Research*, New York, NY: Oxford University Press.

Ockelford, A. and Matawa, C. (2009) *Focus on Music 2: Exploring the Musical Interests and Abilities of Blind and Partially-Sighted Children with Retinopathy of Prematurity*, London: Institute of Education.

Ockelford, A., Pring, L., Welch, G. and Treffert, D. (2006) *Focus on Music: Exploring the Musical Interests and Abilities of Blind and Partially-Sighted Children with Septo-Optic Dysplasia*, London: Institute of Education.

Panerai, S., Ferrante, L. and Zingale, M. (2002) 'Benefits of the treatment and education of autistic and communication handicapped children (TEACCH) programme as compared with a non-specific approach', *Journal of Intellectual Disability Research*, 46(4), 318–327.

Patel, A. (2012) 'Language, music, and the brain: a resource-sharing framework', in P. Rebuschat, M. Rohrmeier, J. Hawkins and I. Cross (eds), *Language and Music as Cognitive Systems*, Oxford: Oxford University Press, pp. 204–223.

Pinker, S. (1994) *The Language Instinct: How the Mind Creates Language*, New York, NY: HarperCollins Publishers.

Pope, A. (1711) *An Essay on Criticism*. London: W. Lewis. Available at http://poetry.eserver.org/essay-on-criticism.html, accessed 27 November 2012.

Powell, A. (2011) 'Music and Williams syndrome: a single-case study exploring emerging savant musical ability', unpublished MSc dissertation, University of Roehampton, London.

Pring, L. (ed.) (2005) *Autism and Blindness: Research and Reflections*. London: Whur.

Prizant, B. and Duchan, J. (1981) 'The functions of immediate echolalia in autistic children', *Journal of Speech, Language and Hearing Research*, 46(3), 241–249.

Quintin, E.-M., Bhatara, A., Poissant, H., Fombonne, E. and Levitin, D. (2011) 'Emotion perception in music in high-functioning adolescents with autism spectrum disorders', *Journal of Autism and Developmental Disorders*, 41(9), 1,240–1,255.

Rimland, B. and Fein, D. (1988) 'Special talents of autistic savants', in *The Exceptional Brain: Neuropsychology of Talent and Special Abilities*, L. Obler and D. Fein (eds), New York: The Guilford Press, pp. 474–492.

Rubin, D. (1995) *Memory in Oral Traditions: the Cognitive Psychology of Epic, Ballads and Counting-Out Rhymes*, New York, NY: Oxford University Press.

Scherer, K. (1991) 'Emotion expression in speech and music', in J. Sundberg, L. Nord and R. Carlson (eds), *Music, Language, Speech and Brain*, London: Macmillan, pp. 146–56.

Scherer, K. and Oshinsky, J. (1977) 'Cue utilization in emotion attribution from auditory stimuli', *Motivation and Emotion*, 1(4), 336–346.

Schoenberg, A. (1967) *Fundamentals of Musical Composition*, London: Faber and Faber.

Serafine, M., Crowder, R., and Repp, B. (1984) 'Integration of melody and text in memory for songs', *Cognition*, 16(3), 285–303.

Simpson, K. and Keen, D. (2011) 'Music interventions for children with autism: narrative review of the literature', *Journal of Autism and Developmental Disorders*, 41(11), 1,507–1,514.

Sloboda, J. (1985) *The Musical Mind: The Cognitive Psychology of Music*, Oxford: Oxford University Press.

South, M., Ozonoff, S. and McMahon, W. (2007) 'The relationship between executive functioning, central coherence, and repetitive behaviors in the high-functioning autism spectrum', *Autism*, 11(5), 437–451.

Starr, S. (1975) 'The relationship of single words to two-word sentences', *Child Development*, 46(3), 701–708.

Sterling-Turner, H. and Jordan, S. (2007) 'Interventions addressing transition difficulties for individuals with autism', *Psychology in the Schools*, Special Issue: Autism Spectrum Disorders, 44(7), 681–690.

Tager-Flusberg, H. (2001) 'A reexamination of the theory of mind hypothesis of autism', in *The Development of Autism: Perspectives from Theory and Research*, J. Burack, T. Charman, N. Yurmiya and P. Zelzao (eds), Mahwah, NJ: Lawrence Erlbaum Associates, pp. 157–175.

Thompson, W. and Robitaille, B. (1992) 'Can composers express emotions through music?', *Empirical Studies of the Arts*, 10(1), 79–89.

Treffert, D. (1989) *Extraordinary People: An Exploration of Savant Syndrome*. London: Bantam Press.

Turner, M. (1997) 'Towards an executive dysfunction account of repetitive behaviour in autism', in J. Russell (ed.), *Autism as an Executive Disorder*, New York, NY: Oxford University Press, pp. 57–100.

US Government Social Security Administration (2012). Available at www.babycenter.co/baby-names-twinkle-99455.htm, accessed 3 February 2013.

Wallace, W. (1994) 'Memory for music: effect of melody on recall of text', *Journal of Experimental Psychology: Learning, Memory and Cognition*, 20(6), 1,471–1,485.

Waltz, M. (2005) 'Reading case studies of people with autistic spectrum disorders: a cultural studies approach to issues of disability representation', *Disability and Society*, 20(4), 421–435.

Watson, K. (1942) 'The nature and measurement of musical meanings', *Psychological Monographs*, 54(2), 1–43.

Welch, G. (2005) 'Singing as communication', in D. Miell, R. MacDonald and D. Hargreaves (eds), *Musical Communication*. New York, NY: Oxford University Press, pp. 239–259.

Wilson, S., Abbott, D., Lusher, D., Gentle, E., and Jackson, G. (2011) 'Finding your voice: a singing lesson from functional imaging', *Human Brain Mapping*, 32(12), 2,115–2,130.

Wing, L. (2003) *The Autistic Spectrum: A Guide for Parents and Professionals*, London: Robinson Publishing.

World Health Organization (1993) *The ICD-10 Classification of Mental and Behavioural Disorders: Diagnostic Criteria for Research*, Geneva: WHO.

Yan, C., Demaine, K., Zipse, L., Norton, A. and Schlaug, G. (2010) 'From music making to speaking: engaging the mirror neuron system in autism', *Brain Research Bulletin*, 32(3–4), 161–168.

Yan, C. and Schlaug, G. (2010) 'Neural pathways for language in autism: the potential for music-based treatments', *Future Neurology*, 5(6), 797–805.

Zbikowksi, L. (2002) *Conceptualizing Music: Cognitive Structure, Theory, and Analysis*, New York, NY: Oxford University Press.

Subject Index

Note: Page numbers in *italics* denote figures and tables.

Author Index